Dawns On

The Credology of Money

Economics Reinterpreted

Cover design: Shakhar Pelled

email: contact@dawns-on.com

Table of Contents

Detailed Table of Contents

List of Tables

List of Figures

INTRODUCTION

This book is a guide to the deep complexity of a shared belief in certain numerical representations.

The belief in money.

It is a belief in something symbolic that humans are capable of identifying, something that will elicit the help of fellow humans everywhere. If you have money, people will help you even if you are not of the same race, religion, gender, nationality or political orientation.

People will receive you with a smile and give you food, lodgings, services and consumer products.

And all you have to do in return?

Flash them a number.

Give them a bit of colored paper.

You do not have to curry favor, suck up, establish ties or resort to any of the myriad gyrations that human beings are wont to direct at each other within the heavy hierarchies of patrons and clients prevalent in all societies throughout history.

They will help you because you pay them.

Money provides every person who has it with access to the great network of service providers and the endless supply-chains of human instrumentality and production.

The belief in money is a belief in which all other systems are embedded, and all aspects of human existence can be converted into its concepts; once money is available, it is ready to elicit the kindness and generosity of people everywhere.

And should you hasten to comment that there is no generosity involved, because we are dealing here with paid services, please consider what you would have had to do a thousand years ago in order to procure even a modicum of what you have in your fridge today, and how you would have gone about "convincing" people to share their produce with you in the past: How many bonds of social obligation and subjugation to patrons would you have had to succumb to in order to survive? And what were the chances that you would have been free persons and masters of your own fate in a world subjected to strict hierarchies in which few were entitled to call themselves "free", and that freedom too was ensnared in rigid and demanding customs.

The universal belief in money, the shared faith burning in the hearts of all humans that money has value, generates the possibility of a unique personal freedom such as was never before seen throughout human history.

This liberating effect also lies at the core of money's subversiveness, as it shreds all fetters of fealty and loyalty that were so vital if one was to survive, replacing them with the power of cold cash to obtain all that is necessary for life while maintaining one's independence.

Money is a complex belief that involves both individual consciousness and social sanction. It depends on such aspects of the human psyche as the sense of ownership and the social approval of ownership, along with disapproval for such breaches of ownership as theft.

Money is a shared belief that does not exist outside of persons; money is an institution of faith[1]. There is no money "out there" beyond human civilization. It is the minds of men that create the symbolic forms of money, and it is the minds of men that assign value to these forms.

[1] This is reflected in the common terms used in economic discourse. Terms such as credit (=*He believes*, Latin), trust, good faith, confidence, and the like.

CHAPTER 1: OWNERSHIP

Our belief in ownership precedes our belief in money: We are capable of associating possessions with people and saying that a person is the owner of something such as Mary's doll, dad's slippers, or Jake's convertible bond. The right of people to hold possessions, to say of something that it is "mine" precedes any monetary transaction, for only an owner is entitled to sell.

Money is contingent on ownership, but ownership is not contingent on money. One may pluck a banana in the jungle, thereby owning it. One may plunder the banana of another, thereby becoming its illegitimate possessor, though not its owner, or one may receive a banana as a gift, thereby becoming its owner for free.

Ownership is a complex phenomenon that includes a personal psychological aspect, the "feeling" or "sense" that something is "mine", and a sociological aspect, the acknowledgement by other people that a certain something is owned by a specific someone, and the recognition of ownership rights as enshrined by tradition and anchored in law.

The psychology of ownership

Ownership is contingent on the ability to own, so the first question that arises in any study of ownership is the idea of the purchasing entity: How are human personalities constituted so that they can eventually claim that certain objects and entities in the world are "theirs", i.e. tied to them in such a way that they have unique rights pertaining to them, such as the right to sell them, give them away, consume them or prevent others from using them. How do human personalities capable of ownership arise?

Even though every personality is unique, the course of human development does include a number of universal stages that are commonly plotted out on graph paper as growth and development curves.

All children share an ancient genetic heritage that allows them to turn over and smile, sit and crawl, stand and walk, and sooner or later, talk.

Once children develop to the extent that they acquire language, i.e., becomes privy to the thoughts of others, one of the very first words that all children utter is the ownership word: "mine".

The perception of ownership is a significant milestone in human development and is critically contingent on the involvement of another person capable of encompassing the child within her own world.

It is important to understand the foundations of personality within the interpersonal environment because money, like language, is a personal idea that is intertwined with the minds of others. There is no language without speakers and no money without traders. Individuals thinking in a language and counting their money have acquired the ability to think and calculate during their developmental journey.

The "I" capable of recognizing an "other" and speaking to him, or of acknowledging the property of an "other" and trading with him, began its journey with a loving mother, and it was the introjection of the mother into the mind of the child that gradually made it possible to differentiate between "I" and "not-I" and establish the child's self-status as an individual.

Right from the first moment after birth, babies seek attachment and yearn to assimilate everything that the mother provides, not just physically but also mentally and psychologically. The baby seeks the mother's gaze. Her personality and love construct his world.[2]

The adults who surround the child and are aware of the meaning of words and intentions. They ascribe meaning to the child's utterances and channel the correlations between speech and reality.

Language is the deep social bridge connecting the inner consciousness of the self with the consciousness of others who are capable of understanding the speech utterances of the self. The self too learns to express its personal thoughts in terms that others can understand, so that the personal and social coalesce in language. As Lyons writes in his book on semantics:

> It is impossible [for humans] to express their feelings and attitudes in language, however personal and spontaneous these attitudes and feelings might be, otherwise than in terms of the distinctions that are encoded in particular language systems... The expressive is necessarily socio-expressive and the personal is necessarily inter-personal.[3]

Thus, when the inner world of a child is constructed in the course of acquiring language, the expansion of knowledge and consciousness that language provides both extends the self into human reality, and assimilates human reality into the "self", a two-way process in which the idea of ownership also appears, as it ascribes tangible parts of reality to the self.

With the acquisition of language, the self expands to hold the world in its conceptual awareness, including elements of reality that are conceptualized as belonging solely to the self, such as "my hand" or "my doll".

We assimilate the objects of our belief-love-attachment into our inner selves, and that assimilation is the foundation of personality. The inter-subjective world of others is reflected in our minds. Our inner personal world replicates and represents inter-subjective reality[4], and all languages are public assets.

---

[2] His work on schizoid mental states led Fairbairn to reject Freud's instinct theory and the concept of the id, and to question the pleasure principle and the hedonistic theory of motivation. He concluded that "the object and not gratification is the ultimate aim of libidinal striving. The infant, a libidinal 'I', was, therefore, pre-programmed to relate to 'the other', i.e., another libidinal 'I', and was primarily 'object-seeking' rather than 'pleasure-seeking. It followed, for Fairbairn, that, at the deepest motivational level, the infant strove to make contact with 'the other', and that the most powerful human anxiety was associated with separation from, and loss of love of, 'the other'.

Clarke, G. S. (2018). *Thinking through Fairbairn: Exploring the object relations model of mind.* Routledge, pp.209-210.

[3] Lyons, J., & John, L. (1995). *Linguistic semantics: An introduction.* Cambridge University Press, p. 45.

[4] The pleasingly unavoidable consequence of this insight is that all forms of philosophical solipsism are but internal mirrors of the discourse that constructed the personality in interaction with a loving mother. In this sense, the insights provided by attachment and object-relations theories refute Descartes' famous "Cogito", "I think therefore I am", because such a claim directly contradicts what we now know about the foundations of the mind, which can never be solipsistic. The existence of other minds it what constructs our minds, so there is no "I am" to think anything before attachment to others catalyzes that I. Descartes

This is the mysterious alchemy of the soul, in which a mind cast into the world at birth slowly absorbs the world of others, absorbs the love and the language and the world views and how to become a person.

All of the mother's cultural heritage, her words and her actions, and who she is, nurture the inner development of her baby's self, the growth of a new 'subject'. As Ogden describes it:

> Mental contents exist in a psychological space that is at first almost entirely interpersonal, only later evolving into a personal internal environment. It is the dialectical interplay of our mental contents and the personal and interpersonal psychological space in which they are lived that constitutes the matrix of the mind.[5]

Speech is the direct extension of infantile attachment. It is the telepathic bridge of love that extends from the baby's mind into the mind of loving others and from their mind into the baby's. This interaction, whereby loving others become beloved others, constructs the inner world of the self from the inner world of others. Love is indeed all you need.

The owning mind

At some point in the development of children, around two years of age, consciousness and ability develop to the point that the child becomes a person projecting a self onto the world. At this stage the child is not only an agent moving and acting within the world but also knows how to call things by their name. The child is now capable of internalizing images of reality and knows the names that others have internalized for those images so that it is now possible to communicate person to person and to tell stories about things that are not actually present when the conversation is taking place.

My mind to your mind.

It is at this stage, when the "I" extends outwards to encompass surrounding reality and enfold it within its awareness through language, that the child begins to grasp the environment as an extension of the self and as "belonging to the I". The self embraces the world with a sense of ownership that is expressed in such words as "My" and "Mine".

The ability of the self to conceive of things as owned by "me" is a fundamental human ability that is simultaneously accompanied by a recognition that other persons have similar abilities and are also attached to various things that belong to "them".

This encroachment of the ego into reality is also the point where the self first meets the full weight of the "opinions of others", who are often unwilling to

---

erred in his conclusion because the existence of his thought does not attest to his own existence but rather to his enmeshment within the world of others. Were we to amend his famous dictum, we could say: "I think, therefore I have assimilated the concepts of others, and it is now clear to me that I exist as they do" (which also turns the entire setup of Descartes' famous proof into something of a red herring). The very acquisition of the concepts that allowed Descartes to speculate in such grand fashion is a social process that depends on the existence of others.

[5] Ogden, T. H. (2018). *The matrix of the mind: Object relations and the psychoanalytic dialogue*. Routledge, pp.7-8.

acknowledge the purported ownership of two-year-olds who call "mine" on everything that meets their rapacious gaze. This resistance marks out the boundaries between "mine" and "not-mine" for the budding "I".

It is a unique human skill, and a pure product of the mind, to agree that something "belongs" to someone. It is also one of those universals that can be found in all human societies. As summarized by Heine in his comprehensive study of possessive constructions in the languages of the world:

> ... all languages that we came across have conventionalized expressions for possession and, hence, possession is a linguistic phenomenon that might qualify as a universal... Such observations also appear to be supported by indirect evidence, for example, by the widespread occurrence both of linguistic items for 'steal' and of the cross-cultural legal relevance of theft.[6]

Ownership not only throbs within language as the direct ability to point to something and say that it is mine, but also on deeper levels that are embedded in grammatical constructions. As Heine writes:

> It would seem that most of the possessive constructions to be found in the languages of the world can be traced back to a small set of basic conceptual patterns... possession is essentially a conceptual relationship pattern... Seiler[7] defines possession as the relationship between a human being and his kinsmen, his body parts, his material belongings, his cultural and intellectual products'. What distinguishes possession from other relational domains such as location, he observes, is that it is biocultural... it is binary, in that it involves two items, the possessor and the item possessed or, as we will say here, the possessee.[8]

Such conceptual-linguistic definitions are easily comprehensible within the developmental understanding of object relations. The primal linguistic structures of possession arise out of the psychological structures through which the infant recognizes its own existence as a separate self within the world, which give rise to more extensive applications in which the "I" is an active agent and not only a possessor.

The conceptual expansion through which an individual slowly forms an identity and separateness from the surrounding world is accompanied by the extension and projection of identity over possessions, and subsequently the recognition and assignment of possessions to the identities of their owners.

At a later stage, the active agency arising from the self is also perceived as "belonging" to the self, so that actions are viewed as the property of actors – a sense of ownership that is vitally important to all economic activities involving labor – as the laborer-owner can sell the self-owned products of self-owned-actions to others.

This is a form of ownership based on creativity, on what the self generates, which is considered as a possession. Whatever people create belongs to them.

---

[6] Heine, B. (1997). *Possession: Cognitive Sources, Forces, and Grammaticalization.* Cambridge University Press, p. 227.

[7] Seiler, H. (1983). *Possession as an operational dimension of language.* (Language Universals Series, 2.) Tubingen: Gunter Narr, pp. 4-7.

[8] Heine, Ibid, p. xiii, p. 4, p. 1.

In slavery, where the self is considered to belong to another, everything generated by the slave belongs to the master too, yet even in such oppressive circumstances, actions are still affiliated with the actor[9], even though the possessions they accrue are transferred to the master because he owns the "owner" of the actions.

The deeper one delves into linguistic studies, the more it becomes evident that the concepts of possession spread over many areas and constitute a crucial cognitive aspect of human conceptualization: Not only does the baby learn to affiliate itself as belonging to its mother, as "mother's baby", but also its mother as belonging to it: "my mother". The many concepts that teach a young person who he or she is, are associated with parallel ascriptions of possession: "Mother's nose", "Baby's nose".

The relationship between 'to have' and 'to be', which has remained a conundrum for Heine[10], may also be understood through the way in which possession arises and expands from the self. It spreads over reality, symbolizing it and assimilating it. The utterance "I have" and the consciousness of "having", and the public recognition of such possessiveness in such utterances as "he has" or "this is his" – are all human thoughts that envelop reality in a way that transforms it into the human mind and its possessions.

The child increasingly acquires the concepts that actualize the potential for personhood by possessively assimilating things into the self, making them part of the personality.

As the child develops, the distinction between self-mine and others-theirs is gradually clarified, and these ascriptions are critical to understanding one's place in the world: I have an ear just like mother's, but this one belongs to me, and that one belongs to mother. This is mother's smartphone, but that is my teddy bear. Sometimes mother shares her food, and then it is my food.

One's entire understanding of one's presence in the world passes through these possessive insights, which project the personality into the world through these categories of possession, even as these very categories are constructed.

This is why, when words arrive, we find that one of the very first words that are universally uttered by children is one that imposes a person's inner world onto reality: "Mine".

---

[9] John Locke captured this in his treatise on the fundamental rights of man: "Every man has a property in his own person: this nobody has any right to but himself. The labor of his body, and the work of his hands, we may say, are properly his. Whatsoever then he removes out of the state that nature hath provided, and left it in, he hath mixed his labor with, and joined to it something that is his own, and thereby makes it his property... It has by this labor something annexed to it that excludes the common right of other men: for this labor being the unquestionable property of the laborer, no man but he can have a right to what that is once joined to".
Locke, J. (1689). *Second Treatise of Government.*

[10] "Among the phenomena that have been named frequently in connection with universal properties of possession, the use of 'be'-verbs... deserves particular mention. These elements, it is argued, are universally associated with possessive constructions... One may wonder, however, what the significance of this observation may be". Heine, B. (1997). *Possession: Cognitive Sources, Forces, and Grammaticalization.* Cambridge University Press, pp. 227-228.

And yet, property, like money itself, is entirely a symbolic attribute, an idea in the minds of people as to the status of certain things in relation to other people. As Bertram notes:

> Because property plays such an important role in structuring our lives and yet also seems mysterious given that it is not an observable quality of objects, the acquisition, understanding, and use of this concept raises interesting psychological issues. How do people acquire the concept and when? How do they make judgments about who owns what, or about whether a thing can be owned at all? How is property implicated in other social relationships and in conflict?
>
> Children pick up the property concept during the preschool years and even quite young infants display some competence with the idea; acquisition of the concept does not seem to be as a result of explicit teaching; children's deployment of property norms is often not reinforced and sometimes undermined by adults[11], yet their attachment to those norms remains robust…At eighteen months, children have a clear sense of themselves as proprietors of objects, asserting ownership by the use of expressions like "Mine!"
>
> By the age of thirty months verbal information alone can establish the association. At the age of about three, children have started to understand the notion that objects they possess might be shared or exchanged with others, though this understanding is imperfect. By the age of five, children understand and experience possession at a meta-conceptual level. They now factor in what others might feel or think when trading with them…[12]

The phenomenon of possession – as recognized by self and others – lies at the very root of the economic world, and is a product of this development in symbolic thought, which represents the world through language and makes it possible for a child to one day say the word "mine" with the intention of deploying the self over something that is out there in the world, which is now somehow connected to the child's personality.

Possession is the spontaneous language that erupts from the minds of two-year-olds regardless of race, creed or gender. If there is something that goes beyond the structure of language that is wired into us, it is this ability to spread ourselves over whatever exists and say: "mine".

A bit later on, this leads to new insights: to the concept of "not-mine" with its far-reaching implications, and the strange process of transfer of ownership, wherein, if I want something that is "not mine", it can become "mine" if the person who is currently applying a "mine" to it, is willing to give it to me, and the willingness of that person to assign a part of reality that is considered as "his" to me, can make that object become "mine".

The teddy bear belongs to my parents, until they give it to me, at which point, it becomes mine. At a later stage, I may have a teddy bear and you may have a toy

[11] Who demand that they "share" or "give" to others.

[12] Bertram, C. D. I. (2013). *Property in the Moral Life of Human Beings.* Explore Bristol Research, pp. 15-16.

dog, and we can decide to swap a bear for a dog, and then the bear becomes yours and the dog is mine.[13]

Wilson describes the natural "rules" of ownership that spontaneously arise in children:

> Parents also don't teach their two-year-olds the following rules of "mine":
> if I like it, it's mine;
> if I see it, it's mine;
> if it's in my hand, it's mine;
> if it looks like mine, it's mine;
> if I can take it from you, it's mine; and
> if I had it a little while ago, it's mine.[14]

It can be easily seen that this universal appropriation of pieces of the surrounding reality arises directly from an expanded sense of self, wherein the child imposes its own internal consciousness on everything in its grasp and within its visual horizon, and finds those very elements that constitute 'reality' as memories and symbolic representations within its mind.

The teddy bear is not only "out there" but also an array of sensory memories and a symbolic representation. It is called "teddy bear" and it is both outside and real and can be grasped, fondled and smelled at any time, and it is also "in here", in the mind where the memories and representations of the teddy bear are stored, and the word "mine" projects these two aspects of the "teddy bear" into the world by publicly linking it to the self.

When a child says "mine" it does not recognize the property rights of others. Infantile omnipotence spreads its net of ownership to all that can be seen and touched.

This consciousness, so blind to the rights of others, is already on the verge of acquiring a new awareness that will be soon be forcibly instilled: the realization that other people exist and that they too are embedded, like the self, in an inter-

---

[13] And yet, even after such a fair "exchange" of bear for dog, it is entirely possible that the original owner will still feel a sense of affinity with possessions that were once "his". An excellent Biblical example is Jacob's acquisition of Laban's property as wages for his work: "…I have been twenty years in your house; I served you fourteen years for your two daughters, and six years for your flocks." (Genesis 31, 41). The legitimacy of Jacob's ownership is repeatedly emphasized, and his wives too exclaim: "Is there yet any portion or inheritance for us in our father's house? Does he not consider us strangers, for he has sold us and devoured our money. All the riches which God has taken from our father, are ours, and our children's." (Genesis 31, 14-16). And yet, even though Laban ultimately allows Jacob to go on his way, it is quite obvious that his sense of ownership persists, and though Jacob's possessions were legitimately received as wages for his labors, still Laban continues to feel that they are "his": "And Laban answered and said unto Jacob: These daughters are my daughters, and these children are my children, and these flocks are my flocks, and all that you see is mine." (Genesis 31, 43). Another unique "possession" in this regard is that of land as a national heritage, wherein even after a legitimate transfer, members of a nation may still consider a land to be "theirs", e.g. Putin and Crimea. It goes without mention that where possessions were plundered, their owners may never despair of them.

[14] Wilson, B. J. (2021). *Respecting Property takes Two.* https://blog.oup.com/2021/04/respecting-property-takes-two/

subjective world, and that they too have a right to lay claim to elements of reality, so that it becomes entirely possible that something may be "not-mine".

If some other person says "mine" in regard to some object, then the only way to recognize "not-mine" is to acknowledge the existence of that other person. Thus, just as the child's ego reaches out to seize the world, it learns that it is not the only ego around, and as the natural drive to possess is quickly curtailed by others, the child learns its place within the world vis a vis other entities inhabiting inter-subjective space.

The rights of ownership mark the inception of morality. Respect for the possessions of others is the original kernel of the knowledge of right and wrong. It is the catalyst of that inner voice which commands a person to respect the property of others, even when they are not present: the conscience that makes people refrain from stealing, and which marks the thief as a wrongdoer.

The deep social belief that one should respect the property of others lies at the root of all economic activity.[15] Even "gift economies", which seem to lack any "commercial" perspective on property, are still based on ownership. It is the Big Man's disbursement of his possessions that establishes his honor. There is no generosity without ownership, for only a gift of my possessions willingly given can be considered generous.

These thoughts and emotions are universal, they constitute the deep foundation that allows the creation of the abstract world of money, and the pan-human faith in the value of money and its unique ability to detach possessions from one owner and transfer them to another.

The child's shift from omnipotence to civil obedience is the very heart of the acculturation process through which social mores and rules are assimilated into the personality, and give rise to the internalized cultural image carried in the heart of each person: the ideas fostered by individuals as regards what is right and good, as well as what is improper and dangerous. This is the rise of the conscience or in psychoanalytic terms, the "Super-Ego"[16]. This is the image of the interpersonal conception of reality as assimilated by each person, and it is often poised to curtail the desires of the avid Ego, not to mention, the unruly Id.

Learning the rules of ownership involves an inherent measure of violence, as it requires "dispossessing" the omnipotent infant self of its chattels and clipping the stripling wings of avarice through the intervention of persons of power and authority.

---

[15] Depending, of course, on who those "others" are. They must be peers. There is honor among thieves and respect among racists.

[16] It is not by chance that this wondrous interiorization of the minds of others into the self has been called "Super-Ego. Before Freud's translator dreamed up these rather pretentious terms, Freud used simpler language to address the various dimensions of the mind's experience. He talked about the "It", the "I" and the "Over-I". Freud's descriptions of these aspects of the self represent a complex dynamic process, and at the heart of this process, whereby the personality rises from its undifferentiated state by assimilating the human treasure surrounding it, one finds the beliefs that the individual adopts through contact with the human environment, such as the prohibitions associated with the possessions of others, beliefs that endow the individual with the ability to recognize the property of others and ultimately navigate the financial world.

The boundaries of possession and respect for the property of others are enforced by those who block the infant's will, long before prohibitions are assimilated and a conscience motivates an eventually acculturated young being to "willingly" refrain from taking the property of others.

Laws everywhere are brimming with the evidence of the fragility of assimilated prohibitions and of the incessant presence of power and authority to sternly enforce ownership rights, wherever the natural tendency to "possess" erupts and tramples the social boundaries that limit an individual's right to expand without regard to others.

Even when this curtailment process is bundled up with exhortations of love that justify the boundaries through the rights of others, i.e., the idea that self-love should be the model for appropriate social behavior in that one should love the other as "thyself" – still this inherent violence that shadows all acculturation processes continues to hover over all economic activities as the powerful dictate to those under their power where the boundaries of ownership shall be drawn and who shall have the right to "own".

Such dictates of power first come from the parents who secure the possessions of their offspring and are empowered by all human cultures to do as they see fit, while children have no rights of ownership at all.

Where a child's property and its ownership are concerned, parents are the ultimate arbitrators, be they stern moralists who impose chores and a paucity of possessions, or pampering coddlers who shower endless gifts upon their children and chase every infantile whim with a butterfly net.

Either way, it is the parents who set the rules.

At the beginning of their existence on this earth, children are wholly owned by their parents, and in many cultures that have not yet been touched by the joys of childhood and the golden conscientiousness of occidental social services, many people remain owned and subjugated to others throughout their lives.

On the conceptual level, the economic world is more primitive and rigid than the world of words and does not require any love or empathy towards the "other". There is no need for a nuanced understanding and a rich vocabulary in order to participate in economic activities.

Since the concepts of possession such as "mine" or "yours" are so primal and basic, they allow the personality to apply itself to the surrounding world, even without naming things. A pig in a poke can be owned even if you don't know the word for "pig".

If the Super-Ego has a stake in reality, it is in the world of economics: The virtues of honesty and integrity, good faith and reliability are prominent features of all economic activity, just as much as the vices of theft and robbery, fraud and embezzlement, and the laws, judges, cops and jailers that safeguard the former against the latter.

It is because of these inherent moral dimensions of the economic world that the responsibility and meaning of possession-consciousness demand strict boundaries between "mine" and "not-mine".

Wilson emphasizes the unique prohibitions that parents impose on their children in order to teach them to become good citizens:

> Human beings appear to be the only species to *teach* their progeny how *not* to acquire things. "No!" is how all parents teach their children the rules of how to acquire—or *not* acquire—things in the presence of other members of their species. Thou shalt *not* steal. Play nice, Johnny.[17]
> No parent in any age or community lets these untaught rules of "mine" stand unchecked. Every generation of parents teaches their children the rules of how not to acquire something. We… teach children when they are allowed to say, "This is mine," and reciprocally, when someone else can say, "This is mine"—that is, when the child must say "That is yours."[18]

Commencing from a very early age, children acquire the abstract concepts of ownership – an imprint of the mind that instills objects with their affiliation to a specific person who is considered their owner. As Wilson writes:

> Even if a pair of Hello Kitty mittens hanging on a wall hook is identical to a pair lying on the floor, a child distinguishes between the two in such a way as to grab the pair that is "Mine!" regardless of which pair is the closest to them. Property is not the effect of leaving the closer pair of mittens on the floor. Property is not the effect of exclusively using the second pair of mittens on the hook. Property is not resisting the dispossession of the mittens within one's grasp. Property is in the original perception that the two pairs of mittens are distinctly different things in the mind's eye. Property is knowing from experience that one pair of mittens is "mine" and the other is, respectfully, "yours."[19]

The fact that possession is the first law of ownership arises directly from the fact that ownership is always associated with a "person". If a person holds an object, the bodily contact facilitates the expansion of the self over its possessions. This seems to be the source of ownership from the outset: If I hold this in my hand, or if I put it in my mouth, then it is part of my body and therefore belongs to me as a part of my self.

A boy may gradually learn that just as his mother, who is an object of his love, remains internalized within him even in her absence, so this sense of ownership remains with the object even when it is detached from him. In this process, wherein the conceptual-mental world gradually enfolds the actual world into itself, the sense of ownership, of the dominion of "mine" over things in the world is contemporaneous with the sense of belonging and affiliation with beloved inner representations: The inner representation of the outside world makes it possible to conceptualize the world and have it continue to exist in the mind even in its absence.

The sense of ownership, however, provides a layer of association that is not possible where the psychological assimilation of beloved objects is concerned: While the real mother becomes increasingly differentiated from the child, in the case of the

---

[17] Wilson, B. J. (2020). *The Property Species: Mine, Yours, and the Human Mind.* Oxford University Press, p. 11.

[18] Wilson, B. J. (2021). *Respecting Property takes Two*. https://blog.oup.com/2021/04/respecting-property-takes-two/

[19] Wilson, B. J. (2021). *Respecting Property takes Two*. https://blog.oup.com/2021/04/respecting-property-takes-two/

ownership of things that the child considers as "mine", the inner representation of such objects is accompanied by an outside ownership that continues to apply even when the object is removed from the child.

This sets up a unique reciprocity with reality: Just as the self bears the object of its ownership within it, so the object belonging to a person, carries that person's "aura" within it, stamping that object as a possession. Owned objects carry some kind of association with the self even when physically detached from the person.

This nature of objects in the world, wherein they can be exclusively owned and remain "attached" to the self so long the sense of ownership persists, lends them the great importance that Winnicott ascribes to the "transitional object": an object owned by the child onto which the child projects thoughts and feelings.

Just as the child assimilates the objects of his affection and they become part of his inner reality, so he projects himself onto his possessions, so that they bear "the stamp of his personhood" as it were. They hold within them the value he ascribes to them and they are affiliated with him. His personality hovers over them like the proverbial spirit of God over the primordial waters, or dwells within them like a Hindu God within its avatar, and in many cases social recognition awards the owner with communal acknowledgement of his ownership rights.

Owned objects remain owned as long as the owner does not relinquish them. This enduring affiliation is bolstered not only by social acknowledgement of ownership, but also by such measures as contracts and laws.[20]

Moreover, on a deep psychological level, the ability of persons to associate themselves with objects that become "owned" by them provides a remedy for the separation anxiety that arises when a child realizes that his mother is a separate entity.[21] Simultaneously with the psychological detachment from the mother comes also the recognition that certain objects remain personally "owned", even when the mother leaves.

Children soon learn that the entire force of their community can maintain their ownership rights once they are acknowledged. Owned objects remain "ours" in a way that the objects of our love can never be, so that physical possessions provide a panacea for the inevitable psychological wounds associated with the separation from the mother.

This is the source of the great importance of transitional objects that belong to a child without dispute and that others refrain from taking from him. As Winnicott describes it:

> Perhaps some soft object or other type of object has been found and used by the infant, and this then becomes what I am calling a transitional object. This object goes on being important. The parents get to know its value and carry it round when travelling. The mother lets it get dirty and even smelly, knowing that by washing it she introduces a break in conti-

---

[20] The ancient halachic concept of "owner's renunciation" is relevant here, as it evaluates the mental state of a person who has lost an object in order to determine if the owner is still "tied" to the object. According to this principle, a person who despairs of ever finding a lost object, is considered to have "renounced" their ownership so that the object acquires the status of "unowned" and anyone finding it can legitimately take possession of it for himself.

[21] The mother too is the recipient of much the same shock when her infant suddenly becomes a vehement shouter of "no", around about the same time as he begins to call out "mine".

nuity in the infant's experience, a break that may destroy the meaning and value of the object to the infant.[22]

The child expands its personality over tangible objects and thereby preserves something of the omnipotent satisfaction of the newborn at the very beginning of life: Even after we have learned to acknowledge the worlds of others and the rights of others, those very others will maintain our rights to our possessions, and these possessions can never be separated from us, unless we do so ourselves.

It is possible that the personality's expansion over its possessions, an expansion of the self that connects pieces of reality to the person, brings about a certain alleviation of the inevitable pain that any person suffers on experiencing separation and loss.

It may be one of the reasons that matters of ownership are accorded such great importance in all human societies. Theft, embezzlement and piracy are abhorred everywhere because they stab at very deep layers of the owner's psyche when they ravage the foundations of ownership.

The consent of others (those same others, who manage such a great part of the child's life, including the demand to separate from the mother) transforms the self's appropriation of possessions into a legitimate moral claim.[23]

There is much in this recognition, in this possessive certitude, that the self finds deeply alluring, thereby giving rise to such well-known epithets as "A lover of money will never have enough of it" (Ecclesiastes 5:10) and leading to the willingness of people to put their lives at risk in order to protect their property from thieves and muggers.

If possessions soothe some of the primordial separation anxiety that is part of the human psyche, then whosoever attempts to dispossess you arouses that anxiety by taking something that is enfolded within your core. Possessions are possessed by the symbolic expansion of the personality of their owner, so that whoever steals them is assaulting the very self.

This strong and intimate attachment of people to their possessions is probably also the reason for the almost universal aversion of religions and spiritual movements towards them. Be they the great creeds originating from India in which disengagement from possessions is an important and crucial step in the journey of any acolyte striving to sever the bonds of attachment; or a Christian striving to avoid the fate of the rich, of whom it is said that: "it is easier for a camel to go through the eye of a needle, than for a rich man to enter into the kingdom of God"[24] or a Jew, who is enjoined to eat bread with salt, drink water sparingly, sleep on the ground and embrace a life of privation.[25]

The love of possessions has been a stumbling block on the ascetic path of the religions. They all share the common belief that life is but a prelude to the next

[22] Winnicott, D.W. (2005). *Playing and Reality*. Routledge Classics, p.5.

[23] And how horrific were the millennia during which slavery was considered legitimate and people could lay moral claim to other people.

[24] Matthew 19:24

[25] Mishna Avot 6:4

world or next incarnation and that "he who hastens to enrich himself will not go unpunished."[26]

Religions, which demand attachments to loftier things and for which the love of possessions is a dire distraction, have long opposed these psychological elements of ownership and the deep ties between a personality and its belongings, but these are the very bedrock of economic life and its focus on the exchange of possessions between persons.

And yet, within economic life itself, in view of this obviously deep and innate psychological attachment of people to their possessions, how is it even possible to exchange possessions? To let go of them? To break that attachment?

How is generosity possible? How is trade possible?

Gratitude and the Sense of Obligation

When the acknowledged owner of a possession gives it to another as a generous gift, such generosity immediately gives rise to both an inner ambition and a social injunction to reciprocate: to repay kindness with kindness.

This may be one of the most essential values of all: that one good turn deserves another, and evil doers deserve revenge. The obligation of a person who receives a favor to reciprocate underlies the moral demands posited by many civilizations.

The relationship created between benefactor and beneficiary is characterized by a deep obligation on the part of the recipient to return the favor received, and a "legitimate" expectation on the part of the creditor to receive reciprocation, and both parties are enmeshed in social expectations to behave accordingly.

A good example of this strong tendency to reciprocity can be found in the famous Chinese web of obligations known as Guanxi, which involves, among many nuanced behaviors, the distribution of hundreds of carefully wrapped gifts to all relatives and acquaintances, business partners and government officials who will repay this good turn in the future.

The Guanxi tradition creates a system of mutual acts of regard bound by meticulously strict rules as to who owes what to whom. According to the reports of persons enmeshed in such systems they impose enormous obligations and exacting expectations for reciprocation, and can be very stressful for those who strive to live up their standards, especially if they fall short. Many Chinese people find themselves in a constant race of repaying favors so as to avoid both public and personal shame.

Guanxi networks are a paragon of how an entire civilization can deeply hone and perfect gratitude and obligation as a central social vehicle that regulates all relationships: reciprocal favors are the central element that holds the Guanxi networks of individuals together, and non-reciprocation constitutes an unforgivable transgression. Everyone is caught in an infinite circle of mutual favors that involves such concepts as loyalty, devotion, mutuality and trust, but also breeds patronage, corruption, cronyism and the distribution of benefits to insiders.

The greatest anger is reserved for peers who do not return favors received, and all cultures have some form of the Biblical verse: "the wicked borrow and do not pay back".[27]

---

[26] Proverbs 28:20

[27] Psalms 37:21

The receipt of a "favor" creates a fundamental imbalance between parties and the receiving party is at a moral disadvantage vis a vis the giving party.

Any exchange of possessions is based on a deep recognition that each of the parties can legitimately attest in regard to his possession that "it is mine". Every economic transaction is based on the recognition of an "other" who "like me" has the right and the ability to extend his personality into the world in such a manner that certain things become his possessions, and once they are his possessions, he is entitled to do with them as he wills. Just as he can move his own hand at will, so he is entitled to use his possessions as he sees fit.

Even though they may not be attached to the owner's body, possessions are still connected to the owner in both his own consciousness and the minds of others who recognize this attachment. Thus, when two people are facing each other in an economic transaction, each inevitably must recognize the personhood of the other and that the other is also a subjective being that has ownership and property rights. Only then, can said other also decide to alienate and transfer his possessions.

Just as society recognizes the right of the parties to own possessions, so society also recognizes their right to alienate themselves from their possessions. This ability to say "this is no longer my possession, I am giving it to you and it is now your possession" is the foundation of all economic activity, even though it is but a shift within the awareness of a person who decides that his self is no longer affiliated with a certain object and that this object can now be affiliated with another person.[28] This act of alienation depends on the public consent of the original owner to give his possession to another and to withdraw from its ownership.

Such is the power of language that is suffices to say "I no longer want this" for a possession to be severed from its owner, whether it be given as a gift, or in exchange for another possession, or simply tossed away into a trash pile.

It is the personal action of a person renouncing a possession that breaks the tie.

Determining value

In order to detach and re-attach of ownership, an exchange must be acceptable to both parties. This is where the **value** of possessions becomes crucial. When a possession is released in reciprocation for another possession, the transaction involves two parties who are relinquishing their ownership simultaneously in favor of a particular recipient, a beneficiary, while receiving a return favor at the same time.

The release of ownership, the giving of the released possession to a beneficiary/recipient, and the reciprocal receipt of a comparable favor, all take place at the same time, and before a favor may be reciprocated, both parties must agree on its value.

How much is a piece of cake given by Donald to Ronald worth?

There is no definite answer to this question as the value of a cake can fluctuate from one person to another and according to different circumstances. If it is a time of famine, such a piece of cake may be of great value indeed, but if it is a dessert after a sumptuous meal, its value may not be so exorbitant.

28

The status of the parties also impacts the value. Is Donald a pastry chef who often gives away his cakes before their expiration date, or is he someone who has never baked a cake in his life, and has made a special effort for you?

Is the recipient hungry? Or perhaps he cannot enjoy the cake at all because of his diabetes but accepts your favor because he fears that turning it down may be construed as a slight?

An endless number of parameters determine the value of the cake for the giver and the recipient, and both parties have to agree on that value before it becomes possible to reciprocate, as each of them must know the value received so that the value required for reciprocation may also be known.[29]

While the objects being exchanged have visible forms, value, like ownership itself, is a figment of the mind. Forms become enmeshed within human minds through the fact that they are both owned and valued, so owners not only own visible forms but also the invisible value contained within them.

Of crucial importance here is that while the form is publicly visible, the value is not. It is in the mind of the owner, and just like ownership must be publicly acknowledged in order to be legitimized. Value must become a public 'price" before the parties can negotiate the exchange.

But how is value ascribed to possessions?

Value is projected onto possessions by the minds of people. While possessions can take any form, the value is instilled into the form in a way that echoes the ancient concept of an "indwelling spirit' prevalent in human religions.

Animistic beliefs that ascribe an "anima" to objects are considered to be the most ancient of human beliefs and may be understood as an extrapolation of the psychological faculties that allow us to recognize the presence of other people has having selves: Just as "I" have a self, and others cannot see that spirit within me, so others too, including objects, have an invisible spirit within them that is invisible to me.

In ancestor worship, the spirits of venerable ancestors are believed to reside in special places created for them within homes, and many polytheistic Hindus believe that the spirits of gods come to reside in their representative statues when a proper offering is made[30].

As far as economic exchanges between owners are concerned, the belief in some invisible quality that only the human mind can perceive is not limited to religion but is also a part of routine economic transactions that ascribe an indwelling value to forms. Value is an ephemeral quantity that only the human mind can recognize.

It is a certain quantity of the something that is being valued, something held within the visible form that is being offered in exchange for a favor. Value is both a personal matter, as owners estimate the value of their possessions, but it is also impacted by the public matter of "price", as people can agree on the worth of something, and the individual is frequently quite impotent when faced with pressures that dictate prices that are at odds with his own evaluation.

---

[29] In modern economies, significant monetary favors are given under contractual stipulations and the application of compound interest that create an imbalance between present and future in the reciprocation of the favor.

[30] Puja, the loving offering of light, flowers, and water or food to the divine, is the essential ritual of Hinduism. https://en.wikipedia.org/wiki/Puja_(Hinduism)

Value residing in forms is measured by numbers, which are the key to the abstraction of forms, as by their very nature, numbers themselves are attached to forms while transcending them: Just as one may count any form, such as three oranges, apples or balloons, so too one can value any form, and that value transcends the form.

The specific form holding value is secondary to the number denoting the value residing within it. The form can be abstracted and the "resident" number can incarnate from one form to another: A banana, an orange and a five-dollar bill – all valued at 5.

The inter-subjectively agreed on "price" differs from the "value" ascribed by an individual, and there is constant interference between the price appraised by others and the value appraised by the self, although the appraisal of others frequently trumps self-appraisal.

Schematically, the evaluation of possessions, may be described as follows:

What you see	What you believe	What you argue over
Form	Value	Price
Objective	Subjective	Intersubjective

Table 1: Form, Value and Price

The abstract numerical idea of money, which appraises the value-price of things, is intimately connected with the constant interaction between self and others: value changes according to price as people become aware of prices and often accept them as guidelines to the values residing in their owned forms. When many people ascribe a value that differs from the one set by the owner, the majority determines the price.

All money consists of an outside form, the ***objective*** form perceived by the senses, an inner ***subjective*** value, which dwells within the form as intangibly as spirit dwells within body, and an ***intersubjective*** price negotiated in the marketplace.

Prices are also fluctuating since they are subject to interpersonal interference between people who are trying to equalize price and value. The price is the essential bridge between the outside form and the inner value. When money is used, the price is what the seller demands in terms of the quantity of the symbolic forms of currency that are supposed to equal the value that he ascribes to the form in his possession.

Rising prices may cause owners of forms to increase their estimation of them, and when the prices of forms decrease, they may force owners to relinquish their possession of forms holding value in exchange for forms that do not properly reflect that value, such as when hungry people pawn their prized possessions.

Price is the point at which the subjective estimation of the value residing in a form meets the judgement of inter-subjectivity, wherein each subjective personality also ascribes a value to the form so that the price ultimately reflects an interpersonal belief that bridges the gap between self and others.

How is price agreed on? How does one arrive at the point where the values equalize in the minds of the buyer and the seller and the parties are willing to exchange ownership?

This point of equilibrium is subject to many forces – from supply and demand to conspicuous consumption, from speculative fervor to market fear indices, from refusal to sell at any price to the winning of competitive tenders and from business cartels to anti-trust regulation.

The most salient factor in all financial transactions is that when the point of equilibrium is reached and the seller and buyer are ready to exchange their respective forms, it is a point in ***time***. The price is the number on which both parties agree at the ***moment of ownership transfer***.

Yet even at that fleeting moment in time when an exchange is made, the money form actually represents the future and capitalizes on the future. It is **a promise of repayment in the future that serves as payment in the present.** All monetary transactions transfer present ownership of a form in exchange for a form that is a promise of a future benefit. That is the central difference between a "barter" economy, in which both parties receive immediate tangible benefits in the form of commodities, and a "money" economy, in which one side of the transaction is a mere promise to render future benefits and services.

And while any commodity can be raised to the role of money, such as cigarettes and chocolate among prisoners of war, money always transcends commodities because it holds a promise for a future benefit.

The price is the aspect that allows the interplay between beliefs regarding present value and expectations of future value. The price is what capitalizes future value in the present. On the part of the seller, the price asked by the form's owner reflects that owner's subjective evaluation of its indwelling value, while on the part of the buyer, the price is what a potential owner, i.e., the buyer, must pay in order to obtain ownership of the form. Both buyer and seller do not only look inwards to their own estimations of value and convictions of desire but also outwards to the many pricing opinions, theories and traditions interspersed throughout intersubjective space, striving to find a middle ground between subjective evaluation and public opinion.

Let's go back to the banana transaction that we used to illustrate the transfer of ownership and examine it from the point of view of value and price.

Donald is the proud owner of a banana and estimates its value as 10, and here comes Ronald holding a coin bearing the number 10.

A denomination of 10 does not indicate a value of 10, but only a monetary form marked as 10. Should this currency be devalued, it is entirely possible that Donald would disagree that a coin denominated as 10 holds equal value to his banana.

Where money is concerned, the number itself is the form, and this is the reason that it is so easy to change the mode of presentation from metals to paper, from cash to card to digital forms, and more. The number is the form rather than the material bearing it, and it is the subjective eye beholding the number that ascribes value to it.

All three aspects of **form**, **value** and **price** are expressed in the transaction. On the part of the seller, the owned **form** is a banana, with a subjectively estimated **value** of 10 and a publicly stated **price** of 10. The public statement of price is separate from the inner value in that it takes many elements into account. It is entirely possible, for example, that the value of the inputs invested in the cultivation of the banana is only 2, but the banana owner estimates the value of his efforts as 8. It is also possible that the banana owner looks around him and sees that sellers of similar bananas are asking for 10, so he realizes that he won't be able to get more than 10, even if he subjectively estimates the value as 12. The owner may also sniff market trends and understand that he can get away with a far higher price than the value that he estimates, so the value of the banana goes up in his estimation.

The external public price is subject to the vagaries of many external pressures and a great deal of bitterness has been expressed by produce growers who found the price of their forms dictated by exchanges, as described by Banner:

> Between the man who produces food today and the man who consumes the food, operates a long and complicated system of buying and selling which has nothing to do with real service to either of these primarily interested parties. The Farmer's Guide cited a local example: "a carload of Indiana eggs sold to a New York wholesaler at 24 ½ cents a dozen, was resold nine times without leaving the cold storage warehouse, until the St. Regis hotel paid 43 cents a dozen for the lot.[31]

This gap between the value and the price is the very difference that all capital markets are involved in, and a great deal of money changes hands not only when actual gaps are found, as in crashing markets, but also in the fervently imaginative search for future gaps.

The gap between value and price becomes especially salient when the level of inflation becomes tangible, and people realize that the value of a coin marked 10 is no longer ten – even if they have been holding that very same coin for a long time and they want to ascribe the same value to it – simply because the monetary form of 10 no longer holds that value in this particular faith community, despite bearing the same name and denomination.

From the point of view of social obligations, the 1st party does the 2nd party a favor and awards it with one of the benefits in its possession, while the 2nd party reciprocates with a benefit of equal value from its own possessions. They exchange mutual favors and each become the owner of the form that was previously held by the other, but both remain, as they were, the owners of the same value.

Forms are exchanged while values are retained.

The value of any economic transaction is retained equally by both parties.[32]

Let's take a baker[33] as an example. By investing time and effort, the baker creates loaves, each of which now tangibly embodies value that is owned by the baker.

If the baker were to eat the bread himself, the forms would be gone along with their value, but were he to sell the loaves, he would retain the value, which would now be embodied within the symbolic forms of money, while the loaves would be

---

[31] Banner, S. (2017). *Speculation: a history of the fine line between gambling and investing*. Oxford University Press, p.115.

[32] One of the great distortions of prevailing economic practice, with many destructive consequences, is the failure of the GAAP in general and of double-entry bookkeeping ("DEBK") in particular, to account for this win-win situation. Instead, DEBK prefers to offset the values against each other, so that instead of an outcome of 2 wherein each party retain 1 unit of value, the GAAP outcome is 0. What the GAAP conceal is a transaction in which both parties are pleased to retain the very value they had from the outset, while gaining a new form they covet. No tit for tat obligations were incurred, and both parties have squared off. Each got what the other got and equivalence has been achieved.

[33] An imaginary baker, for now that we have highly roboticized and computerized baking conglomerates, the idea of a human laborer as the owner of the value inherent in a loaf of bread becomes problematic. Who actually owns the bread? Shareholders? A lending bank?

transferred to buyers, who are now placed in the original position of the baker, as they can either consume them or sell them on, thereby creating additional copies of the value originally created by the baker.

Once sold, the value originally generated by the tangible forms of the loaves is transferred into the symbolic forms of money, and may now be replicated further in other forms and transferred, stored or replicated without limit.

Say you have 10 units of whatever currency is trusted in your environment, and the price posted for the bread is also 10. This means that in that point in time, the value in your 10 units of currency is equal to the value of the loaf you want to buy. When you exchange your monetary form for the bread form, you retain the original value of 10, but you now have it embedded in the form of a loaf, while the baker-seller also retains the original value of 10, but it is now held in the symbolic form of money.

Once you eat the bread, and the value will be gone, absorbed into you.[34]

However, until the point of consumption is reached and it is ultimately removed from the world, the bread form may generate additional value, for every time it is sold its value is replicated. Every transaction creates another copy of the bread's value onto a monetary form.

The person who bought the loaf from the baker may extend the chain further by cutting up the loaf and selling individual slices to the poor who can't afford a whole loaf. Say the loaf was bought for 10 units, and its new owner cuts it into 20 slices, which he sells for the "low" price of 1 unit each. Even people who don't have 10 units to buy an entire loaf can manage to somehow scrape together enough money to buy a slice or two. The buyer turned seller thus gains 20 units of value from the same loaf of bread.

In regular bookkeeping parlance we can say that the bread-slice seller has made a profit of 10 units, because he paid 10 units for the original bread, but the product has in fact released 30 units of value now copied onto money, for the 10 units paid to the original baker and the additional 20 units paid to the slice-selling entrepreneur all continue to exist in the world long after the bellies of the poor have digested their meager fare.

This "released" value, may even be greater if the baker sells it first to a wholesaler who will add to its price before he sells it to a retailer, who will again add to its price, thereby increasing the value eventually stored in monetary forms.

Even though the loaf has been consumed, the monetary form encasing its original value persists beyond the consumption of the bread. There may undoubtedly be owned forms in the world that incorporate the value replicated from ancient loaves sold by ancient bakers who passed on the value extracted from their loaves to posterity in durable forms.

In this sense, money is essentially **value freed from its connection to tangible reality** in a way that allows it to be reused, pooled, collected, transferred and more.

---

[34] A more pedantic accounting could perhaps be made of the life sustaining value of the caloric content thus obtained, but if you are unemployed or have nothing to sell, then, according to prevalent economic doctrine, the value of your life becomes economically "worthless", so that the value of the bread is completely removed.

It is very difficult to destroy value once it has been successfully embodied in a symbolic vessel: it can be given away, it can be gambled away, it can be stolen, or lost in some transaction, and more, but in all of these scenarios, the value itself is not lost, it only exchanges owners.

Once it has been extracted from the tangible world in which loaves are baked and consumed and transferred into the symbolic world of money, value will persist in its existence so long as the faith of the community continues to support it.

The inner values on both sides of a transaction are only equalized at a specific point in time and this equality is fleeting. The form in one's possession can lose or gain value at any time. The values of loaves and currencies fluctuate constantly, and the only thing that remains stable is the ownership of a value containing form.

So long as you are holding a form, be it a loaf or a banknote, its value may go up and down but your ownership remains stable. You can do with your form as you will.

The symbolic currency forms are provided in a range of denominations that facilitate the equalization of the agreed value at the moment of exchange, when the ownership of forms is switched.

Although it is customary to call the owner with the monetary form "the buyer" and the other owner, "the seller", these terms are misleading because both parties have a form containing value that they wish to exchange. If one party owns a banana and the other party owns a monetary form denominated as 10, the first party wishes to "buy" the banana, and the second party wishes to buy the monetary form denominated as "10", to the same extent as they both wish to "sell" their forms. The exchange is symmetrical.

Table 2 summarizes the conservation of ownership of value while forms are exchanged.

Before		Transaction	After	
John owns a form (a banana) with an inner value of 10	Jane owns a form (a banknote) with an inner value of 10	The parties agree on a price of 10	John owns a form (a banknote) with an inner value of 10	Jane owns a form (a banana) with an inner value of 10
Ownership of 10 is retained throughout				

Table 2: Conservation of Value Ownership

The above table demonstrates how ownership is the root of all money.[35] Money represents ownership copied onto an abstract form that society recognizes as retaining ownership: It is a belief in ownership reified in a currency upheld by an entire community of believers.

So long as a community believes in the power of its currency forms to retain ownership of value, the owners of the currency forms can easily exchange them for other forms that retain equal value. Whether such value is embedded in commodities

[35] This may be one of the reasons that economic thought is so often obsessed with the idea of self-interest. It is the dominion of a self over value that underlies all commercial activities; the concept of something that is "mine" and not "yours", which I, having dominion over it, can transfer to you.

or in labor, in tangible or intangible forms, value is always the property of an owner clothed in some external form.

Currencies are unique in that they transcend the origins of human ownership as an extension of the self and become an extension of intersubjectivity. If what makes a form “mine” is an awareness of the self within the social context of others, then money is a shared awareness that value can be transferred and assigned from one owner to another in a way that preserves the value in a form that is intended from the outset for a future exchange with other forms.

Rent is a unique innovation of the human mind, wherein ownership as an extension of the self, replaces the self so that instead of usage of the exertions of the self itself, as in labor, the extended self now offers usage of its owned forms, without the self being involved in such usage beyond the fact of ownership.

Through the consensus that the property of others is sacrosanct, ownership itself requires people to pay for the use of forms that are owned by others. Amazingly, no toil or sweat are required. The acknowledged, ownership of a form, made possible by the firm belief of a community in the extension of a person to possessions, is sufficient to create a “usage” form, to be exchanged for monetary forms.

Where the classic capitalist use-case of an industrial plant is concerned, ownership is the core engine driving it all: The “capitalist” only has ownership. He owns the machines, but does not operate them, he owns the products but does not produce them, and he ultimately owns the symbolic values generated by all this in the form of “profits”.

Thus, not labor[36], which is the toiling of the self, but pure ownership, an extension of the self, lies at the core of capitalist value production, and that ownership is sustained by public consent.

In modern versions of capitalism the fact that ownership is the engine of all financial transactions becomes increasingly evident: There is no tangible “possession” of the various instruments of debt that constitute the financial world, and the ownership of one financial instrument is often hedged against another, so that one finds ownership of disembodied “profit” and “loss” that have never had any association with anything tangible.

One can discern the centrality of ownership and the insignificance of possession in every routine transaction at a grocery store. Even when a customer is holding the products in his hands, and places them one by one on the conveyer belt at the point of sale, they are not considered to be his. Nor are they considered to be owned by him after passing each and every item through a barcode scanner, nor are they his even as he places them one by one in his own bags.

Their ownership is only considered transferred after their price has been accepted as the value inherent in their forms and an exchange was made with an equal value embedded in monetary forms.

The groceries are only considered owned by the customer when the printer spews the official receipt testifying that the value of the grocery forms has been fully reciprocated with equal value in a monetary form.

---

[36] In fact, the only reason that labor produces value is that the laborer retains natural ownership of his labors.

The receipt itself is a legal document that reflects the communal consensus acknowledging the exchange of ownership. Only when it is issued is the ownership of the grocery items believed to have shifted to the person acquiring the tangible forms and the party dispensing the groceries is now considered to be the owner of the monetary forms incorporating value equal to the prices specified on the items.

The physical possession of the items is completely subsumed in their abstract ownership – and should the customer fail to reciprocate – should his card be declined or his pockets turn out to be empty, the items will be taken out of his bags and returned to the shelves, since they were never his, even though he physically handled them.[37]

Price and Inter-subjective Space

The interaction between the elements of the fundamental triad of Value, Form, and Price determines the point at which ownership of a form is relinquished and acquired.[38] After each party goes off with its own form and value – the price no longer plays a part – it is only relevant at the moment of transaction, and as a point of reference in subsequent ownership narratives such as: "I bought this fantastic hat at a garden sale, and it only cost me 10!"

Prices are produced in the interference zone between the subjective and the objective. They constitute an argument between believers over the shape of reality. They are the hope of gamblers and speculators, and the despair of slumps, recessions and busts. They are the mirages of inflationary economies and the unreachables of deflationary ones.

Pricing is ever a social action and always dependent on the minds of others. Often, it is impacted by such considerations as prestige and envy, and often exploitative of the fundamental ignorance of the individual, who does not know if the price is 'right', and can only look to others for direction.

In facing the world of others, the individual puts a "mask" on the value, which is the price. The price tells others what the individual purports the value to be. It defines for others the quantity of currency forms required to equal the price of the form available for ownership transfer.

Even though the price is an external expression of value, it is often taken by people at face value as the value. The denominations of currency forms (when they are being used as the "quote" currency to "fill" the price) parallel the "price" so that

[37] Is entirely possible that such an eventuality may be accompanied by more than a modicum of shaming, because of the taint of theft hovering over one who had "bagged" products that did not belong to him, and it has become evident in retrospect that he does not have the means to legitimately acquire them.

[38] In this we depart from the common definition of money as a "means of exchange", for money is not used to exchange but rather to copy value from one medium to another, wherein the critical dimension of the uprooting and transfer of ownership is also present. The two additional features commonly attributed to money, "unit of account" and "store of value" flow directly from the dynamics of form, value and price: the accounting is a number that reflects the price, making it possible to "copy" it to a corresponding number denominated in monetary forms, and the store of value is the owned value-preserving essence of money rather than a separate quality.

value expressed in price is exchanged for value expressed in denominated currencies.[39]

Just as the personhood of an individual is opaque to others and represents itself to them in certain ways, so value too is opaque and represented in price. This makes prices subject to the vicissitudes of representation, especially the difficulties involved in gauging the authenticity of others. People are constantly striving to divine "true" motives and "true" values[40].

Individuals may use prices to determine their beliefs about value, conflating value with price, such as in the case of brands or conspicuous consumption, where the high price constructs the value, or in the case of common staples in regard to which "everyone" knows the price.

Maxwell describes four widely accepted approaches to price, all of which are contingent on intersubjective consensus:

> **Competitive-based pricing:** Basing price on competitors' prices (also called *market-based pricing*).
> **Cost-based pricing:** Basing price on costs plus profit (also called *cost-plus pricing*).
> **Customer-based pricing:** Basing price on what a customer is willing to pay (also called *demand-based, value-based, dynamic,* or *yield pricing*).
> **Custom-based pricing:** Basing price on what is traditional in an industry.[41]

It can be seen that "reasonableness", i.e., a good argument to convince the payer that the price is "right", is crucial in getting people to accept the price. All of the various forms of pricing are based on such arguments.

Competitive based pricing is limited to markets that already exist in which there is more than one supplier of a certain commodity. This type of pricing means that both sellers and buyers constantly survey the behavior of others and adjust their prices according to what others do.

Cost based pricing is the most prevalent in classical economics, and is in fact based on a fairness argument: If one invests such and such, one should at least get the investment in return plus something for one's trouble, so that the price is contingent that "something extra", on which people must agree.

However, this argument is always subject to much contention around the question of how much a person should earn? Subsistence? Comfort? Wealth? Unjust enrichment? The "cost" side is also obscure: What is included in cost? Just the financial costs? Or also the ecological and social costs as in full-cost accounting, triple bottom line accounting or sustainability accounting. Again, it is consensus that drives both accounting and price.

---

[39] Such terms as value, worth, price, etc. are often conflated, thereby making it difficult to distinguish between inner "value" and external "price".

[40] Just as they frequently resolve this problem of reliability by relying on the opinions of trusted others and figures of authority.

[41] Maxwell, S. (2008).*The price is wrong : understanding what makes a price seem fair and the true cost of unfair pricing*. Wiley & Sons, p. 178.

Customer based pricing is based on the simple equation of "have money will buy" and is a path that leads to inflation: the more money flooding the market the higher the prices, as prices expand to absorb as many currency forms as possible.

Custom-based pricing is the classic pretext of "this is how it is done" which seems to be a sub-category of what the buyer is willing to pay, except that in this case the buyer justifies what he is willing to pay by pointing to custom. On the seller side, this type of pricing can enforce price stability against various market forces, as the seller sticks to the customary price even when greater profits can be made. From this point of view, adhering to custom may also be perceived as demonstrating virtue, as in the Talmudic story of Rav Safra explicating the verse "He that walketh uprightly, and worketh righteousness, and speaketh the truth in his heart": [42]

> Rav Safra had a donkey for sale.
>
> A man came along and asked him how much he wants for it, but Rav Safra had just reached a passage in his devotions where he was prohibited from speaking.
>
> The man asked: will you sell it to me at such and such a price?
>
> Rav Safra did not respond.
>
> The man thought that Rav Safra was unwilling to sell at this price and offered a higher price.
>
> Rav Safra did not respond.
>
> When he finished praying and could speak again, Rav Safra said to the man: "I had already decided in my heart to sell you the donkey for the first price you mentioned. I will not charge you more."[43]

A distinctly contra-inflationary position, which also undermines the accepted economic dogma of rational self-interest.

Imagined Pricing – Real Consequences

Prices behave very differently when one leaves the terra firma of the lives of men and floats up into the higher reaches of the realms of affluence, which are populated by the great imagined prices of the rich: all you have to do is believe.

In the stratosphere of affluence, a house appreciates by 100,000 Euro since it was bought four years ago. It's just standing there, the house, but in the minds of affluent others it is undergoing the mighty magic of price appreciation.

The property has not moved or changed.

It just is.

It has not even been bought or sold. All that has changed is the minds of the people.

The obverse is also true: When people no longer appreciate a property, its price dwindles and wanes. Hundreds of villages have disappeared from the Bulgarian hinterland through depopulation. Properties stand empty, of no worth to anyone.

Where have all the people gone?

Gone to nice flats in Berlin.

If a "market" is led to believe that prices are higher, then they are higher. People will insist on the higher price when selling, and if they can't get the price they will

---

[42] *Psalms* 15:2 KJV.

[43] TB Tractate of *Bava Batra* 88a.

refrain from selling, until someone despairs and sells for a lower price, at which point a rumor of lowered prices may spread.

It is only when you want to actually use money in a transaction that things become problematic. It is at this point that symbolic belief interacts with reality. So long as the money is only on the books, you can be as rich as Croesus, but when you come to spend it, then the market prices will determine the value of your money, its buying power.

CHAPTER 2: THE ROOTS OF MONEY

Even though monetary forms obey the tripartite rules of form-value-price like any tangible form, they have certain unique characteristics produced by thousands of years of evolution, which began with the "neolithic" or "agricultural" revolution, when many people stopped moving about the earth in small groups of hunters and gatherers and began to establish permanent settlements around agricultural enterprises.

There is an interesting and rather sharp divide separating the hunting-gathering that characterized human existence for most of the past, as humans relied on the benevolence of nature[44], and the civilization that is the cradle of our own, in which humans dominate nature and domesticate natural beings according to their needs. This revolution did not take place so long ago. It appeared throughout the world no more than about 12,000 years ago.

This is the stage at which humans emerged from a state in which we merely picked the fruit within the terrestrial garden and began to toil with the sweat of our brows in order to coax the earth to stop bringing forth thorns and thistles, and yield instead the bountiful crops that have allowed the population of earth to expand from hundreds of thousands to the current billions.

According to available archaeological findings, this revolution involved the first cultivation of various wild strains of grains, and the same phenomenon occurred in diverse places all over the world. The targets of domestication were different in every place: In the fertile crescent we find such well-known cereals as wheat and barley, in China they tamed rice and millet, while in Mexico it was all kinds of gourds and the ancient ancestors of maize.

This is the critical revolution that established the patterns of human life that persist to this day, by allowing people to congregate in large permanent habitats and benefit from cooperative enterprise, as well as the ground-shaking ability to accumulate surplus possessions, yielding a great plentitude of goods that could sustain an increasing number of people and a growing complexity of permanent habitats.

This was undoubtedly the time in which economic relations began to prevail, as the earth, which in the past was but a range for wanderings and gatherings, attained new significance as the basis for permanent settlements and cultivation of orderly crops. All of a sudden, there was no better benefit than holding onto a piece of land where one could build one's home and grow some crops. Particularly important in the context of the development of money as a form of promise was the fact that every bit of land represented the potential for generating the future benefits of its produce.

Great shifts in the social structure of human societies followed the advent of agriculture and especially the appearance of power structures, in which owners at the top of the social pyramid utilized the toil of many people to create a surplus that could be traded with fellow owners.

---

[44] In fact, this state can be estimated as extending over millions of years, if one takes into account all the hominids that subsisted in undomesticated nature before the advent of homo sapiens.

The most valued possessions became the land and the manpower to cultivate it, both owned by the powerful, and both capable of producing future benefits, which though yet unknown could nevertheless be estimated on the basis of past experience and future hopes.

In agriculture, produce arrives a long time after the investment and is dependent not only on a great deal of patience and toil but also on a bit of luck, so that augury, prophecy and sacrifices to the gods became a significant part of human existence everywhere.

Certain crops must be sown and reaped at known times, so the seasons became regularly repeated self-fulfilling prophecies. The future begins to be inscribed in consciousness as something that can be foreseen with some level of certitude, even if at the present moment it only exists in the minds of the people waiting for its fulfillment.

Once people stopped wandering around in the wild, and began raising crops and husbanding animals, the ability to foresee with some assurance what we will eat tomorrow was bolstered. If you were raising wheat and sheep, you would probably be eating bread, cheese and mutton. Most importantly, yields could be foreseen and promised to others as a future benefit.

Yet the needs of expectant folk are many, and even as their eyes are raised to the future, there is no respite from necessity. Even though one is looking forward to receive a great benefit from a field of wheat that has been carefully tilled, sown, irrigated and weeded, and even if all goes well and the future bounty is plentiful, still at the present moment the earth has merely swallowed up the seed and there is nothing to be had.

So, people began to promise future produce to those who had surplus they could share in the present. Thus were the first loans made: favors were given on credit, trusting that they will be repaid, and the first inscriptions of the future reciprocation began to appear.

Such a forward-looking transaction is quite revolutionary in that the bestower of the favor is willing to accept a mere "promise" to reciprocate one day, and the main feature of that "promise" is that it is not given on a mere handshake, but is inscribed and documented in a way that preserves it as a tangible form that bears the promise with it.

The oldest forms of such promises were found in spherical clay envelopes that were discovered in some of the most ancient neolithic sites – right at the very beginning of human agriculture.

These envelopes contained tokens that documented each owed good in its own right: "To create a record that represented 'two sheep', two tokens each representing one unit [i.e., one sheep] were used".[45]

Significant efforts were made to preserve these tokens in the best and most precise way:

> To ensure that tokens were not lost or altered in their type or quantity, they were placed into clay envelopes shaped like hollow balls known as bullae. Ownership and witness seals were impressed on bullae surfaces,

[45] https://en.wikipedia.org/wiki/History_of_ancient_numeral_systems#Clay_tokens.

> which might also be left plain. If tokens needed to be verified after the bulla containing them was sealed, the bulla had to be broken open.[46]

This was the most ancient form – before writing – of tangible promissory notes. The shape of each token represented a tangible form, such as a ball shape for a sheep, or a conical shape for a phial of oil. The number of tokens was equal to the number of promised forms, and the tokens were placed together in a clay ball that sealed them until repayment day, at which time these clay envelopes were smashed and thrown away – very similar to the custom that prevailed after paper was invented – to rip up a promissory note once it had been paid.

This is the reason for the mysterious concentration of clay ball fragments in trash areas and their greater numbers during the times of harvest – when people would repay their debts.

This practice of tokens wrapped up in clay envelopes subsequently led to a critical intermediate step on the way to the invention of writing:

> Tokens began being pressed into a bulla's outer surface before being sealed inside, presumably to avoid the need to break open the bulla to see them. This process created external impressions on bullae surfaces that corresponded to the enclosed tokens in their sizes, shapes, and quantities.[47]

Economic transactions began assuming strange shapes in which symbolic forms became intertwined with tangible ones: Give me this benefit now, and when I gather my crops, I will return the favor. In order to make my promise clear and tangible for both of us, please accept this small clay form, shaped as a ball, and it will tangibly represent my promise to give you a lamb in the spring.

These ancient tokens already prefigured the abstract tangibility of modern currencies. These forms, which eventually developed into inscriptions on flat clay tablets and then into promissory notes and other symbolic documentary forms, transformed the future promise into a tangible good in the present.

It was at this stage that the development of numeracy began to co-evolve with the creation of surplus, which made it possible to discount the future and sell things on credit. The ownership of value, the documentation of value and the development of numeracy are all tightly intertwined at the most ancient root of money.

Money and the development of numeracy

The discovery of clay bullae is one of the most exemplary stories of archaeological research, and is highly significant in the development of the monetary phenomenon in human life. It was Denise Schmandt-Besserat who found tiny "tokens" within the most ancient archaeological collections. She describes the thrilling discovery of the bullae, which were in fact "hollow tablets":

> When opening the hollow tablet, the excavators found it to hold forty-nine counters which, as stipulated in the text, corresponded to the number of animals listed. This hollow tablet constitutes the Rosetta stone of the token system. The counters (Akkadian, *abnu*, translated as "stone"), the list of animals, and the explanatory cuneiform text leave no possible

---

[46] Ibid.

[47] Ibid.

doubt that... counters were used for bookkeeping... Short cuneiform notes... referred to *abnati* were "deposited", "transferred," and "removed".[48]

Maurice Lambert... clearly identified that the first impressed signs of writing were reproducing the shape of the former tokens: "the writing was a copy, here as in other places, of what existed in reality". [49]

To recognize that the tokens constituted an accounting system that existed for five thousand years in prehistory and was widely used in the entire Near East was to be my own contribution. I was also able to draw parallels between the shapes of the tokens and those of the first incised signs of writing and establish the continuity between the two recording systems. [50]

The tokens were a primitive system of counters. One of their most awkward features consisted of indicating numbers in one-to-one correspondence: Three ovoids equaled three jars of oil. Also, each category of goods necessitated a special type of counter; for example, jars of oil were counted with ovoids and measures of grain with cones. This was the case because there were no tokens standing for 1, 2, 3 that could be applied to a variety of items. Instead, each token stood for a unit of goods... one-to-one correspondence, object specificity, and tying together the notions of the item counted and that of number.[51]

Tokens appeared in the Neolithic village... about 8,000 BC, coinciding with the first sign of agriculture. The synchronic occurrence of tokens and plant domestication... was not fortuitous but demonstrates that the new economy based on agriculture brought about the need for accounting. In fact, in each of the five sites that yielded the earliest tokens, the invention of clay counters was consistently related to evidence for harvesting and hoarding grain... The link between cereal consumption and keeping records of quantities of grain explains the fact that spheres, cones and flat disks, probably standing for measures of cereals, were among the most common early Neolithic tokens. [52]

For thousands of years, commencing from the appearance of the first permanent settlements of ancient agriculture until the appearance of writing in the first civilizations, a period lasting from around 10,000 BCE to around 5,000 BCE, these tiny tokens served to represent tangible goods in a no less tangible fashion: an oval token represents a phial of oil, a cone represents a sheep – which directly draws the value ascribed to things into the things themselves and hosts the value within the form, so that when one had to promise a sheep – a cone shaped sheep token could be given – and the value of a sheep accorded to it.

---

[48] Schmandt-Besserat, D. (1992). *Before writing, vol. I: from counting to cuneiform (Vol. 1).* University of Texas press, p. 9.

[49] Schmandt-Besserat, Ibid, p. 9.

[50] Schmandt-Besserat, Ibid, p. 10.

[51] Schmandt-Besserat, Ibid, p. 196.

[52] Schmandt-Besserat, Ibid, p. 168.

These were the ancient forms of money before we were able to count, before it was possible to encode values through the abstract form of the ten numerals, now universally utilized by mankind. Yet these ancient tokens represented a crucial step in the birth of money even before counting for they made that crucial cognitive leap that became the foundation of all human economic activities: the transfer of value from tangible forms to symbolic forms. The tangible replicated within the minds of men.

Schmandt-Besserat suggests the following chronology for the subsequent development of abstract counting:

> Circa 8000-3500 B.C.: Counters of multiple shapes indicate a system of concrete counting.
> Circa 3500-3100 B.C.: Markings, impressed in one-to-one correspondence on envelopes and tablets and fusing together the notions of product and number, suggesting that concrete counting still prevailed.
> Circa 3100 B.C.: Numerals were invented. They were the first symbols expressing numbers abstractedly – independently from the item counted.
> ca. 3100-2500 B.C.: Archaic numerations for counting various categories of items still lingered, showing that the transition from concrete to abstract counting lasted over several centuries.[53]
> Pictography brought about the abstraction of numbers. The last tokens and the first pictographs of Uruk conveyed the same information concerning the same goods, for the benefit of the same southern Mesopotamian bureaucracy. Writing did so, however with a different degree of abstraction. The scribes recognized that three jars of oil, three animals, and three bushels of grain were all instances of "threeness". They invented symbols to express these abstract concepts. Numerals constitute the first tangible evidence for abstract counting.
> The tokens are unique in prehistoric assemblages in documenting the evolution of cognitive skills… the steps from tokens to writing reflect the development of signs always further removed from real goods. Numerals represent the first mathematical symbols and first signs expressing abstract concepts. [54]

In the context of our own analysis of money, it seems that the symbolic forms paralleled the forms that they symbolized in a perfect representation of exchange: a form for a form, a favor for a favor. Except that the favor contained in the symbolic form is to be redeemed in future. In this way the ancient forms conserved the value of a form within an abstract version of the form itself.

The clay envelopes made it possible to preserve the tokens of "debt" until the debt had been repaid with actual goods, at which time the envelopes were broken and the tokens within it discarded. As time passed, the contents of the envelope were stamped onto it so that it could be kept until the time of redemption while still providing a reminder of what was in it. It was simple enough to press the tokens themselves into the envelope, thereby imprinting it before they were closed within it.

---

[53] Schmandt-Besserat, Ibid, p. 197.

[54] Schmandt-Besserat, Ibid, p. 197.

The system of markings on envelopes ushered in a new phase of the token system. At first, the impressed notations were ancillary to the counters, but in the course of time they challenged and eventually supplanted them. This occurred when solid clay tablets bearing impressed signs replaced the hollow envelopes holding tokens. These impressed signs still perpetuated the shape of the tokens, but they assumed an entirely new function. Whereas the markings on envelopes repeated only the message encoded in the tokens held inside, the signs impressed on tablets were the message. The first tablets were a decisive step in the invention of writing and amounted to a revolution in communication technology. [55]

Around 3100 B.C., the accountants of Uruk invented the first numerals – signs encoding the concept of oneness, twoness, threeness, abstracted from any particular entity.

This was not a small feat, since numerals are deemed to express some of the most abstract thoughts our minds are able to conceive. After all, "two" does not exist in nature, but only groups of two concerete items, such as two fingers, two people, two sheep, two fruits, two leaves, or even sets of heterogenous items such as one fruit+one leaf, and so on. "Two" is the abstraction of the quality of twoness shared by such sets.[56]

The invention of numerals made a breach in, but did not put an end to, the age-old principle of one-to-one correspondence. It was a major break with the past that pictographs encoding commodities were no longer repeated as many times as the number of units inolved. One-to-one correspondence continued governing the use of numerals however. "Nine" was represented by nine wedges, fifty by five circles and so on. For instance, the tablet of Godin Tepe Gd.73.295 bearing the notation "33 jars of oil" displayed a single pictograph standing for "jar of oil" and expressed "33" by three impressed circles (10+10+10) and three wedges (1+1+1). This archaism, in turn, was perpetuated for centuries in the Sumero-Babylonian arithmetical system.

In fact, this system persisted up until the invention of the modern decimal system, and some use is still made of Roman numbers even to this day. [57]

The ability to count, which lies at the very heart of our use of money and our ability to compare the values of different things, did not appear overnight. In his research of the historical development of numbers and counting, Menninger points out that numeracy took a different path from the development of language:

> We must make sure not to overlook… the recognition that spoken number words and written numerals, curiously enough, do not coincide. Written number symbols are definitely not mere representations of number words…our researches have shown us that the laws that govern early numerals, ordering and grouping, do not in fact correspond to the rule of the number sequence, which is stepwise gradation. Hence, the writing of

[55] Schmandt-Besserat, Ibid, p. 129.

[56] Schmandt-Besserat, Ibid, p. 192.

[57] Schmandt-Besserat, Ibid, p. 193.

numerals is not merely the representation of the number-word sequence. [58]

And thus, one of those paradoxes of cultural history comes about, in that the Romans, who possessed such a subtly and precisely ordered, flexible verbal number sequence, which differs from our own only in minor details, used a system of numerals so crude and cumbersome that it is hard to see how it could be a product of the same culture:

Four thousand	Eight hundred	Seventy	Nine
MMMM	DCCC	LXX	IX

as contrasted with 4879. [59]

If, for example, we symbolically wrote numerals for the units, and T, H, and Th for tens, hundreds, and thousands, our number would be written: 4Th 8H 7T 9, and it would exactly represent the manner in which we speak this number… This is precisely what Chinese does; it writes the number words with an ideogram that at the same time is its numeral:

4	Th	8	H	7	T	9
四	千	八	百	七	十	九
szu	CH'IEN	pa	PAI	ch'i	SHIH	chiu

Chinese representation of the number 4879[60]

Whereas for us the written word "four" and the numeral 4 are two distinct and separate ways of representing a single concept, Chinese has only the one: Number word and numeral are identical. This accordance of spoken number words and written numerals is unique, the only known instance in world history.

This phenomenon described by Menninger is easily explicable in light of Schmandt-Besserat's findings:

The tokens were symbols, independent of phonetic, and they could be shared by people speaking different languages. Again, tokens can be compared to our numerals, which originated in India and stand for the same concepts for innumerable people who express them in different languages.[61]

As to the development of modern numeracy, it had to wait until quite recent times, when a "positioning" system was finally introduced.

The Indian numerals do not indicate the rank of a number by a special symbol but merely by its position: 4879. Thus, the number ranks are not named, they are a nameless "positional" system of writing[62], so to

[58] Menninger, K. (2013). *Number words and number symbols: A cultural history of numbers*. Courier Corporation, p. 78.

[59] Menninger, Ibid, pp. 78–79.

[60] Menninger, Ibid, p. 79.

[61] Schmandt-Besserat, Ibid, p. 152.

[62] The namelessness of decimal positions is also an interesting case in point. The positioning system is learned sometime during childhood then never mentioned again. The core technique of this universally used number system remains in the minds of the beholders of numbers. The position is never expressed. A 4 in the 4th position to the left is simply expressed as four thousand.

> speak...The essential difference between the two systems of numerals lies in their possession, and respectively their lack, of a symbol for the rank, or order, of a digit.
> To express the quantity 4079, the Indian number system must expressly designate the missing hundreds (by the symbol for nothing, zero) - something that the spoken number words do not do. The Chinese, on the other hand, can omit it altogether by writing 4Th 7T 9.
> Our numerals do not have the same origin as the phonetic alphabet we use in writing and printing. Our letters are not akin to our numerals. One would naturally be inclined to suppose, in all innocence, that the human mind, when it took the trouble to record its ideas and concepts, would have devised similar systems of writing words and numbers, "seven" and "7." But this did not happen, neither in our western culture nor anywhere else in the world. The early system of writing numerals is everywhere the older of the two sisters.[63]

Unnoticed, it turns out that our number system is a pictographic lingua franca! What is the following number?

5

Oh, it's the number five! Also knowns as חמש, пет, cinque, etc.

The numerical symbol has become a widely accepted pictogram of the well-known quality of "fiveness". This is a form to which language is only subsequently applied in order to provide an appropriate label, so that it has a different name in each language.

It took more than a thousand years until the innovation of modern numerals spread throughout the world and everyone began using the decimal system in which the quantity and position of 10 symbols can express an infinity of numbers, and yet this developmental separation between numerical representations and the words expressing these representations – leading to the existence of a universal pictographic symbolic language understood by all – is one of the most ancient and fundamental aspects of money, which enumerates value in all languages.

Once it became possible to record value with abstract numerical symbols, the way was open to the creation of money as a unique form intended to encapsulate value. A form that also underwent gradual abstraction before it could be represented by pure numbers.

The abstraction of money

In a confluence between the emergence of numerical literacy and the needs of commerce, it is "weight" that filled the central role of estimating value. The unity of form and value developed significantly in precious metals, which could be weighed, thereby providing a tangible expression of the "value" ascribed to their form. The weight was the value.

Weight is close to the essential value of objects since it too is invisibly inherent in things. To this very day, physicists have not been able to fully explain the force of gravity acting on the matter of the universe. Just as values are hidden in forms, so gravity is hidden in matter, and contrary to 'value' which forever remains within the

[63] Menninger, Ibid, p. 80.

consensual consciousness of people, weights can be publicly measured, thereby indicating the "value" in a visible way. This was the reason that precious metals were so successful as money throughout history. "Abraham weighed to Ephron the silver… four hundred shekels of silver, current money with the merchant."[64]

Any trader could weigh silver and gold, and the evolution of money was forged by the international accessibility of the concepts and practices governing the weighing and inscription of money.

At some point, the weighable forms of precious metals began to be packaged in pre-weighed coins. There was no longer any need to be a merchant or carry a pair of scales around with you, since the weight, and thus the value, of each pre-weighed coin, was imprinted on it and visible to all.

The new coin forms had both a weight and a numerical denomination that corresponded to that weight, and since the weight of the metal and the denomination assigned to the coin corresponded to each other, it became conceptually trivial to compare the weight being weighed with the number being counted, until eventually, the numbers and the counting became sufficient information.

Although the first orderly coins based on weight are already found in the archaeological record some four hundred years before his time, there is no doubt that Alexander the Great was the progenitor of the first "currency" in the sense of standardized forms passing easily from one owner to another and accessing the entire wealth of an empire. In his own lifetime, Alexander established more than twenty mints that minted millions of coins as part of an intentional policy to establish an orderly monetary form throughout the empire, with an emphasis on providing a sufficient quantity of smaller denominations for the needs of daily life.

The tangible connection between weight and value was maintained throughout, wherein the drachma, weighing 4.3 grams, served as the point of comparison for all other coins, which were multiples of its weight, from the tiniest of coins weighing no more than 0.09 grams (1/48 of the weight of the drachma) and up to the massive deca-drachmas weighing 43 grams – 10 times the weight of a drachma. The system in its entirety was able to cover the entire scope of daily needs by providing a full spectrum of weights that could be easily added and subtracted from each other.

The Coin	Name	Weight	Relative to the Drachma
	Dekadrachm	43 grams	x10
	Tetradrachm	17.2 grams	x3
	Drachma	4.3 grams	=
	Obol	0.72 grams	1/6

[64] Genesis 23:16 KJV.

	Tetartemorion	0.18 grams	1/24

Table 3: The Coins of Alexander the Great[65]

It is estimated that Alexander minted tens of millions of such coins in his own lifetime and they are prevalent in museums and private coin collections all over the world. As can be seen in the above table, they are organized in strict hierarchical order, and the transition to a symbolic form is made naturally via the evident "value" of the coin – its weight.

This critical shaping of the shining silver desired by all into compact forms with a fixed weight, was an all-important transition that shifted from tangible money, with a weight that can be felt by the body, which was a form with a physical mass equal to its value, to the abstract representations of the same value.

Once people became used to the coins and to their value when making transactions without the need to whip out a pair of scales, and the felt value of the coin and the belief in the value of the coin were both applicable to the same outward form of the coin, it ceased being just 4.3 grams of silver, and began to be a drachma.

One drachma buys so and so and is worth such and such in obtaining the benefits provided by other believers in the drachma, and this value is now wholly assigned to the nominal form "drachma", in the belief that the value is indeed inherent in that name.

Even as it became such a critical step in the development of modern currency, the widespread belief in the value of pre-weighed coins was also cynically abused by sophisticated minters, who quickly learned to empty their coins of gold and silver by creating much cheaper alloys, while at the same time leaving the representational denomination of the coin as is. Public faith in the value of a coin continues to accept it has having its denominated value, even when it is emptied of precious metal.

A person who is unaware that the form has been emptied, will continue to use a coin as money, and will not feel the difference. So long as ignorance is preserved, a monetary form purporting to be gold is of no less value in trade that a form that actually contains gold. The crucial factor determining the value of a coin is the existence of a durable form that is believed to contain an agreed value, rather than the value of the metal from which the coin is made.

The same community that ascribes value to a gold coin can also ascribe value to a gold-less coin, and to use it for the selfsame commercial purposes. It is neither gold nor silver that constitute money, but a durable widely accepted form considered by the community to have value that constitutes money.

This custom of "packing" monetary forms that are considered less valuable, such as silver alloys, into other monetary forms that are accepted by a community as valuable, i.e., the denominated face-value of a coin, is not relegated to the distant past alone. The fiasco of the subprime mortgages is a salient example of the same practice not so long ago, as "trash" mortgages, i.e., mortgages that were empty of the value of the lender's solvency, were repackaged as sophisticated financial

[65] Based on en.wikipedia.org/wiki/Ancient_drachma – where one can find the full hierarchy.

instruments and sold to buyers who did not know that their instrument had been emptied of value.

So long as suspicion and disillusionment have not awoken the general public to suspect its money, the money will continue to function properly. We really don't care if a coin is golden or not, so long as it is accepted as currency by all members of our community, just as there was no real problem with the securitization of the subprime mortgages, so long as any skepticism or mistrust were held at bay.

Paradoxically, as far as coins are concerned, it was the very embezzlement of their metallic content that constituted an important stage in the development of money, as it quickly became evident that only experts and merchants dealing directly with coinage, recognized the problematic coins and quickly hedged their investments, but the rest of the community blithely continued to use the coins as if their denomination did indeed reflect their value. This paved the way to the modern forms of money that no longer contain any inherent value. The value of modern currencies is generated by the trust awarded to them by their respective communities, so that the external form and inner value become fused. What is the value of a ten-cent coin? Ten cents.

In the 1970s, the producers of money ripped off the band-aid and stopped pretending that the money they were producing was worth anything more than the value ascribed to it by the public. The public continued to respect the money because its producers continued to point to it and say "this is money".

Since the form was a matter of convention, as was its value, and since its denomination, which signifies the scope of the favor that it can be used to return, is also a matter of convention, then it was always possible to agree on any conceivable form, so long as it was universally accepted, to the point that current forms are mere numbers on a screen.

The Emergence of Money from Debt

The development of money from debt took place simultaneously with its development as a growing abstraction from physical objects. The invention of writing and numbers were a direct consequence of the relations between benefactors and beneficiaries, who quickly became creditors and debtors.

The recording of debts evolved into a monetary form in its own right, so that it became enough to point to a written form. The lender could hold the written promise of the borrower as a valuable form in its own right, and the borrower could be released from the bonds of gratitude by disbursing his debts with precision.

Money is the inevitable outcome of this process: a debt appraised as a number and inscribed in writing becomes money. That is the nature of money from its initial appearance to date. When you give someone a dollar bill, you are giving them a promissory note to be paid by the community of those who place their trust in the dollar.

Written and stamped things are akin to scripture in being regarded as deeper proof of ownership, and they have transformed the belief in the ownership of forms of value into a belief in inscribed forms testifying to ownership and value.

Subsequently, once the institution of inscription became the focus of faith in money, it became possible to strip away any tangible forms and leave the inscription of ownership in its purely symbolic form, without any underlying "fundamental asset". Gold is no longer necessary; the written form is enough. Wholly symbolic forms are believed to contain differential value according to the differential belief in their value.

When legitimate ownership is supported by legal inscriptions it elicits a deeper measure of faith since the law itself is legitimized by a strong intersubjective faith in its legitimacy. Canonized records have greater standing in the faith of the many, so that the great economic question of "who does this value belong to?" is best answered by pointing to an official record or inscription which attest to ownership.

Ownership itself is solely legitimated by belief.

The central role of persuasion in perpetuating inequality arises from the fact that if people believe that something does not belong to them, be it land, machines, money or the very commodities created with their participation, they will behave accordingly. They will pay rent to landlords for the privilege of having a roof over their heads, they will accept wages that are dissociated from the actual value that their products incorporate, and they will work for decades to pay interest on money loaned to them that has long since been spent.

Historically, it was the ability of the affluent to trade in debts, i.e., to rent their capital or to purchase the debts of their peers, which ultimately led to the increasing abstraction of monetary forms and the rise of the modern capital economy in which a small lucky percentage of the population live on cloud nine, while the rest of the populace continue to labor within the reality of needs and scarcity.

The modern debt-based production of money

In a similar vein to King David's morose lament, "I was shapen in iniquity; and in sin did my mother conceive me,"[66] the original sin of the large sums of money flooding modern economies is their conception in debt. Just as biological conception is the very basis of life itself, so debts and obligation are the universal basis of human relationships. Money has developed naturally from these binding ties, so that its wondrous rise to the role of promoter of human liberty and creativity, not to mention the catalyst of across-the-board cooperation between all peoples, is even more surprising than the rise of that ancient warrior-lamenter from the abyss of iniquity.

The monetary forms created by debt begin their journey as a means of encumbrance, but continue as a means of liberation, even though at present, these liberating qualities are but the foam on the deep and enslaving abyss of debt burden.

The creation of monetary forms through debt is an amazing magic trick that has not received sufficient attention. There is no need to hide doves in kerchiefs or bunnies in a cylinder hat. All one needs is a firm system of faith and the stroke of a banker's pen.

The secret of this magic is wondrously simple.

A citizen comes to a bank and asks for money.

The banker is happy to accommodate him, but only on condition that he repay what he is given with interest.

The citizen agrees. The future will take care of itself. Why delay gratifications when you can have cash in hand immediately.

---

[66] Psalm 51 5 KJV.

The banker takes a pen and writes: We hereby give John Hope 100,000 monetary forms, and John Hope will repay us that amount plus 10% annual interest[67], in installments over 20 years.

The banker now writes minus 100,000 in John Hope's account. The bank now owes John Hope 100,000.

The bank now writes an asset in the amount of $231,605.19 on the bank's books, which is what John Hope now owes the bank.

If he pays the paltry sum of $965.02 per month for 20 years, he will discharge that debt.

John Hope exits the bank with a song in his heart and money in his pocket. Since the only way to use that money is give it to others, 100,000 monetary units have thereby been added to the economy, along with a ticking time-bomb of an additional 131,605.19 (231,605.19 -100,000) that will be needed if John is to discharge his debt.

But wait, wait! Where did all this money come from? Where was it before? Did the banker whisk it out of his back pocket? Does his desk drawer have a false bottom?

No at all.

It was truly magic! Creation at the stroke of a pen.

Purely symbolic ownership lies at the core of this money production mechanism. Banks own a legitimized, government-sanctioned right to create, ex nihilo, a four-fold "ownership" of "asset" and "liquidity" at one and the same time: the bank becomes the owner of an asset inscribed on its books along with new money created in this act and directly transferred to the borrower, who now becomes the owner of both the money and a debt greater than the amount received from the bank, as it includes both principal and interest.[68]

The bank creates ownership of a money amount, X, the principal, but transfers that ownership to the borrower in exchange for a virtual "asset", the future return, recorded on its books, which equals the principal + interest, i.e., X+Y, while the borrower obtains ownership of the immediate amount, X, but is obligated to provide the bank with ownership of the greater sum of X+Y.

Moreover, the borrower's ownership of X is wholly contingent on payment of X+Y, and should the borrower fail to pay, the bank is entitled to collect the debt from other borrower assets and from guarantors, in its move to restore its ownership of X+Y, as well as collect an additional plethora of fines, penalties and foreclosed assets.

It can be seen that as far as the bank is concerned, the only action required of it was that involved in making records on its books, which create and assign ownership, and that it remains the true owner of the money it produced even as some of it winds its way into the economy through the borrower's spending.

It is the borrower who feeds the newly made money into tangible reality, as he uses the monetary forms created by the bank to make purchases.

---

[67] Aye! There's the rub! "Annual" means it's compound… oops.

[68] This additional money can only be obtained by an additional act of ex-nihilo money creation by a bank, and this is why all modern markets are doomed to periodic crashes – generated by the infinite demands of compound interest.

The following table summarizes the encumbrances involved in the creation of money. It can be seen that the only party that is in debt is the borrower. The bank has acquired a tidy asset, and the ultimate recipient of the newly manufactured money has no obligations tied to it.

The bank has 231,605.19, the recipient of the new money has 100,000, and only the borrower is left to bear the burden of finding additional money to pay the bank. You will note that in that single act of creation, the bank has generated 331,605.19 and that the borrower now has to find other sources of money to repay the bank.

First Round	Second Round	Third Round and on
No debt	Debt	No debt
The ownership of the asset is created simultaneously with the creation of the monetary form. The bank creates ownership of two forms that contain value: The asset now recorded on its books, and the monetary form given to the borrower.	The borrower becomes the first owner of the monetary form created through the loan and enjoys all the advantages of the Cantillon effect[69], but at the same time has incurred a debt towards the bank far greater than the money received.	As the borrower now uses the monetary forms he has received from the bank acquire other forms, the monetary forms are no longer bound by debt and are free to serve in their usual role in the economy of paying debts, replicating values, offsetting obligations and switching ownerships.

Table 4: Monetary forms created by debt

The nature of debt is the creation of a form that captures future value. The future lies at the very heart of debt, and debt itself creates a monetary form that already holds the entire future value that the debtor will produce as he repays his debt. The debt creates immediate cash based on the lender's faith in the future solvency of the borrower.

It is important to note that the true fructifying value of monetary forms is separate from their origin in debt, and that while that origin remains inscribed in "books" and enforced under laws, once the money is created it is "free".

Once the borrower starts to expend his newly minted money, he enjoys its true power to open up new vistas of human enterprise, as demonstrated by its amazing effects when it is unencumbered and circulates with great abundance.

North writes of one historical case in which the 'debt' aspect of money was not well-policed, and the monetary forms created by bankers were instrumental in creating and supporting an entire civilization of enterprise:

> Banks emerged to finance new markets, rising and declining according to their success in generating economic activity. At times this would be a loose system where money was made available as required to finance economic activity, such as in the nineteenth-century American West, where approximately sixteen hundred local banks issued some seven thousand paper currencies to meet market conditions. The pioneer estab-

[69] Whereby initial recipients of new money can spend it before inflation (caused by the addition of new money) sets in.

lishing his farm could be assured of cheap credit from a local bank that could easily go bust, leaving him with his farm and no debts. [70]

Obviously, banks are not eager to go bust in order to support farming enterprises, and they have done a great job of consolidating their power, so that even if the farmer goes bust, his debt will remain on the books, while the bank has become too-big-to-fail and will never go bust.

Nevertheless, at the height of the housing boom, before the Fed shut down the festivities with its crippling interest hike, the economy behaved in much the same way as it did in the old days of bountiful entrepreneurship in the Wild West. There was plenty of money and nobody was worried that they wouldn't have enough to pay it back, as they could periodically "refinance" assets that were continually appreciating.

Debt is the main engine of money generation in all modern economies. Debt remains the enslaving noose around the necks of most people on earth, and is the destabilizing force periodically shaking economies, even as it serves as a great conduit for the transfer of wealth to the wealthy, as commercial banks create more and more credit money in order to collect value from debtors. Modern money is born in debt, and if you are not a 3rd round recipient you will have your cross to bear.

The ancient networks of human bondage - the ties of commitments and promises that underpin all human social interaction - are still the foundation of the debt economy and the progenitors of money. Only when money reaches the hands of the 3rd owners, does a quantum leap occurs in which it becomes an instrument of discharging one's obligations on the spot – the exact obverse of debt creation.

Have credit card? Create money!

The invention of consumer credit cards has allowed the masses to participate directly in the creation of money through debt as they go along.

Your credit "line" or "limit" is the ultimate amount of money that the bank will allow you to create. Neither the debt nor the money exist, until you make an actual purchase, but when you pay with your credit card, the money is instantly created along with the debt. The plus and the minus are simultaneously created with the card owner's future in the middle: The plus on the vendor's books, the minus on the credit-card company's books, and the future obligation of the payer-borrower based on the bank's faith in the payer-borrower's future.

The new money created via card is recorded on the books of the point of sale at which you perform the purchase, and the debt that was created by expending that money is recorded as a plus on the books of the credit card company as well (since you now owe it money, your debt is considered an asset), and only you, the happy holder of the card, are saddled with a minus on both ends: The money is gone, and you now have to find more money to pay your debt.

You can of course console yourself with whatever you purchased with that money. If you bought a sofa, you can just sit on it and rest, and if you bought some food, it will hopefully comfort you.

---

[70] North, P. (2007). *Money and Liberation: The Micropolitics of Alternative Currency Movements*. University of Minnesota Press, pp. 6-7.

Nevertheless, once the money is in the account of the recipient, it is immediately freed from the circle of debt and can be used for any purpose without incurring any further liens. Most importantly, even if you were to renege on your debt after maxing out all your credit cards – the money that you created with your credit cards remains in the economy, it is completely separate from your "bad debt".

For the bank granting the loan, the debt creates "value" in two ways: first by financing tangible goods in exchange for a future obligation, and then, should you default on that obligation, by repossessing those tangible goods.

As Joseph writes:

> When defaults occur, the most common step is repossession. In this, the same banking system that created money out of nothing and loaned it at interest can now take ownership of *physical* assets, such as houses or cars... what we really have is a structurally induced transfer of wealth from the lower class to the upper class, for guess who owns the banks?... remember, in real life the money for the loan was created out of thin air, whereas the property is real. [71]

In the hands of a bank, the collaterals provided by borrowers are the means to immediately realize the bank's investment. It sells money to the borrower via the loan, and in exchange the borrower provides it with conditional ownership over some form of collateral such as the house that was bought with the money he borrowed. In this manner, it is the bank that actually owns it all.

The borrower's ownership of the money is fleeting. After he purchases the house, the money is no longer his, and he must now pay back a far larger amount. Should he fail to repay the loan, his ownership of the house will also be shown to have been contingent, because from the moment that the house was encumbered as collateral, the bank became ipso fact the owner of the house and can foreclose on it in the event of default.

The problem though, is that the more money people receive to buy houses, the higher the prices of houses go in the usual inflationary process that raises prices in the presence of a great deal of money (never fear, this will not impact the inflation targets, since houses aren't included in such measures as GDP or CPI). The people who bought houses with loans can see the value of their asset appreciate and feel that they have at last joined the wonderful world of the affluent in which inflation is transformed into appreciation.

However, they soon discover that they continue to be part of the regular economy because all that money they received is now worth less, and at the whim of the government, the interest rates may increase to the point that they cannot repay the loan, and all the assets that they had will be transferred into the hands of the bank.

This is how the cycle of house ownership goes:

The borrower wants to buy a house.

The bank issues a loan (thereby creating the money) in exchange for a lien on the house.

The bank pays the money, usually directly to the seller of the house, and the buyer of the house is now indebted to the bank.

---

[71] Joseph, P. (2017). *The new human rights movement: reinventing the economy to end oppression*. BenBella Books, p. 131.

In practice, the bank is the one purchasing the house, not the borrower, and the bank will one day give the house to the borrower if the debt is paid.

The borrower, who brokered the deal between the seller of the house and the bank, now becomes the contingent owner of the house.

The seller of the house received the money, and the bank received a lien on that house, and if the borrower acquits himself with honor and perseverance, he may one day own that house, but as of now he is just a go-between.

The bank and the seller of the house are those who actually profit as they are paid in full: the house-seller gets the money now and the bank will get the (same) money plus interest once the debt is paid. Only the middle man, the borrower, remains in a limbo of contingency for the next thirty or so years as he toils to get the money to pay off the loan and get actual ownership of the house.

The middle man's only benefit from the transaction is that he gets to use the asset. He can live in the house or rent it out to others. But he cannot sell it without the bank's approval. Also, he lives in the expectation and hope of one day actually owning the house.

This is the main paradox and stumbling block of all "free" economies:

All interfaces with tangible forms are finite.

All interfaces with intangible forms are infinite.

The significance of this is that a person can only earn a limited amount of money in order to cover his debts, but the liability, especially where compound interest and linkages are in the picture, can increase without limit.

The debtor, on his part also provides something that has not come into the world yet: his future efforts. So, the **bank trades money it doesn't have for a life that has not been lived yet** – and the forms of value that mediate these two intangibles are the "hook" into the real world that provides these pure fictions with traction, and tangible reality is ultimately moved by these manifestations of faith.

The two worlds, the tangible and the symbolic, are superimposed.

In the **tangible** world, people work and pay some of their wages as tenants, whether of the person who officially owns the house, or of the bank who holds the house as collateral, and in the **symbolic** world, the bank holds all: the debtor's debt as an asset and the debtor's house as collateral.

Inevitably, at some point, there comes a day when the abstract world of symbolic monetary forms creates some turbulence that overturns the fragile cart of the tangible. Perhaps some sober-faced economists at the federal bank decide that prices are too high and know the old trick of making money more expensive by raising interest rates. When interest rates are raised, borrowers can no longer afford their loans, so are obliged to sell the houses for which they borrowed the money. The crash will not be late in coming. If everyone is selling their houses, house prices go down, and tremendous debts accumulate.

Money remains with the affluent, while the non-affluent are only given a chance to own it by repaying a loan. Should they fail to meet their obligations, their collaterals will be foreclosed.

In many ways, taking a loan is a kind of inverse gamble, in which, according to the risk, the borrower gambles on his future after receiving an immediate "payout" from the bank, and he now places small "bets" every month in the hope that he can continue holding onto that money. He is gambling on his future solvency. Should he lose that gamble, he will lose the "win" that was only given to him conditionally.

Borrowers too can make money in a similar way to how they received it, by manipulation of accepted economic beliefs and by shifting ownership in creative ways to generate income. Let's take as an example, a leveraged short position on a currency.

A speculator receives a large loan in the currency that he wishes to short. For example, Soros borrows 3 billion pounds. Soros is the first recipient and therefore obligated to repay 3 billion pounds to the owner. At the same time, since value is replicated, he is now also the owner of 3 billion pounds which he can dispose of at will. So, he sells his 3 billion pounds off in exchange for 9 billion German marks, retaining the value but switching forms.

He now waits awhile as the Bank of England goes through its political gyrations, until people lose faith in the form of the GBP, while the German mark form continues to enjoy the faith of people in its value. When the value of the pound drops so that the form of the pound contains less value than it did before, Soros can now buy 4 billion pounds with just 9 billion marks.

9 billion abstract monetary forms called "marks" now contain value equal to 4 million abstract monetary forms called "pounds".

Soros now pays off the debt of 3 million GBP to the originator of the loan, and is left with a cool billion pounds in hand. He is also the beneficiary of the Cantillon effect vis a vis the pound, since it will take some time until the depreciation of the pound leads to price increases throughout the British market, so that a billion pounds initially wields considerable buying power.

Without the constant interplay of value, form and price, all this would not have been possible. Debt, though, adds the dimension of the future into the mix. Soros borrowed specific forms (pounds) and repaid the same forms, but in the interim he transferred their value to other forms (marks) that retained the value while the value of the pound depreciated. When Soros bought pounds again, he had to purchase a lot more in order to contain the same value.

The essence of debt is a belief in some future value, which motivates the lender to cede ownership of forms to a borrower. The ownership preceded the loan. The new forms of debt are also based on this belief, but it creates ownership at the same time as it creates the loan, so that institutions not only create fiat money, but also fiat ownership.

In classic Schrödinger's cat fashion, ownership is replicated and transferred at the same time, thereby making the first recipient both owner and not-owner. Soros held 3 billion GBP forms of which he was not the owner, since he only "borrowed" them and had to pay them back, but he was also their owner, since he could dispose of them at will. This was done by doubling the forms created – assets on the lender's books and money in the hands of Soros.

After the entire transaction had been carried through, Soros remained sole owner of the balance of one billion pounds. The double ownership had been cancelled out by repaying the obligation, and the balance remained with Soros.

The truly amazing innovation here is that the entire play took place in completely intangible forms. Neither lenders nor borrowers, nor buyers nor sellers, laid hands on a single tangible form. It all took place in the interplay of mental obligations and beliefs, never touching anything tangible.

Interest Rates – Promises promises

Interest rates are a major driving force of economic activity, as people seek out the best and most reliable promises, which are usually inversely related: the greater the reliability, the more stingy the promise, and the more extravagant the promise the lower the reliability.

Such promises, backed by both the ability to create money ex nihilo and the power to collect taxes, are the bread and butter of governments in their attempts to manipulate their economies, hiking up interest rates to combat inflation or taking them down to fend off a recession, and making all manner of interest manipulations in order to curb the volatility of markets.

Governments everywhere are the most reliable debtors. If the US government promises you a 2% coupon on a bond, you can usually rely on that and expect to receive those two percent in future. But if a commercial mortgage-backed bond offers you 10%, well… you can rely on it in a boom economy, but when the bust comes, your entire holding may be wiped out. After all, the government creates the money so can easily generate enough for your 2%, but the commercial people have to use the money already available in the economy, or even get new money via loans, a completely different proposition.

Faith in the future can both invigorate and dampen the economy: when faith imagines a bright future the economy breathes freely and money flows into the economy, and when faith imagines a darker future, the economy falters as people take their money out of it, thereby desiccating once exuberant blooms within the yellowed pages of accounting ledgers.

The promise of interest is a key rhetorical tool in shaping beliefs in prices, and many issuers of financial instruments create forms around specific promises of future interest.

Bonds are an excellent example of a financial instrument that captures future values by promising interest. Bonds repackage the future payment streams of a debtor and parcel them off in currency-like denominations

Even though they are wholly symbolic, bonds are also similar to more tangible forms in that they are bought with the money. In a sense, when one buys bonds, a fiat currency is chasing a fiat commodity, or rather existing monetary forms are used to buy up future monetary forms in an attempt to equate the value now with some future value.

Bonds have an important place in the transfer of original ownership of money into the economy, as governments create both bonds and money ex-nihilo and exchange one for the other – in a way that pushes present money into the economy in exchange for future obligations.

Bonds are a good way of monetizing the future, mostly because the same authority backing government bonds is the one that is also backing the currency.

The entire existence of bonds is based on the belief in a promise to pay made by a respected authority that can be counted on to keep its word.[72]

In the example below, the value of the bond is set at 100 while the initial sale price is 113. Whoever buys it for 113, knows that at redemption the payment received will be only 100.

Type of bond	Bond "Coupon"	Inner Value	Market Price	Bond Face Value[73]
	Future Belief	Value	Price	Form
	Fixed	Variable	Variable	Fixed
Government Bond	5%	113	113	100

Tim Benett of MoneyWeek offers a clear explanation for the form of bond face value: "Think of it as like buying vegetables… it's a kilo of carrots, whether you are me, the grocer, or my next-door-neighbor… the price is negotiable. The fact that it is a kilo of carrots isn't, but the price is… gilts work like that: the symbolic value is 100 pounds, but the market price can be different".[74]

It is here that one can most clearly see how in the absence of a credological investigation that distinguishes the beliefs underlying economic entities, there is a deep confusion between the fixed external (par or face) form and its ever-changing value and price.

In fact, it is at this point that one can clearly see how language has enfolded reality in its embrace – for a commodity form such as a banana, and the forms of financial instruments such as bonds, stocks and the money used to buy them, are all made of the same cloth. For human beings, reality has long since been enveloped by the nominal, by the naming of things that allows them to take their place in subjective and inter-subjective consciousness.

When one refers to a banana it is to the banana of the mind, the language label, the nominal name-tag that conceptualizes it as a banana, so that in this sense it may be said that the epithet "banana" given to a certain yellow commodity is the form of the banana rather than the banana "itself"[75] – for forms too are "imagined" entities in their role as vessels for the indwelling value and as containers to which the negotiated price may be attached.

Thus, what is being traded and bartered as a form is the nominal concept of "banana", which is equivalent to the denominated "face" of a banknote, or the "par" number used to constitute the form of a stock or a bond.

The distinction between numbers used as the "name" that constitutes a form and those used to determine its value or price is quite common in many areas, and is the first knowledge that is imparted to neophytes in their initiation into a profession,

---

[72] In the 2008 meltdown it was discovered that the true collateral was in fact the "word" of the rating agencies, which was nothing less than a promise that promises would be kept, but couched in an objective-seeming symbology of a trio of letters suffixed by pluses or minuses, to give it a good sheen of believability.

[73] The analysis presented here is based on the excellent explanation provided by Tim Bennett of MoneyWeek - https://youtu.be/AqTjNU7mQZQ

[74] https://youtu.be/AqTjNU7mQZQ?t=208

[75] Indeed, the Kantian Ding an sich, according to the school that holds it to exist (for people do eat an occasional banana…).

such as the "nominal" scale in statistics, "char" strings in programming or the "text" data type in a Microsoft Excel spreadsheet.[76]

Thus, the forms constituted by denominations of bills, bonds and other financial instruments should have been more appropriately referred to as simply the "par", the "face" or the "nominal", without adding the words "value" or "price" that obfuscate the issue.

The "face" or "par" of a bond is its form, since it is stable and unchanging over time, while the price and value fluctuate, and just as you would buy a more tangible commodity form, so you can buy a bond form constituted by its "par", using currency forms to ultimately equate the indwelling value of the bond with the indwelling value of the money forms. The price on both is external and when it is equalized, ownership can be transferred.

This is, of course, very much what happens in the forex markets where the base-currency becomes the form, while the quote-currency is used for pricing, and the market forces of intersubjective jockeying to agree on the internal value of the form is reflected in the ever-fluctuating price.

Now enters the element of belief in the future. Why exchange the intangible forms of currency for the equally intangible forms of bonds and other financial instruments? Moreover, thanks to inflation, the currency today is probably worth more than what it would be worth at some point down the road. It turns out that beliefs in a darker future are conducive to bond holding: because of fear of having their surplus completely wiped out, people are happy to buy some low risk, low yield instruments that can assure them of retaining some value should the market take a cataclysmic turn for the worse.

Derivatives

At the heart of the factors leading up to the Great Recession of 2008 one finds an infinite variety of debt manipulations, ownerships, and many forms of packaging and distribution. The new forms of debt that arose over the decades preceding the Great Recession are unique in the history of mankind in that they took the basic patterns of debt creation, gambling and speculation into new worlds where no man had gone before.

During the years in which the housing and ancillary mortgage markets boomed, in fact since 9/11, the interest rates had been extremely low. This meant that commercial banks provided copious amounts of this "cheap" money for consumption, packaged in various forms of credit. At the same time, the low interest rates meant that banks were always on the lookout for more profitable loans on which higher interest rates may be charged to account for "risk". They found a way to do so by issuing loans to lenders with low credit ratings, who became known as "subprime lenders", since the "risk" involved in such lenders meant that they could be charged higher interest rates. As is always the case, those who have less always pay more.

---

[76] Anecdotally, Biblical first man's first act was the "calling of names", i.e., the nominal labeling of reality: "...whatsoever Adam called every living creature, that was the name thereof." (Genesis II 19 KJV).

Yet, just as much as banks love profits, they are also risk averse, so they sought ways to both have the cake and eat it and get rid of the risk associated with the subprime loans by selling them to others.

This was done through repackaging the loans in what became known as Collateralized Debt Obligations or CDOs, in which "good" (low risk, low interest) mortgages were mixed with "bad" (high risk, high interest) ones. The banks called such packages "diversified" and colluded with rating agencies to give the entire package a high credit rating (on the basis of the "good" mortgages that they contained).

In view of the lucrative interest rates offered by these CDOs (on the basis of the "bad" mortgages that they contained) the banks sold them to a great many investors who were looking for ways to make greater profits in a market with very low interest rates.

When the banks succeeded in selling these loans, they received large inflows of cash, which they immediately used to make additional loans to "subprime" (i.e., higher paying) borrowers, which fed more cash into the general market.

In this way, a great "cycle" of cash flows was established that provided the non-affluent with increasingly liberal loans, and the affluent with increasingly lucrative returns.

Everyone was happy.

These were perfect upwardly spiraling cycles.

In addition to the packaging and reselling of the debt itself – another new instrument was developed to mirror it – the CDS – the Credit Default Swap, as described by Pinsent:

> The seller of the contract assumes the credit risk that the buyer does not wish to shoulder in exchange for a periodic protection fee similar to an insurance premium and is obligated to pay only if a negative credit event occurs. It is important to note that the CDS contract is not actually tied to a bond, but instead references it. For this reason, the bond involved in the transaction (the insured CDO) is called the "reference obligation."[77]

In other words, the CDS, the insurance, was no more than a pure piece of gambling. It is a side bet on the chances that the "reference obligations", i.e., the CDOs, will tank.

These financial instruments capitalized on the nature of insurance as an inverted debt and a form of betting on outcome, and sold a vaunted "safeguard" that would apply in the event of defaults on the mortgages. This additional instrument of faith was also a form of "benediction" that would assuage any doubts about the value and validity of the CDOs.

Thus, the banks were in fact selling a double bet: CDOs that capitalized on the belief in an eternally blooming house market, and the ability of people to pay their debts, and CDSs, which did the exact opposite by betting on insolvency, thereby "securing the risk" by providing a counter-bet as a form of insurance.[78]

---

[77] Pinsent, W. (2018). *Credit Default Swaps: An Introduction.* https://www.investopedia.com/articles/optioninvestor/08/cds.asp

[78] It was ultimately revealed that the "insurance" was no more than lip-service, since neither the insurers nor the banks believed that the Real Estate market would indeed collapse (for it

In a business based on reliability and trust, the CDSs served as a sophisticated infallibility insurance – for even if you made a mistake, there was no mistake: should your CDO collapse, your CDS would immediately cover the loss. The CDSs themselves were sold over-the-counter like bearer bonds and became a "currency in their own right".

The whole venture was colored by a "double bookkeeping" frame of mind, since it looked pretty good in the symbolic world of balance sheets to see how CDOs offset themselves against CDSs, neatly cancelling out the risk, while in actual fact the risk was doubled as it was copied onto two different types of mirror-image instruments: interest bearing debt and premium paying insurance.

The holders of the debt still bore the same risk of default, and the insurers betting against the same default now bore it too.

Part of the huge meltdown was the collapse of the insurers, as Amadeo succinctly summarizes:

> On Tuesday, Sept. 16, 2008, the Fed announced it was bailing out insurance giant, AIG. It made an $85 billion "loan" in return for 79.9% equity, effectively taking ownership. AIG had run out of cash. It was scrambling to pay off credit default swaps it had issued against now-failing mortgage-backed securities.[79]

It is helpful to keep in mind that this entire system, which disrupted the lives of millions, of the entire world, resides mostly in the mind. Except for a few outliers that snaked their way into empirical reality, such as houses that people actually lived in, everything else was just numbers in the minds of men.

The mortgages, the interest, the financial instruments, the CDOs, the CDSs, the bets, the insurances, the swaps, none of them were ever more tangible than printed paper, and mostly they were just virtual forms flitting across screens and bandied about with great fervor. The transactions, the signings, the risk, the gambles and the promises – all remained within the realm of the symbolic.

Unfortunately, though, not everything that happens in the symbolic stays in the symbolic. After all symbolic "assets" are erased from the balance sheets, the residual price is ultimately paid in tangibles, and by people who only have tangibles to rely on, i.e., the non-affluent who are now divested of all symbolic surplus.

All this was supported by a thick web of trust. Everyone relied on the tangible value of real-estate, which became very much akin to gold in partial reserve times: a very expensive form that was difficult to move, but was used as a basis for issuing various bearer bills, which then took on a life of their own and were traded independently.

This was supported by the assurance of not only insurance in the form of CDSs, but also of rating agencies which gave their stamp of confidence to the various instruments.

---

was deemed "Safe as Houses"), and when it ultimately crashed, there was no money to cover the promised insurance payout and the U.S. government was obliged to buy up the insurer.

[79] Amadeo, K. (2019). The Stock Market Crash of 2018. *The Balance.* https://www.thebalance.com/stock-market-crash-of-2008-3305535

As few thought to "look inside" the package as would have asked to visit bank vaults to inspect the actual purity of the gold when gold was held in reserve. Money is all about trust. Certainly, you don't look a symbolic gift horse in the mouth.

In faith as in faith, the charismatic authority of the leader is always the ultimate bulwark of the true believer, and since all the financial giants of the economy were happily on board, what believer would entertain heretical doubts? As Amadeo writes:

> Collateralized debt obligations and other derivatives were so complex that it was difficult for investors to determine what the real value should be. As a result, investors paid whatever the seller asked, based on his **sterling reputation**.[80]

Faith in the future and betting on the future lay at the very center of this system. Commencing from the first mortgage loans that monetized the future of the borrowers and gave them large amounts of money to buy houses, through the bought houses themselves, which now became collateral in the hands of the bank and the subsequent re-monetization of these mortgages as CDOs, which then figured in the forward-looking calculations of professional fund managers whose careers were increasingly contingent on their ability to look into the future, and culminating in the CDSs at the very top of the soothsayers pyramid, which purported to cover every conceivable and (in particular) inconceivable future, but placed their bets on the conceivable while collecting premiums from the rubes who wanted to bet on the ridiculous odds of the inconceivable - everyone in the chain was busy with the future – and since the future is yet to be – and everything we think about it is but an article of faith, it becomes the perfect ambience for the growth and development of more and more intangible symbolic instruments.

In the period preceding the crash, the Fed changed its policies and created the crucial factor which put the people who were actually paying the mortgages under. Although this critical factor was central in the calculations of those who were betting against the market, and was obviously instrumental in triggering the collapse, it is rarely mentioned in analyses of the crash, even though the question almost begs itself: why did people, who had been paying their mortgages regularly, suddenly begin defaulting?

It turns out that the Fed was following its "inflation targeting" policies, and probably a little concerned over the general exuberance of the economy (if everything is flourishing what would the Fed have to tinker with?). The Fed was also busy with the "future", and painting various imagined scenarios, in which inflation played a central role.

Convincing itself that it was staving off future inflation, the Fed moved to place a chocker on market liquidity, and thereby struck against the weakest link in the chain, the people who actually paid the mortgages, triggering the collapse of the market[81]. Here is a report from 2006:

---

[80] Amadeo, K. (2020). 2007 Financial Crisis. Explanation, Causes and Timeline. *The Balance.* https://www.thebalance.com/2007-financial-crisis-overview-3306138

[81] This was certainly not the first time in history that government austerity measures crushed an economy.

> Fed policy-makers boosted their target for the federal funds rates to 5.25 percent, as had been widely expected, putting the overnight bank lending rate at its highest since January 2001... Several investors have been concerned that the Fed will cripple economic growth .... For consumers, the Fed funds rate affects rates on a variety of loans, including credit cards...[82]

Although it is customary to blame the low credit rating of the sub-prime borrowers and the risky behavior of the lending banks as the causes of the crisis, the actual proximate cause were these pernicious tweaks provided by the Fed, which pushed borrowers over the edge as their mortgage payments jumped up beyond their earning capacities. This horrendous and fateful policy, which sent the entire world into a slump, was so damaging that the Fed refrained from again raising interest rates for almost a decade.

In fact, for seven years. In response to the Recession, it set those rates to zero at the end of 2008, only hesitantly raising them again in 2015.[83]

It seems that the rest of the economy was operating under a different image, where the borrowers were considered from the outset "unfit" and the system considered "brilliant" for outfoxing this unfitness by hedging the bets, collateralizing the risks and insuring the downsides...

What actually happened up until the crash was that the non-affluent, who are usually strapped for cash and would not even dream of buying something as expensive as a house, could now become property owners.[84]

Most historical descriptions of the crash tend to gloss over the contribution of the Federal Bank to the collapse, but it is obvious that had the Fed provided QE to the now bankrupted homeowners, instead of the "too big to fail" debt packagers who had benefited from the arrangements, everyone could have been happier: The homeowners could have kept their homes and the lenders could have continued enjoying their payments, and it is possible that the market would have "failed" to crash.

Even though the injection of huge amounts of Quantitative Easing into the marked seems to be an imprudent move in view of the Fed fears of inflation that had perpetrated the debacle from the outset, QE poses less of an inflation "risk" since by being placed directly in the hands of the affluent it only serves to calm market jitteriness, but causes little change in demand. A poor man made suddenly rich, may buy a house and increase his spending exponentially, but a rich man made richer, only adds the extra to his existing wealth. The sudden influx of a great deal of additional wealth has no significant impact on the demand of the affluent. What matters it if their accounts are at a hundred million or two hundred million, they're not going to rush out to spend the extra money on groceries or a roof over their

---

[82] Wong, G. (2006). Fed hikes rates again Central bank policy-makers raise key rate to 5.25%;. CNNMoney.com staff writer (June 29 2006). https://money.cnn.com/2006/06/29/news/economy/fed_rates

[83] See Cox J. (2015). Fed raises rates by 25 basis points, first since 2006. *CNBC*, https://www.cnbc.com/2015/12/16/fed-raises-rates-for-first-time-since-2006.html

[84] The movie "The Big Short" provides some interesting interviews with the non-affluent who had enough ready cash to make the pre-hiked-up-interest-rates mortgage payments and were buying house after house in a bid to cross into affluence.

heads. Money coming into the hands of the affluent makes little difference and can be absorbed in balance-sheets without stimulating the economy, hence the stagnation of the economy despite persistent injection of QE into the hands of the affluent. It just doesn't "trickle down"[85] into the general economy, a situation very similar to Sieroń's "imagined" situation (after Hume):

> Imagine a situation in which people who were the first to receive new money decided in solidarity to destroy it all. In this case, their increased buying power would not materialize in the market, so it wouldn't bump up prices.[86]

Once upon a time one could laud the capitalist system as enriching the entire populace even as it enriched the rich more, but this argument has been deflated in a roboticized economy. The trickle-down effect, if there ever was one, is obviously tapering off: If robots are sowing and reaping, money will flow to robot owners, who are most probably affluent themselves. As all menial labor is displaced by "robotial" labor , wealth will circulate within an increasingly closed affluent system.

---

[85] Contra various exuberant supporters of the "trickle-down" approach, which obviously inspires the providers of QE, and which economist J.K. Galbraith has dubbed the horse-and-sparrow theory: 'If you feed the horse enough oats, some will pass through to the road for the sparrows.'

[86] Sieroń, A. (2019). *Money, inflation and business cycles : the Cantillon effect and the economy*. Routledge, p. 15.

CHAPTER 3: THE CONSEQUENCES OF MONEY

Capturing life efforts

Once a community adheres to a durable monetary form, it becomes possible to capture the values held by perishable forms. The value of an apple, soon to be consumed, or of a fleeting hour of toil, many now be captured in perpetuity.

This phenomenon of copying invisible value into a durable form became the key to all economic development as it now became possible to capture the values of all the myriad forms of passing favors and perishable goods by which people benefit each other.

Efforts expended in work disappear from the world as they are being carried out, but when such efforts are considered worthy of remuneration, their value may be caught by a monetary form.[87] The value captured in money is preserved and may now be copied to other forms without limitation, even though the value of the effort for which payment was received is gone once the effort is ended.

As an example of the way in which the value of life-efforts is captured, let's take a profession that has gone extinct sometime in the 1980s following automation: the defunct job of movie projectionist. It used to be a technician's position involving knowledge of electricity and mechanical maintenance. In the 1940s people studied for this profession in technical colleges.

The projectionist would sit in a booth above the movie theater and handle the machines that projected the film. He would load heavy 1,000-foot reels of 35mm film into special brackets, then thread the film along a complicated path of pulleys and rollers. He would maintain the incandescent carbon arc needed for the projector light, and switch between two machines in order to seamlessly start a second reel as the first was finished. He also had many other tasks such as machine maintenance, splicing the films, and rewinding the films back on the original reel once they had been projected.

He was not producing anything.

He was providing a service.

Once the movie was over, the service was over.

The life-effort exerted by the projectionist was gone.

All that was left was a notation of hours "worked", which at the end of the month would be totaled and multiplied by the wages per hour, and the projectionist would get a check inscribing the amount, which he would then take to the bank, which copied the amount into its own ledgers, and notified the paying bank that it should deduct the amount from its ledgers. The check was marked "paid" with a large well-inked rubber stamp.

As far as the value of the projectionist's efforts is concerned, nothing occurred beyond various "inscriptions": the paying bank wrote a minus, the receiving bank

[87] The fact that work itself does not retain its value, even though that value is transferred to a monetary form (cut and paste, instead of copy-paste) has led many classic economists, including Smith and Marx, to assume that "work" is the basis of all value. It goes without saying that work is no different from any other thing to which people assign value.

wrote a plus, and the projectionist now proceeded to convert this record into currency forms of various denominations, some of which he converted into commodities – such as foodstuffs, and when he ate the foodstuffs their value was lost – but the value of the monetary forms that he left at the supermarket in exchange for his groceries was not lost – it continued on its way to the supermarket's bank.

The monetary forms used to capture the value of the projectionist's life efforts spread through the economy as they were repeatedly used in other transactions. The flow of money just went through the projectionist, motivating him to action and allowing him to feed himself, and little of it remained with him.

The value created by his life-effort ended with that effort, but its replication in a monetary form continues to exist long after the projectionist had "eaten" his wages.

The profession of projectionist no longer exists. A computer took over that position. The movie house owner had an initial large outlay to buy the new machines, but only low maintenance costs since then. Also, a single computerized projection machine positioned in a central projection room can handle a number of movie theaters simultaneously. The human projectionists were let go.

All humans are commodities to each other and benefit each other as they benefit their own selves. Anything human can be commoditized, but the deep faith that allows extricating value from commodities and transferring it to symbolic forms, makes it possible to disengage a person's utility from a person's being.

A hand, an eye, an ear, are all accouterments of "being", and yet they are commodities in that they provide value. The ability to perform services with the body is the most basic form of commodity. Watchers rent out their eyes and washers their hands and backs. The very concept of "labor", which so many economists have considered the quintessence of "value", hinges on the utility of the body for generating value – and yet this value goes far beyond classic definitions of "labor", for the loving embrace of a nanny can be sold for money too, as can the attentive ear of a therapist.

The benefit of wage labor lies in its ready commoditization of people in all those areas where there is no tangible product, from the services of a lawyer to the care provided by a welfare worker. In the present age, with the decline of human involvement in production following automation, there is an increase in the importance of all the professions that are essentially services provided by one human to another.

At the other end of the spectrum are the perishable goods of human consumption, the food that is consumed and gone, and the many tangible forms, like prescription glasses, that are consumed by an individual and subsequently discarded, ultimately losing all value as they are buried in landfills.[88]

This also illuminates the expanding gaps between the rich and the poor. The poor are stuck with the perishable forms of their life-efforts, while the rich hold the

---

[88] Nevertheless, thanks to the fundamental aspect of free agency underlying all storage of value in forms, all objects may continue to function as forms of value because of the freedom of individuals to assign value. Objects that have become worthless in the eyes of one individual may still be considered valuable by another - so one often sees people sifting through the trash of others or collectors rummaging in attics looking for objects that one's grandmother had already discarded. However, food is consumed and gone, and once its physical shape no longer exists, its usefulness as a form of value is also gone.

eternal forms of money. Money may shift from one owner to another, but it never disappears from the world. The total amount of money held by humanity always expands and grows to hold more and more value.

The consensual community-based belief that a value of 5 is captured in a form denominated as 5 establishes that value forever. This value can be passed on to other monetary forms – such as added to 19 other forms marked as 5 and exchanged for a single form labeled 100. It can also be deposited in a bank and its value copied to a digital representation in a numbered account.

People born into affluent families own all the value accumulated by their ancestors, and those who are born to a leading marauding nation, such as the English, enjoy a heritage of tremendous accumulating values. Anyone walking around London will quickly sense the rich layers of acquisition accumulated through multi-generational colonialist plunder and the transatlantic slave trade. We may gratefully credit the British with the great innovation of abolishing slavery, an institution that was taken for granted throughout history[89], but the value accumulated over centuries of shameful practices still remains. Wealth, once captured in durable forms, may exchange hands and "run away" from you, but remains, in itself, imperishable.

Networks of cooperation

Between the two poles of value production and value consumption, the monetary form stores and replicates value along the entire chain of human economic interactions.

As a concrete example of how value stored in monetary forms flows through the human world, constantly replicating itself[90] as it passes from one owner to another and from form to form, let us now track the progress of a can of tuna through a supply chain and see how every node within it replicates and retains value while transferring ownership.

It is impossible to point to the origin of a particular chunk of tuna that ultimately ends on a consumer's plate. The tuna is a very large creature, so a single fish may be the source of many a chunk. If the drained contents of a can of tuna weigh 4 ounces while a single tuna fish weighs anywhere in the range of 50 to 2000 pounds, depending on species, then hundreds or even thousands of cans may originate from a single tuna fished out of the sea.

The ultimate simplicity of buying a can of tuna at a supermarket masks the great human productivity underlying it and the maverick inventiveness of humanity that created every step of the process.

---

[89] Perhaps we should doubly thank the British. Sometimes only the deepest horror and the most blatant injustice can shock people awake. The horrific excesses of the transatlantic slave-trade finally led to the recongition that slavery is an abomination. Who knows if we would not have been otherwise stuck forever with the gentler and far more insidious Muslim version of slavery, which persisted for may years, until finally abjured under Western pressures in the 20th century.

[90] Many economic problems can be attributed to conditions arising when such replication is blocked by either the absence of a sufficient quantity of monetary forms, especially smaller denominations, to allow full human participation, or when monetary forms are kept out of the market through hoarding or by government policy.

Humans had to learn to fish such large specimens as a tuna, which requires seafaring boats and the cooperation of many fishermen. This was followed by all the great historical developments of the fishing, canning, distribution and marketing industries, that are ultimately supported by your little payment of symbolic embodied value at a local supermarket.

Such a supermarket too, involves the participation of many people in its own right: There are the people who set up this specific store. There is probably a company that runs it, and perhaps your local branch is part of a chain of supermarkets. They are probably an incorporated company limited and have investors, and many people and a great deal of money were involved in the incorporation itself. They bought this building, and someone built it, perhaps a private contractor or a construction company. There were lots of officials involved in the regulation, zoning and licensing. Then a lot of people were involved in setting up the shelves and everything else required for the physical infrastructure of this shop.

In order to ultimately sell a single can of tuna, it is necessary to employ a great number of people. If it's a big supermarket there are probably cashiers, inventory control clerks, shelf stockers, managers at various levels and so on, and that's even before we get to the actual product. This is just the vehicle that makes the product available to us as we walk into the supermarket or even if we buy online from that supermarket and people will be running around between the shelves and getting our package ready, and then someone will deliver it to our door.

The physical infrastructure is there to support the entire process by which the tuna is brought to us on a "silver platter". We didn't go out and fish it out of the sea. Our food is not procured through hunting-gathering but through networking, and the network depends on all these people working together, and the one medium that unites them all is trust in the monetary forms of embodied value.

The entire supply chain is united by money: Money for wages, money to buy produce, money to pay for the building, money paid to all the people who have cooperated in creating this point of sale. All these people accept value embedded in symbolic forms in payment for their involvement. They are all motivated and organized together through their consensual trust in the particular embodiment of money that serves as their local currency, which mediates between all the parts of the system so that they can work together to bring a bit of tuna to your table.

When you purchase a can of tuna, the ownership of the can and its value is transferred to you, while the ownership of the symbolic forms of value you provided is now transferred to the store, and merged with its receipts.

If we move upstream, we see that some of the embodied value will again be replicated in paying the wholesalers who supplied the supermarket with the tuna. In these transactions, the supermarket gets the tangible forms of tuna cans for retail sales, while the wholesalers get a replication of the value of the shipment in symbolic forms.

The wholesalers themselves carry out transactions with a number of suppliers, and these intermediaries will also receive copies of the value replicated from the payment that you made when you bought the tuna. These may include a shipping company that brought the cans from overseas, so you have all those ships and the people operating them. Perhaps, too, there is a tuna canning factory in some other country that is involved, and they accept a different currency of symbolic forms, and the party making the forex conversion will also take a little bit of replicated value.

Ultimately, at the very end of this chain you will find the person who actually took the tuna out of the water, who replicates the value of the tuna fished in whatever currency form was paid for it.

The tuna industry comprises all these countless of people, who all work harmoniously together thanks to their shared belief in the value of money.

Much of this network involves free initiative and enterprise: Who set up the tuna company? Who set up the company that makes tuna canning machines? What about the graphic artist who made the logos for the tuna cans? Did he or she study in some design school before they set up shop? All these people are embedded in an enveloping system of trust that allows them to find their place within reality, whereas that reality is borne by this consensual faith in money that sends its tendrils deep into the daily life of each and every person.

The monetization of value is the true lingua-franca of the world, as it easily crosses boundaries between cultures. Some of the people in the tuna production chain may be living in quite diverse cultures. Perhaps the fisherman is fishing in the Sea of Japan? Or perhaps he is actually a Norwegian sailing the North Sea? Who knows? Are there even tunas in the North Sea? Perhaps then in the Indian Ocean? Could the fisherman be Hindi? Perhaps he is very xenophobic and won't like us at all. He could be a Muslim, a Christian, a Hindu, a Buddhist or a confirmed atheist. It really doesn't matter. It could be a man or a woman, a patriot or a turncoat – it matters not.

Whoever they are, their faith in the value embodied in monetary forms enables them to work together with others without regard for race, creed, color, gender, or anything else.

Faith in money unites us all in a single fabric of trust that allows whoever you are and wherever you are to participate in the livelihood of others, and to share with others this creation of our world as we freely transfer value from tangible forms into symbolic ones and vice versa.

CHAPTER 4: MONEY AND CIVIL RIGHTS

It was the struggle of elite groups over their economic interests that historically led to an increased measure of freedom and recognition of rights. When it becomes impossible to take by force, despots are obliged to share their power:

> The Magna Carta was agreed to in 1215 as a compromise between the king and the magnates, restricting the king's power and giving the magnates protections against the financial exactions and related abuses they had experienced in the past... In a Parliament held at Oxford in 1258, they forced the king to agree to a new charter that enhanced the rights provided in the Magna Carta, more fully curtailing the means that could be used by the monarch in raising funds.
>
> More important, to deprive the king of support among the commons, which included many knights and royal officials, the Oxford charter committed the magnates to extend to the (upper) commons rights similar to those that the nobles had extracted from the king for themselves. Finally... in 1296 the king accepted a new charter, providing guarantees against arbitrary taxation, a key step toward acceptance of the idea that there should be no taxation without representation... In the reigns of each of these kings, their financial pressures forced them to extend the property and other individual rights to the nobility, and eventually to what we may consider the upper middle class.[91]

It is not every day that those in authority are willing to dilute their power and let others enter their inner circle. In fact, even five hundred years after the achievements of the Magna Carta, the right of franchise in 18th century England was still reserved to owners of property and they were the ones that set the agenda.

It was only in 1918 that all English men over 18 and all English women over 30 got the vote, and it was only in 1969 that both men and women became eligible to vote at 18. Throughout most of history most men, women, and youngsters were disenfranchised and had no say in their fates, not to mention those classes who not only lacked property but were themselves property.

The increased participation of a greater number of people in "ownership" is the hallmark of greater human prosperity, as human potential requires a robust material platform in order to develop fully.

The widespread dissemination of anonymous means of payment took place simultaneously with the rise of new political views, as described by Leithart:

> political writers tried to imagine states where obligations of gratitude no longer played a foundational role. Personal bonds of loyalty were damaging to the common good of nations and kingdoms, and thus political life should be founded on, and run off of, different principles than families and networks of friends. Power should not be beholden to favors or those who can bestow them; no one should be able to dangle a debt of gratitude

---

[91] Landes, D. S., Mokyr, J., & Baumol, W. J. (Eds.). (2012). *The invention of enterprise: Entrepreneurship from ancient Mesopotamia to modern times*. Princeton University Press, p. 538.

over the head of a ruler. What this required in practice was the destruction of medieval aristocracies, whose power was all but entirely dependent on gift alliances.[92]

The basic human sentiments of gratitude and indebtedness have not disappeared, but they have dissipated into an ever-growing system of reciprocity mediated by the symbolic forms of money. These made it possible for people to immediately discharge their gratitude: They could use money to repay the exact value of what they received, thereby relieving themselves of any long-term obligations. Money immediately discounts future obligations.

Once money flows within an economy, it is no longer a promissory note, but rather a note preventing indebtedness. The note bearing the injunction to "pay to bearer" relies on the great web of faith in the ability of money to efficiently capture and cleanly copy any value, and to transfer its ownership so that no further obligation exists. Cash is anonymous money supported by a community of faith that believes in the soundness of the money. You can trust anyone belonging to this community to respect your money and relinquish ownership of valuable things in exchange for it.

The role of banks in providing access to money

The achievement of universal access to large quantities of monetary forms was a protracted historical process. The first banks, which appeared among Italian traders about seven hundred years ago, initiated the modern monetary revolution by entering the market as a third party willing to immediately return a favor to a benefactor in exchange for the gratitude of the indebted party.

If and when the debtor returns the favor one day, he will no longer have to return it to his original benefactor, but rather to that third party, the bank, which has already repaid the debt, and is now the one that must be repaid.

Thus, was modern cash born: Affluent persons with deep pockets stepped into the shoes of the original recipients of favors and repaid those favors immediately, thereby discharging the obligation towards the original benefactor, while the obligation of the beneficiary remained in place, even as the original benefactor was replaced with a new one.

This substitution of one creditor for another and the immediate repayment of the original debt while transferring the obligation to a new creditor, teaches that human respect for the fulfillment of obligations is so ingrained that the sense of gratitude is capable of displacement from the original benefactor who benefited the original beneficiary to another benefactor, thereby also providing the original beneficiary with an added benefit by discharging his obligation towards the original benefactor.

Thus, from the very inception of banking to this day, "debts" are sold as assets and transferred from one party to another, and money itself, in all its many forms, is a promissory note to "return favors".

Whosoever holds a monetary form holds a promise to return favors, and can now receive such favors from countless people who would be willing to benefit him in exchange for just such a promissory note. Any supermarket would be willing to give

[92] Leithart, P.J. (2014). *Gratitude : an intellectual history*. Baylor University Press, pp. 9-10.

you the benefit of a banana, in exchange for such a monetary form that promises that it too, in its turn, can receive a favor.

Wealth itself may be defined in terms that are reminiscent of "gift economies", which certain anthropologists love to present as a counter-example to monetary economies, for the amassing of wealth as measured in monetary terms is no more than the amassing of such promissory notes to receive favors from anyone who is willing to exchange favors for such promissory notes.

The banks were quick to establish mutual ties and create a robust network of immediate disbursement for parties doing favors, regardless of the form of the obligation that had to be repaid:

> The Amsterdam Exchange Bank (Wisselbank) was set up in 1609 to resolve the practical problems created for merchants by the circulation of multiple currencies in the United Provinces, where there were no fewer than fourteen different mints and copious quantities of foreign coins. By allowing merchants to set up accounts denominated in a standardized currency, the Exchange Bank pioneered the system of cheques and direct debits or transfers that we take for granted today. This allowed more and more commercial transactions to take place without the need for the sums involved to materialize in actual coins. One merchant could make a payment to another simply by arranging for his account at the bank to be debited and the counterparty's account to be credited. [93]

The bills of exchange also became means of buttressing trust. Metallic currencies frequently lost the trust of the public because one ruler or another may have excessively adulterated his silver or gold. But now the problem of unreliability was drowned in the great sea of banking trust.

The old Italian bankers had created a means of assuring a form of trust that transcended the actual currency: Trust in the value of the bank itself, the value of the human institution that wrote the bills of exchange. Trust was shifted to the source of trust rather than the tangible material on which it was originally foisted. The material was stripped away and trust remained.

This arrangement, however, was restricted to a very limited number of members: just the bankers who were within the inner circle of this economic elite:

The bills themselves circulated among merchants as a kind of paper money. Although the activities and services of the banks remained confined to a relatively small number of people and did not involve the average peasant or city dweller, the banks had, in effect, found a way to put more money into circulation.[94]As the forms being exchanged became less tangible, for they were but exchanges of promises to return a favor one day – the importance of the tangible forms held by the bank (such as bars of precious metals) declined, and the typical characteristic of modern banking known as "fractional reserve" began to flourish. According to this system, the number of favors that a bank could disburse to others (who would then owe it a favor) exceeds the number of favors that the bank had actually received (the deposits of precious metals held by the bank).

---

[93] Ferguson, N. (2008). *The Ascent of Money: A financial history of the world.* Penguin, p.48.
[94] Weatherford, J.M. (1997). *The History of Money.* Crown Publications, pp. 74-75.

> By lending amounts in excess of its metallic reserve, [the Swedish Riksbank] may be said to have pioneered the practice of what would later be known as fractional reserve banking, exploiting the fact that money left on deposit could profitably be lent out to borrowers. Since depositors were highly unlikely to ask en masse for their money, only a fraction of their money needed to be kept in the Riksbank's reserve at any given time. The liabilities of the bank thus became its deposits (on which it paid interest) plus its reserves (on which it could collect no interest); its assets became its loans (on which it could collect interest). [95]

This was the birth of "fractional reserve" banking, in which a small number of tangible forms kept in reserve can be used as a jumping board for the creation of a great deal of money through debt.[96]

As Weatherford writes:

> Under the new system a bag of a hundred florins that might once have sat idle for years in a noble's strongbox could now be deposited for safekeeping in an Italian bank that had access to branches across the continent. The bank then lent the money and circulated the bill of exchange as money. The noble still had his one hundred florins, which were now on deposit in the bank; the bank had one hundred florins on its books. The merchant who borrowed the florins was richer, and the person who held the bill of exchange now had one hundred florins as well. Even though only one hundred gold coins were involved, the miracle of banking deposits and loans had transformed them into many hundreds of florins that could be used by different individuals in different cities at the same time. This new banking money opened vast new commercial avenues for merchants, manufacturers, and investors. Everyone had more money; it was sheer magic. [97]

So began the great age of completely abstract monetary forms supported through faith in their value.

Now everyone truly <u>believed</u> that these bills were worth 100 florins, and so long as they believed that, an entire world of economic expansion became possible!

Money was freed from the constraints of the illusion of its materiality, although hundreds of years would pass before even those 100 golden florins that served as a fiction of collateral would be removed. [98]

The innovation of replicating money via notes of exchange, which were the precursors of what would one day become state-printed banknotes, embodied the newly established trust in the institution of banking itself. The affluence was now embod-

---

[95] Ferguson, N. (2008). *The ascent of money: A financial history of the world.* Penguin, p. 48.

[96] An important point to remember at this juncture is that modern double-entry bookkeeping is still focused on balancing the account and fails to show this proliferation of money, which disappears behind the veil of an accounting system that only documents differences rather than accumulation.

[97] Weatherford, J.M. (1997). *The History of Money.* Crown Publications, pp. 75-76.

[98] And yet, the recognition of the arbitrary infinite availability of money still encounters deep resistance to this day and motivates governments to undergo all kinds of convolutions and contortions to maintain a sense of monetary tangibility.

ied in trust. So long as you believed that the bank was solvent, it could print as much money as it needed.

In our present era, the entire edifice of the global economy is contingent on trust in the soundness of financial institutions. This leads many prophets of doom to decry the entire fiat-based economy as a Ponzi Scheme. Of course they are right, and this directly leads to the question of authority. A government has the authority to run a Ponzi scheme, not so private individuals.

It is the prerogative of power.

Old Carlo Ponzi failed because he could not produce additional money. He was a mere user of money, not a producer, and once he ran out of investors, he ran out of money. States creating fiat money have no such limitation. The establishment Ponzi scheme can go on forever.

The reason that Ponzi schemes sometimes operate over long periods and everyone is happy is that so long at the so-called "bubble" does not burst, everything is fine. There is no backing for money beyond the pouring of liquidity backed by sheer trust – and what if people realize this? What will they do? Make a run on gold? There is nowhere to go. They must continue to trust, and we are all in this together, we are all interdependent in the intersubjective world of others, and only our continued mutual trust makes the human economic world exist.[99]

This understanding opens a way to a different approach to the weaknesses of the market. Volatility is simply a result of backsliding in heart, of losing faith in the soundness of the system. It is so easy to doubt and think that there may no longer be "100 florins" in the bank, and once doubt creeps in, it ultimately leads to what happens when you have runs on banks, and the market slides into a liquidity crisis because people are certain that their underlying assets are being taken away, and they are usually right for their wealth was an ephemeral inscription based on some fractional reserve, some "100 florins" replicated without end, and when their faith wanes, their "assets" evaporate.

Even the assets that serve as reserve, even the original "100 florins", in all their gilded weight, are but the reification of faith in their value, and they too are worthless without intersubjective faith in their value, so that the extension of that faith to the innumerable additional loans that create money is but a natural development of the strange miracle of symbolic Forms accepted by all as tangible reality.

The innovations of modern banking slowly rolled across Europe with promissory notes, until in mid-18th century London a central bank was given the authority to issue bank notes: "A distinctive form of promissory note that did not bear interest, designed to facilitate payments without the need for both parties in a transaction to have current accounts."[100]

The invention of cash![101]

---

[99] When that trust is shaken, the world teeters on the brink, although it seems now that governments have learned some of the lessons of history, and in the Great Recession, the G20 came forward to bolster trust in the underlying asset (which was trust itself) by creating huge quantities of money ex nihilo.

[100] Ferguson, N. (2008). *The ascent of money: A financial history of the world.* Penguin, p. 49.

[101] Though its days may now be numbered!

No need for a bank account. All you need is carry around a banknote issued by a recognized bank. This idea of "pay to bearer" was a new level of abstraction for "currency". It was no longer necessary to identify the recipient. The promise to deliver money became money in its own right.

The advantages of the easy proliferation of money

In the 18th century, Benjamin Franklin wanted to print a lot of paper money because he already understood that it really doesn't matter what the currency is. All you need is trust and any form will do to capture and convey this mutual trust, if, as we now know, disembodied numbers can do this, then certainly paper was sufficient for the task.[102]

The fiat money regime prevalent throughout the world today is a natural progression of fractional reserve banking, but it was only at the beginning of the 1970s that monetary forms finally shed their illusory guise as a tangible thing and were publicly exposed for the intangible consensually agreed-on symbolic forms that they always were.

In this sense "fiat" is still a misguided term, for it is not the fiat of the sovereign that dictates the value but the willingness of citizens to accept the fiat and agree that this indeed is "money".

Fiat money constitutes a true reflection of the nature of money. It has no pretentions to be linked to anything tangible. It blatantly, impudently admits its absence of intrinsic value,[103] and yet insists that it is the currency and every single denomination is full of value, and whether you like it or not, you'd better believe it.

Governments print money, point to it as being valuable, and everyone agrees. Not just within the society directly ruled by that government, but all of humanity, all people everywhere, respect that currency, as exchange rates are used to compare the fiat money of different countries.

People respect currencies according to the power of the governments backing them, with the dollar having reigned supreme for many years. In many countries where the locals distrust their own currencies, the phenomenon of currency substitution[104] is prevalent, especially dollarization, where economies, such as Ecuador, or Panama distrust their own coin and prefer the U.S. dollar exclusively, while other countries, such Argentina or Zimbabwe use the dollar alongside their own currencies.

Fiat money is just currency without the illusion of intrinsic value. It embodies values symbolically and transcends even the paper that it is printed on – for most of it is now just numbers on monitors – which can be converted into printed paper – for

---

[102] Franklin, B. (1729). *A Modest Enquiry into the Nature and Necessity of a Paper Currency.*

[103] Right in the face of all tangibilists, who hate it deeply and pine for gold. Tangibilists come in all shapes and sizes – and have history, tradition, and even the Bible to point to. Many of them refer to metal specie as "natural currencies" as if the belief in gold is more natural than the belief in the American dollar.

[104] For a map, see https://en.wikipedia.org/wiki/Currency_substitution.

those people who prefer holding onto something,[105] or sadly, the more impoverished non-affluent who have little access to banks and plastic cards.

The famous economist Milton Friedman wrote about the revolutionary nature of fiat money:

> It is worth stressing how little precedent there is for the present situation. Throughout recorded history, commodity money has been the rule. Money, in the sense of a medium of exchange and unit of account, has commonly consisted of a claim on a specified physical quantity of a designated commodity.
>
> The end of specie standards and the emergence of a world monetary system in which every country has an "irredeemable paper money" has produced two very different streams of literature: one, scientific; the other, popular. The scientific literature, dealing with monetary reform and the government's role in providing outside money. The popular literature is alarmist, and "hard money," essentially all of it based on the proposition that… the world is inevitably condemned to runaway inflation unless and until the leading nations once again adopt commodity standards.[106]

Even though it has been many years now and governments have shown that they are able to manipulate their fiat money in such a way as to stabilize the economy, they were unable to do this skillfully. It is still a work in progress, but there is obviously no turning back, because commodity money itself was a different kind of "fiat", which depended on faith in metal and on the manipulations of its availability.

We remain fiat, because we have ultimately always been "fiat" believing in the value of what others consider valuable, even though self-appointed prophets of doom continue to issue books under such strident names as "The Non Repentant view of the Economy" or "The Non-Politically Correct View of the Economy", which are mostly concerned to decry fiat regimes as hoaxes.

The present economic systems undoubtedly involve a lot of pain and a lot of conflict, and considerable lack of clarity, yet there is progress in a direction of greater empowerment of individuals, enfranchisement of people who were before barred from entering the market. There is no need to return to something that has never been real and ultimately proved itself to lead to great panic and loss. As we saw in the Great Depression, those harking back to tangibility were those who broke the economy.

Today, even fiat money is but a drop in the great ocean of intangible wealth. The banknotes and coins in circulation are just a fraction of the actual quantity of money in the economy, about 5%. Ingham gives an even lower percentage:

> Portable things that we take to be money are still used in 85 per cent of all transactions but now amount to only 1 per cent of the total value of monetary transactions. In other words, actual media of exchange are now a relatively insignificant element of most monetary systems; but con-

---

[105] Perhaps akin to people who prefer reading print books rather than read them on their smart-phone, but the words only represent the thoughts of the author, which transcend the material used to represent them.

[106] Friedman, M. (1985). Monetary Policy in a Fiat World. *BOJ Monetary and Economic Studies.* September.

> sciousness of money is still formed to a significant extent by the small-scale transactions.[107]

Ingham summarizes some of the core problematics of received economic dogma, which somehow manages to simply ignore the abstract manner in which money is actually created, and illuminates the doctrinal underpinnings of the yearning for tangibility:

> The most startling paradox… is the fact that the mainstream, or orthodox, tradition of modern economics does not attach much theoretical importance to money… Two assumptions in orthodox economics account for this counter-intuitive position; both are fundamentally mistaken. First…it is maintained that money is a commodity… in the sense that it can be *understood,* like any other commodity, by means of the orthodox methodology of microeconomics - 'supply and demand', 'marginal utility' and so on. The *analytical* structure of the modern orthodox economic analysis of money is derived fundamentally from the original Aristotelian commodity theory in which money is conceptualized as a 'thing' that acts as a medium of exchange because it possesses value… In this conception, although 'cash' is now reduced to insignificance, there can, nevertheless, be a 'stock', or 'quantity' of 'things' that 'circulate' or 'flow' with varying 'velocity'. But, as we shall see, these metaphors are as misleading as the underlying theory on which they are based.[108]

Moreover, as Ingham succinctly points out, some of the more callous austerity policies are not the product of anything "real", but are social constructs reified within economic dogma to assume a reality of their own

> The production of the supply of money is always subject to rigorous control, and is not permitted to respond freely to demand. The scarcity of money is always the result of very carefully constructed social and political arrangements. [109]

[107] Ingham, G. (2004). *The Nature of Money*. Polity Press, p.6.
[108] Ingham, Ibid, p.7.
[109] Ingham, G. (2004). *The Nature of Money*. Polity Press, pp.7-8.

CHAPTER 5: THE CONSEQUENCES OF MONEY

Beyond tangibility

What we believe about the world determines our interactions with it. There is no need to quote here the many examples of religious dogma constructing reality, from run-of-the-mill ad-hoc explanations up to and including Papal Infallibility, but in "science" too, it is trust in the theories espoused by various disciplinary consensuses that envelopes all of our conceptions of reality. As Shapin describes it:

> Most of our formal knowledge of the natural world is derived from no other source than what scientists tell us, or, more precisely, from what is told us by their apparent spokespersons... If indeed we know these things at all, we take on faith the principles of aerodynamics and hydrostatics, the role of DNA in heredity and development, the chemical structure of benzene.[110]

We in fact believe what scientists "come to believe", and this becomes our representation of reality – mediated by trust and belief in the consensus of our many peers that these beliefs do reflect reality.

Where money is concerned, more than any other belief system[111], empirical reality is completely swallowed up in the symbolic to the point that we are willing to convert all forms, be they tangible or intangible, into the denominations of currency forms. We are secure in the belief that the value incorporated in the monetary forms we have received is fully transferable to other forms that contain value, in future transactions.

The potential that money represents for future interactions, a potential that is sheer hope based on a deeply held faith, is more important than any immediately tangible utility, for all is convertible to money and money is convertible to all. Money is literally the embodiment of a preference for a bird in the bush over a bird in the hand. In fact, we quite happily relinquish our bird in the hand in exchange for the promise of a future bird.

Even the great housing bubble, which had something tangible (houses) at its core, did not actually concern houses, but their further embodied value, securitized debt tranches, that represented some future obligation to pay higher and higher returns. Most of the financial part of the economy is constructed of similar self-inflating money, where the owner of a financial instrument is holding a form with a capacity for self-increase.

Both the affluent and the non-affluent share a common belief in the ability of monetary forms to hold value. The entire human world is stable in its belief in money. Even if currencies have many different forms, they can all be converted into each other, so that the core virtual value freely flows from one form to another, be it the currency of different countries, or any other physical or symbolic object that

---

[110] Shapin, S. (1995). "Trust, Honesty, and the Authority of Science." Institute of Medicine. *Society's Choices: Social and Ethical Decision Making in Biomedicine*. Washington, DC: The National Academies Press, p. 390.

[111] Science does have religion's alternative narratives to contend with.

people attach value to: all forms can be exchanged with the intangible symbolic forms of money.

All surplus is accumulated in the symbolic while life-efforts[112] and consumption constantly flow in and out of the symbolic and are in fact conceived of in symbolic terms. Everything that is embedded in reality, all those tangible things that an individual can encounter directly: A piece of fruit, a roof over one's head, shoes for one's feet, are all wrapped up in the belief in the value held by symbolic forms, all are sustained within the symbolic network which allows all human needs to be obtained from other humans who share the belief.

Even though we are ostensibly all born into tangible reality, where everything in our lives is at first tangibly available and the abstract concept of money and its use only slowly develops over time, ultimately, we grow to live within the belief in the symbolic, utterly conceptualizing reality in its terms.

As in all matters of belief, be it religion or science, our theories about the world, or beliefs about how the world is, especially when intersubjectively shared, have a tangible impact on reality. We literally live within the intersubjective world of others as represented in our minds, for there is no perception outside of our minds and no understanding outside of our conceptions of the world, and the belief in the transmutability of value from one form to another becomes the fundamental economic infrastructure of our lives.

There is a clear-cut distinction between the non-affluent who hasten to convert tangible forms into symbolic ones and back again, instantly converting the value embodied in whatever symbolic monetary forms they have into such tangible forms as food, clothing, residence, etc., and the affluent who retain huge surpluses of symbolic monetary forms which they only occasionally utilize to acquire tangible forms, but more usually just hoard or use to obtain more symbolic monetary forms, without having to pass through tangible reality.

When you buy value embodied in shares and wait for share prices to go up, you never leave the symbolic. When you buy a painting for 80 million dollars, you have co-opted the crazed artist's masterpiece into the world of symbolic financial instruments. It has become another store of symbolically embodied value; Stored not in the actual tangible picture but in the universal belief in the value of a Van Gogh. It is not the Portrait of Dr. Gachet that stores the huge symbolic value ascribed to it, but the intersubjective consensus on its value, as expressed in auction, which buoys it on the symbolic aspirations of the affluent.

Banks, risks and rating agencies

The success of a bank is measured by the extent of the debts that it gets to collect and call assets, banks are always seeking to expand the circle of borrowers among the less-affluent, even though the risk of default is greater among them.

---

[112] The term "life-effort" is preferable to the term 'labor' as the latter is skewed by the speculations of economists who disenfranchise the great bulk of actual life-efforts exerted in the economy for subsistence, such as the tremendous investments involved in housework and child-rearing, not to mention the many government enterprises that do not get to be included in the GDP.

In a world of symbolic fiat money, banks are constantly descending into the real world in search of the "gold" behind the symbolic money, i.e., the real actual capacity of a borrower to repay his debt, because only if a bank can point to the "reserves" of its debtor, can it justify recording that debt as an asset on the bank's books.

Thus, the borrower's ability to repay the debt, the collaterals that he provides and the guarantors that he corals to vouchsafe payments have replaced the now-extinct fractional reserves.[113] Instead of holding a reserve in the bank's vaults – the reserve has now been outsourced to the borrower's real world.

This situation gives rise to a constant conflict between the bank's desire to lend money (thereby creating it in the economy) and its wariness in regard to the assets securing the loan. When governments had a less stringent hold on banks, it was possible to find extensive funding for many risks because the banks were ready to produce money even when the collaterals were less than robust, but once central banks have become the rule, the demand for secure collaterals has become stricter as part of the regulatory environment, so that fewer people can receive loans, and less new money is fed into the economy.

The balance of collaterals and risks provides justification for the pricing of loans. Collaterals are often more tangible assets, while the risks are no more than a bunch of beliefs, estimations and concerns provided by certain "accredited" agencies and popular pundits – matters of pure faith.

In this manner, virtual "risk" becomes the counter balance of tangible "collateral". The risk is a self-contained narrative in its own right, used to justify higher prices for higher "risks". "Credit rating" is a rating of faith that monetizes it and converts it into symbolic quantities.

Since belief in value is the core generator of value, and trust in money is what makes it money, evaluators of reliability have assumed a significant influential role in modern economies. Rating agencies routinely quantify trust and distrust. Lower ratings mean greater risk of breach of trust.

The agencies rate the extent of the distrust that debtors will be able to generate enough value to meet obligations, as well as the extent of distrust in regard to financial forms of value, based on the rating of distrust towards the financial institutions and governments creating the monetary forms.

In this way, the monetary forms themselves come to embody value in direct proportion to the robustness of the economy producing them and the stability of the governments and banking systems generating them.

The genius of the modern economy is that it has not only learned to quantify trust and distrust, but also to value distrust more highly than trust, by adding a "premium" on the risk of breach of trust.

It is the investors who buy high-risk financial instruments who stand to gain the most, while less ardent believers who stick to cash or buy low-interest high-reliability bonds may lose their money to inflation, which is but the general rising

[113] Even the last vestiges of tangibility pretense have been shredded with the final demise of the fig leaf of reserve banking as the Fed dropped all reserve requirements: "The Board reduced reserve requirement ratios to zero percent effective March 26, 2020. This action eliminated reserve requirements for all depository institutions." https://www.federalreserve.gov/monetarypolicy/reservereq.htm

tide of distrust in the value of symbolic monetary forms, which is so paradoxically created by a glut of forms.

Thus, distrusted financial instruments have become much sought after by affluent investors with great surplus or gamblers with great audacity and a leveraged credit line. BBB rated bonds pay higher returns than AAA rated ones, since being unreliable, their buyers are given an additional financial incentive to buy them.

The reward of "blind faith" in a risky bond may often be destitution, but for many of them, it is possible that "blind faith" in one scheme or another breeds great profit, for it is the very concentration of a plurality of humans on a single endeavor, product, or theory, which gives such an endeavor, product, or theory their power.

Where finance is concerned, all processes are circular: trust in money creates money and trusted money creates trust. If you believe it, it will come, and it will come because you believed it.

Patron-client patterns in the absence of money

Socialist systems, established on the basis of certain speculative thoughts on the nature of man, history and the economy, were determined to abolish ownership of private property, and remove the central role of money. They can therefore serve as an excellent "laboratory" for examining the question of what happens to the basic human drive to reciprocate favors when ownership of private property is blocked and money stops filling a major role in the relationships between people.

In his brilliant monumental work on the "socialist system" Janus Kornai analyzes the human dimensions that flourish under regimes that receive their inspiration from Marx, with a particular focus on "the social relations between people, and... the relations of superiors and subordinates, of those exercising and those obeying power. What molds these relations, and what influences do they have on economic activity."[114]

These relations are saturated with a hierarchical ideology in which the leaders of the people are at the apex of society and know what is right and proper, and many of the citizens fervently adopt this ideology and view it as a superior system.

> The adherents of the official ideology are imbued with the Messianic belief that socialism is destined to save mankind. The conviction that the socialist system is superior to the capitalist is one of the most important ingredients in the ideology.[115]
>
> The official ideology states that socialism is a purer, nobler system that ensures social justice and equality. People themselves are transformed under this system, as they place themselves, voluntarily and increasingly, in the service of the common good, so conquering their own selfishness and individualism. This idea appears in Stalinist ideology, but it plays a particularly crucial role in Maoism.[116]

---

[114] Kornai, J. (1992). *The* socialist *system: The political economy of communism*. Princeton University Press, p. 12.

[115]Kornai, Ibid, pp. 50-51.

[116]Kornai, Ibid, p. 52.

All of the various "popular" organizations established within socialist societies as representatives of various sectors, only serve to affirm the truth uttered by the deeply adulated supreme leaders:

> The mass organizations' main function ultimately becomes one of conveying the ideas and intentions of the party to "target" sectors of society (the workers, youth, women) corresponding to the sphere of each organization. As Lenin put it, they are "transmission belts" between the party and the masses.[117]

Once private ownership is cancelled, and all property is owned by the state, an urgent need arises to manage areas that are often in private hands in countries where private ownership is allowed, and are managed within financial frameworks in which people exchange monetary forms for the various services and products that they need. Under the socialist regime, private individual desires are considered selfish, so it is the party that decides what services and products are needed. As a consequence, a hierarchical bureaucratic apparatus expands to regulate social relations via transmission from superiors to subordinates, as Kornai describes:

> The influence of the bureaucracy spreads to such traditionally private spheres as culture, religion, the life of the family, how many children people have, the relations of a household with its neighbors, how free-time is spent, the choice of career and employment, and much more...Every economic transaction qualifies as a matter of concern to the party and the state...[118]

Once the favor-returning action of money is disallowed, human patronization patterns spontaneously re-emerge. In the absence of money, the ancient feudal patterns of patron-client relationships become dominant and the importance of personal ties increases.

The Soviet system was widely organized on the basis of patronage- clientelism wherein senior officials cultivated support networks among officials of lesser rank.[119] Russia is governed to this day by members of the old communist aristocracy – Putin's clients and cronies who occupy positions bestowed on them by their patron.

This may also be key to understanding why the socialist system was so enthusiastically adopted in China, for the Chinese Guanxi system of patronage was already in place, so that the Soviet method was easily mapped onto it.

It is not independence that is rewarded in the education of children everywhere, but enthusiastic obedience and dedication to fulfilling the wishes of the parent, teacher and master. Hierarchical organizations have always significantly benefited those who obeyed the powerful.

---

[117] Kornai, Ibid, p. 40.

[118] Kornai, Ibid, p. 46, ibid fn 21.

[119] Consideration should perhaps be given to any system in which money is not part of an exchange of favors, in order to assess the extent to which it is subject to the problems associated with patronage. There is no doubt that academic institutions everywhere are subject to this problem since one cannot advance without the patronage of more senior academics who recommend and foster the advancement of those among their more junior peers who provide loyalty and support for the agendas of the senior academics, thereby solidifying their academic standing and political power.

In the coercive hierarchies that characterize humanity throughout history, a special place is reserved for the faithful and devoted slave, the obedient and attentive child and the loyal worshipper who is overjoyed to fulfill the wishes of his Lord: "Hath the Lord as great delight in burnt offerings and sacrifices, as in obeying the voice of the Lord? Behold, to obey is better than sacrifice, and to hearken better than the fat of rams."[120]

In similar vein to these traditional systems, which are characteristic of religions to this day, the socialist method also generates a traditional social hierarchy that obligates the believer to obey his elders and betters and relinquish his views for theirs.

> The classical system has a paternalistic nature self-evident from what has been said about self-legitimation: those possessed of power are convinced they know better what the interests of those whom they rule demand. The bureaucracy stands in loco parentis: all other strata, groups, or individuals in society are children, wards whose minds must be made up for them by their adult guardians. [121]

Only the powerful subversive effect of monetary forms on all hierarchical systems makes the development of the new existential phenomenon of personal freedom possible.

When it becomes impossible to reciprocate favors by paying for them, the beneficiary of the favors loses some of his freedom, and becomes subject to the type of benevolence that knows what is good for you better than you, as may be seen in the classic position of socialist leaders vis a vis "the people":

> The major criteria of selection are political reliability, loyalty, and fidelity to the party and its ideas… Berlin, personifying the paternalistic dictator, phrases his line of thought like this: "easy for me to conceive myself as coercing others for their own sake, in their, not my interest. I am then claiming that I know what they truly need better than they know it themselves... Once I lake this view, I am in a position to ignore the actual wishes of men or societies, to bully, oppress, torture them in the name, and on behalf on their 'real' selves.[122]

It is very easy to fall into this patronizing trap, and there is hardly a political system that does not suffer from some level of patronization, since people who "know better" or have received specific training and are therefore "better qualified" make decisions for the ignorant and the unqualified. History is full of hair-raising stories of abusive practices that were deemed good and worthy, causing untold suffering until they were eventually abolished, at best.

As described by Kornai:

> The virtues of discipline are closely linked with those of willing sacrifice. Individuals must be prepared to subordinate their own interests to higher interests, as defined in a specific situation by the bureaucracy. If need be, they should take on extra work outside the officially prescribed working hours. If need be, they should renounce the pleasures of improving their

---

[120] 1 Samuel 15:22 KJV.

[121] Kornai, Ibid, p. 56.

[122] Kornai, Ibid, p. 57 fn. 15.

material standard of living. If need be, they should accept the subordination of family life to state interests, for most of the time of all adult family members is taken up with work and political activity. In this respect again, the official ideology embraces a kind of "military spirit"; all citizens should feel they have been mobilized. Metaphors taken from military life are common: "the labor front," "hero of socialist labor," "the battle for production," and so on. The building of socialism is likened to a long campaign in which all must do their duty. Those who do not (or are suspected of not doing so) are cowards, deserters, or traitors. [123]

Kornai points to the importance of private ownership in fostering responsibility, because owners value their possessions and take care of them: "property rights arc full if, and only if, the utilization of the property affects the owner's own pocket,"[124] Kornai describes the ownership situation in the socialist system:

> None of the profit from the state-owned firm passes automatically into the pockets of members of the bureaucracy, and, conversely, they need not contribute out of their own pockets to any of the state-owned firm's losses. Since the connection between the "personal pocket" and the residual income of the state-owned firm is entirely absent, those who otherwise have the deciding voice in how the residual income is used are not real owners at all from this point of view. The automatic, spontaneous incentive noted with private property does not apply. Society must rely wholly on artificial incentives.[125]
>
> The depersonalizing of property becomes extreme. Whatever state-owned firm one takes as an example, there is no individual, family, or small group of partners to whom one can point as owners. Since no one can pocket the profits and no one need pay out of his own pocket for the losses, property in this sense is not only depersonalized but eliminated. State property belongs to all and to none.[126]

Kornai points to the way that various forms of private ownership and private enterprise seem to develop naturally:

> The various forms of private ownership, including capitalist ownership, develop and gain ground basically as a result of spontaneous economic processes. This transformation is paralleled in the legal system, which protects private ownership and enforces private contracts. Though the regulations of the state give a greater boost to capitalist ownership in certain periods, one certainly could not say that the state had organized capitalism's development and stabilization. [127]

In contrast, under a socialist regime, a concerted and focused effort is made to thwart the human tendency to own personal property:

> Those in power are convinced that elimination of private property serves the people's interests, and that the peasants serve their own interests by

---

[123]Kornai, Ibid, pp. 58–59.
[124]Kornai, Ibid, p. 65.
[125]Kornai, Ibid, p. 74.
[126]Kornai, Ibid, p. 75.
[127]Kornai, Ibid, p. 87.

giving up their independence and entering the cooperative. Their backwardness and shortsightedness prevent them, however, from recognizing their own interests, which is why they must be compelled, even if they resist the change. One purpose for which the power is needed is to force people against their will to adopt a way of life that eventually will be for their own good. A system of values is being discussed that deeply influences the adherents of the Communist party, from the top leaders down to honest, enthusiastic party members who hold no function in the apparatus. This conviction spurs them to work, make sacrifices, and accept unpopular tasks, and to implement their program regardless of whatever mass resistance they meet.[128]

As Korani clearly demonstrates, the main difference between socialist and non-socialist systems is the role of money, which replaces the ancient hierarchical relations of patronization that are the inevitable consequence of the attempt to manage a society from the top down.

> Subordinates have several kinds of motivation for carrying out the superior's commands, the most characteristic being the effort to win the superior's approval, receive the reward offered, and. avoid the penalty threatened for noncompliance…[129]

Inevitably, when one cannot pay for favors, one is obliged to return them in kind! As Kornai writes:

> It is worth mentioning at this point deeds based on mutual assistance and favors… The manager of one firm will help the manager of another by supplying a component, for example, hoping that he can expect similar support next time. Friends will help build somebody's house, each one knowing he can count on similar assistance when he needs it. This reciprocity mechanism helps to fill the gap left by the frictions of bureaucratic coordination and the narrow scope left to the market mechanism.[130]

Here is the wonderful paradox of mutual assistance that flourishes pleasantly when life is hard. This is precisely the mutual aid that monetary systems undermine, because money quantifies everything and copies everything to the abstract option of "returning the favor" by just paying for it, so people ultimately prefer to hire help for pay and be rid of any post-favor obligations than to return to the classic heart-warming system of one good turn deserves another.

By uprooting private property, the socialist system intensifies generosity and revives all these classic systems of mutual aid; the warm and caring arrangements rooted in the plight of the many. In this regard, the socialist systems are an engrossing historical experiment that allows us to look on economies that uphold private ownership from the "outside".

> It is unique in history for a central power to have intervened from above artificially by means of legal regulations in the development of society to decide that a particular main type, market coordination, should vanish, or

---

[128]Kornai, Ibid, p. 88.

[129]Kornai, Ibid, p. 92.

[130]Kornai, Ibid, p. 106.

> at least be confined to insignificant positions, and replaced by centralized bureaucratic coordination. This was a fundamental change that did not occur spontaneously. It was carried through by the central decisions of power, and by fire and the sword. It was then followed by numerous concomitants that arose spontaneously without any central decision expressly being taken; the atrophy of self-governing forms, the dwindling of enthusiasm for voluntary work for the community, and relegation of family and community life to a subordinate role. And there was another concomitant: a spontaneous self-generation, self-propagation, and excessive expansion of bureaucratic mechanisms that went beyond the expectations even of those who initiated and directed the epoch-making changes. [131]

In fact, the monetary systems of capitalism are the first and only in history that have undermined such stifling structures of patronage. By providing room for self-interest and private property they have subverted the discipline that is typical of tight systems of patronage. When money is drained from the system, relationships revert to systems of control, and the control exerted by a socialist system is obliged to be very meticulous:

> Thousands upon thousands of functionaries in the party apparatus, the state administration, the firm and cooperative managements, and the mass organizations negotiate, calculate, renegotiate, and recalculate before the millions of planning commands finally emerge at all levels.[132]
> The starting point for discussing implementation of the plan is that implementation is compulsory. This principle is so important that some authors have referred to it as the most characteristic feature of the system by attaching such names to the system as "directive planning," "imperative planning," or "command economy".[133]

An interesting example of the wastefulness of such “command economies” are China’s ghost cities. Built at the command of the masters, they have created a tremendous surplus where no demand yet exists:

> Thousands of villages have been swept off the face of the earth; hundreds of new cities and myriad new towns have taken their place, well in advance of the populations and businesses that are intended to fill them. While many of these are currently lingering in the void between construction and vitalization, the question is rarely if, but rather when. When will these places attract sufficient population and commercial base to function fully?[134]

Command economies exert a characteristic influence on the personality of the people enmeshed within them, as Kornai notes:

> All these circumstances affect directly the daily management of affairs, and perhaps even more important is the long-term effect on the character

---

[131]Kornai, Ibid, p. 109.
[132]Kornai, Ibid, p. 114.
[133]Kornai, Ibid, p. 114.
[134] Shepard, W. (2015). *Ghost Cities of China: The Story of Cities without People in the World's Most Populated Country*. Zed Books, p. 198.

> of each member of the bureaucracy. It is unwise to criticize upward, come out with unusual ideas, or take initiatives. It does not pay to think for oneself or take risks on one's own. A subordinate wanting to do something should "cover himself" in advance by obtaining his superior's prior approval and spreading the risk over as many superior leaders as possible... Since most people have at least some vanity, it is also worth flattering the superior. These character traits develop not only after the individual has entered the bureaucracy. From the outset those with these attributes gain entry and above all advance quickly in their careers. The character-forming and training effect, and the selection criteria of bureaucratic control, reinforce each other: servility and a heads-down mentality prevail.[135]

When people cannot use money to buy what they need and what they choose, but instead bureaucratic systems determine what they need for them, the number of services and products available to the public decreases, as no one is thinking up new ways to be useful. This is how a "shortage economy" is created, in which people wait in long queues for the allocation of services and products. Kornai writes the following on the consequences of such a shortage economy:

> The shortage phenomena and the uncertainty of obtaining supplies induce the buyer to hoarding, that is, to build up large input stocks. Buyers make up for the absence of mobilizable producer reserve capacity by themselves producing the inputs they lack, if need be. This occurs even in the household in the form of handyman, do-it-yourself activity, and is thoroughly typical of the producer firms in classical socialism... Wherever possible an engineering works makes its own components and has its own foundry, and even its own building department, because it does not believe any outside firm will deliver a part or a casting, or provide a construction service on time or in an orderly way.[136]

Thus does the coerciveness and inefficiency of the patronizing command system give rise to its obverse: self-reliant people who do not rely on the system but on their own powers. It does not breed any technological sophistication, but it does encourage self-reliant self-starters.

Capitalist systems are far more fragile in this regard because they rely on extensive cooperation between a great many different and very sophisticated parts. Breakdowns in supply chains can lead to problems which people in socialist countries would not even conceive of. At the level of the individual, the Soviet system is much simpler and hard to break, as it is very nearly broken anyhow. The parts are simple and easy to assemble, like Lego Duplo versus the sophisticated Lego Technic of capitalism.

In a capitalist economy even a blocked toilet or the need to install an electrical outlet can be big problems for people who rely on the skilled services of easily-available specialists.

Kornai makes an interesting comparison between a "seller's market" that characterizes "shortage" economies, where the seller has the upper hand, and a "buyer's

---

[135]Kornai, Ibid, p. 121.
[136]Kornai, Ibid, p. 249.

market" that characterizes capitalist economies in which the buyer has the upper hand. In a seller's market, the buyer makes an effort to look for products and is willing to settle for almost anything if only to have something; in a buyer's market, by contrast, the sellers court the buyers and convince them to buy their produce.

As Kornai writes:

> Human contacts suffer damage that is statistically invisible but all the graver in human terms. Often the seller (or, in the case of a rationing system, the bureaucracy's official) is unfriendly and rude, while the buyers must grin and bear it, lest they get even worse treatment next time. The defenseless consumers frequently find themselves in demeaning situations. [137]

It is particularly interesting to look at two differential economies, one that encourages private property and one that discourages it, which have developed from an identical point of origin. Kornai writes:

> Consider North and South Korea, which were in the same economic position after the Second World War, The South resembled the North not only in its point of departure but even in certain features of its political and administrative structure applying in the postwar period: it was ruled by a relentless dictatorship that brooked no opposition; the bureaucracy of the state played a big part in running the economy, intervening in decisions on foreign trade, investment, the extension of credit, and so on. Yet the difference is fundamentally significant: the official ideology in South Korea differed utterly from North Korea's; the possessors of undivided political power, far from intending to eliminate private property, cooperated with it and sought to assist its prosperity. Although a big part was played by bureaucratic coordination, there was no mention of abolishing the market, which operated with great vitality. As time went by, North Korea finally came to display all the classical system's essential features, while South Korea, after decades of suffering and sacrifices, developed a political and economic system that increasingly resembles Japan's path of development and differs ever more sharply from North Korea's. [138]

This is the bottom line: When one cancels private property mediated by monetary forms that allow people not only to hold private property but also to exchange it, multiply it, change it and alter it in all of the creative ways that money makes possible, the result is social stagnation.

As Kornai sharply comments, the fact that there are capitalists in a market economy is not the most important point, the essential matter is the democratization created by money and the extensive freedom for an autonomous existence that does not depend on the good graces of people or is forced to submit to their commands:

> In reality the fact that economic actors maximize their profits is not the most important attribute of a market mechanism based on private ownership. The major features are decentralization, free entry, and free competition. [139]

---

[137]Kornai, Ibid, p. 307.

[138]Kornai, Ibid, p. 369.

[139]Kornai, Ibid, p. 406.

> Another very strong inducement to join the private sector is the desire for autonomy… Private entrepreneurs find it gratifying to be their own masters. That applies not only to rich, highly capitalized proprietors but to the owners of the tiniest family workshops or peasant holdings.[140]
> Many people commit themselves to a private business even if the rewards are meager and uncertain, because they do not want a boss breathing down their necks, and independence has great intrinsic value for them. The knowledge in itself that there is the chance of private enterprise and that an individual is able to leave the public sector and seek prosperity and a career elsewhere raises one's self-respect. The expansion of the private sector increases the opportunity for citizens to choose, and ultimately the liberty of individuals.[141]
> Private enterprises need no central command before entering into market-mediated relations with each other and the households. It happens self-evidently and spontaneously; all that had to be done for the market to develop was to lift or at least ease the prohibitions.[142]

After having experienced the entire range of economic regimes from the communist regime in the fifties, through the period of socialist reforms, and eventually the indulgent capitalist regime in the US, where he spent his later years, Kornai's conclusion is that capitalist and socialist markets have certain inherent qualities:

> I would like to spell out only one virtue of capitalism: its innovative and dynamic nature. In the first part of the essay, I argue that rapid innovation and dynamism are not a random phenomenon, which may or may not occur, but a deeply rooted system-specific property of capitalism. The same can be said about its opposite, the socialist system. Its inability to create great revolutionary new products and delay in other dimensions of technical progress are not due to some errors in policy but, rather, is a deeply rooted system-specific property of socialism.[143]

The socialist method teaches us important lessons regarding freedom and possessions. The option of owning personal possessions allows every person to become an entrepreneur. Sometimes, perhaps even frequently, a person may waste his time on nonsense and squander his freedom to own on products of ostentation and prestige, but other times he may invest in his own personal capital and that of his children through education and self-improvement, or in beneficial enterprises, inventions and environmental improvements, and all the myriad things that people can do to benefit others when they have control of their own possessions.

The great lesson to be learned from the Soviet experiment is that the freedom to own personal possessions is the key to all human prosperity, and plentiful money in the hands of the public is the best way to achieve this.

Whenever money, capital and personal possessions are disempowered, the tribal power, the power of nepotism, increases instead – because without money, people are forced to meet their needs by courting personal favors, and one requires a great

---

[140]Kornai, Ibid, p. 434.
[141]Kornai, Ibid, pp. 434–435.
[142]Kornai, Ibid, p. 448.
[143] Kornai, Ibid, p. 4.

many personal favors and a very wide-branching network of patronage in order to acquire a number of benefits that a free market provides quite easily.

In both milieus, a person must do many things and the world of debt surrounds people on all sides, but the psychological and practical approaches are different because the obligations are also different. Under capitalism, you have anonymous debts to credit institutions and banks; under communism your creditors have a face – it is the face of your patron.

The crucial question is always: Who will own the surplus? Who will decide what to do? At this moment in time, we are witnessing the bear inklings of the tremendous potential inherent in the personal freedom to control one's disposable income. Economic freedom is the only true human freedom, because true enslavement is the slavery imposed by reality itself and the necessities and vicissitudes of making a living.

Only when sophisticated cooperation is achieved, is it possible to create extra plentitude: the surplus that allows a standard of living that is less enslaving. When the surplus is managed by a minority, as it was throughout most of human history, distortions are created that detract from freedom and block entrepreneurship.

Only when money is available to all to do as they like, can the true spirit of entrepreneurship arise among the tangled weeds of conspicuous consumption and the pursuit of prestige.

Like all things in life, there is far more potential than actualization. Millions of seeds carried in the wind will one day give rise to but a small number of fruit, but where freedom exists, some may enjoy the wind under their wings and innovate and initiate new ideas and projects, while in places that impose strong limitations on the individual, people will tend more to emulation (which can be controlled and regulated) than to innovation (which is far more dangerous).

CHAPTER 6: ECONOMIC DOCTRINES

For hundreds of years, thinkers have intensively studied the issues surrounding economic transactions between people, and have offered many descriptions and theories that eventually became principles of faith in their own right and deeply influenced attempts to regulate the economy and rectify some of its more blatant ills.

Most governments today rely on the theories of academically trained economists, and some of these theories have achieved the status of universally held doctrines. Special importance is attached to these beliefs because they win official support from the authorities of each country and serve as the basis for the economic policy imposed on the population. Some of these doctrines have caused a great deal of suffering.[144]

A great many royal vestments proved to be non-existent after the crisis of 2008:

> The dominant strain of academic economics, and of policymaking orthodoxy, not only failed to see the crisis coming but asserted that better policy and increased financial sophistication had made financial crises far less likely than in the past. The president of the American Economic Association, Robert Lucas, was confident in 2003 that "the central problem of depression prevention has been solved." The IMF was sure in 2006 that financial innovation had "increased the resilience of the financial system" and made commercial bank failures less likely.
>
> Ideas matter. They strongly influence the assumptions with which policymakers approach practical policy choices. They define other ideas as unsound, not worth considering, taboo… In two key ways the dominant strain of modern economics ill served our understanding of financial and macroeconomic instability. Finance theory assumed that human beings are rational and financial markets efficient, and macroeconomics largely ignored the details of the financial system.
>
> But underlying these specific failings was also a methodological and philosophical bias— a preference for mathematical precision and elegance at the expense of realism and a desire to arrive at certain answers…[145]

Even the most bizarre doctrines, and humanity has known a few, contribute to social order. The fact that a doctrine is shared and believed by a community establishes the cohesion necessary for social function, even if that dogma eventually undermines the very society that stubbornly adhered to it, as evidenced by the consequences of the socialist dogma discussed above.

---

[144] As pointed out, for example, by Bertran et al.: "policies geared towards the poor are often driven by normative assumptions, rather than empirical facts, in ways that may miss the intended beneficiaries."

Bertran. M., Mullainathan, S. & Shafir E. (2004). "A behavioral-economics view of poverty". *The American Economic Review*. 94 (2): 419–423.

[145] Turner, A. (2017). *Between Debt and the Devil*. Princeton University Press, p.242.

Theories, even when quite wrong, always have their impact on reality. As Soros[146] wrote:

> The behavior of people—exactly because it is not governed by reality, is easily influenced by theories. In the field of natural phenomena, scientific method is effective only when theories are valid; but in social, political, and economic matters, theories can be effective without being valid. Although alchemy failed as science, social science can succeed as alchemy.[147]

It is not the "truth" of a belief that matters but its tangible consequences for human life. A belief in witches endangers independent women with a mind of their own, a belief in the "free market" can litter the streets with the homeless, while a communist belief is liable to foster penal colonies in Siberia.

We have a bias of thinking of beliefs as being true or not, but the truth or untruth of a doctrine can only be verified if we are open to the refutations of empirical reality, and dogmas are wont to deny reality in the name of a higher "truth".

Often, rather than reality impacting the "truth", it is beliefs, as universally adopted narratives, that can paint pictures with dire consequences for real human lives by impoverishing various aspects of reality, by marking out certain areas of reality as unsuitable, as dangerous, or as having some "natural" attribute or other that is proclaimed to dictate a certain attitude.

Economic beliefs have shaped not only policy but the very reality of economic agents, and have led policymakers down certain paths that are often at odds with what is actually happening in human lives and what would benefit these lives. Moreover, when reality is found to contradict prevailing economic dogma, it is simply denied. As Fine and Milonakis describe how since

> The first principle of Economics is that every agent is actuated only by self interest… In so far as economic agents were in reality motivated by 'sympathy with each other's interests', [it was] held that they were emphatically not 'economic' agents.[148]

Fine and Milonakis also point out that "orthodox" economics have applied:

> a prodigious reductionism across a number of dimensions. The individual was reduced to a given set of preferences… The technical assumptions necessary for this exercise to be accomplished, together with aggregation over individuals for general equilibrium, were simply assumed to be – and have become taken for granted as – a conventional wisdom. [149]

Once this one-sided economic axe had been ground, it was possible to hack away at all kinds of things that failed to comport themselves according to economist axioms, such as products that do not behave according to supply and demand, which were easily circumvented by making up all kinds of ad-hoc exceptions such as

---

[146] The ultimate pudding-proofer of economic acumen.

[147] Soros, G. (2000). *Open Society Reforming Global Capitalism.* Public Affairs, p.47.

[148] Fine, B. & Milonakis, D. (2009). *From Economics Imperialism to Freakonomics: the Shifting Boundaries between Economics and Other Social Sciences Economics As Social Theory*. Routledge, p. 11.

[149] Fine & Milonakis, Ibid, p. p. 5.

"Giffen Products" or "Veblen products" to maintain the fictions and avoid their empirical refutation.

The method becomes the message and the aspiration to present something tight and powerful with a good logical argument overrides any empirical evidence capable of refuting or refining the theory.

The mathematical models developed by economists make it possible to become even more deeply immersed in abstract mathematical games that remove any conflict with reality through various reductive assumptions.

Funnily enough, the very reliance of monetary forms on the web of social trust refutes accepted economic doctrine in the most fundamental way. It was the shared trust of people who were sharing a world of faith that created a deep social faith in the integrity and trustworthiness of their fellows, and gave birth to the modern world of citizenship and equality.

Money embodies trust in its forms, and it is that trust, which ultimately fostered capitalism. The divorce of the field of economics from reality is so far-reaching that the very core of economics, money itself, is considered to be irrelevant to economics. As Ingham succinctly points out:

> The 'neutrality' of money is the second paradoxical tenet held by orthodox economic theory… it is held that money is a 'neutral veil' over the workings of the 'real' economy… Indeed, money is not even accorded an analytical place in some of the most prestigious mathematically sophisticated models of the economy…[150]

Lawson too writes about the deep dogmatic rift between economics and reality:

> The feature of modern economics which is remarkable here is the minimal concern that is shown either for tailoring methods to insights available regarding the nature of the social world, or for explicitly determining the sorts of conditions under which chosen methods would be appropriate… Rather, methods and procedures are formulated according to the nature or degree of their technical sophistication, or their conformity with *a priori* conceptions of proper practice.[151]

Leontief points to the way in which mathematical methodology has become a sophisticated means of circumventing the need to address reality:

> Economists developed a nearly irresistible predilection for deductive reasoning. As a matter of fact, many entered the field after specializing in pure or applied mathematics. Page after page of professional economic journals are filled with mathematical formulas leading the reader from sets of more or less plausible but entirely arbitrary assumptions to precisely stated but irrelevant theoretical conclusions... [152]

Leontief describes the specific methodologies adopted by economists to bypass the need for empirical inquiry:

> Nothing reveals the aversion of the great majority of the present-day academic economists for systematic empirical inquiry more than the

---

[150] Ingham, G. (2004). *The Nature of Money*. Polity Press, p.8.

[151] Lawson, T. (1997). *Economics and Reality*. Routledge , p. xi.

[152] Leontief, W. (1982). Academic Economics. *Science*, Vol. 217, Issue 4555, pp. 104-107, p. 104.

methodological devices that they employ to avoid or cut short the use of concrete factual information... They first of all resort to "aggregation." The primary information, however detailed, is packaged in a relatively small number of bundles labeled "Capital," "Labor," "Raw Materials," "Intermediate Goods," "General Price Level," and so on. These bundles are then usually fitted into a "model," that is, a small system of equations describing the entire economy in terms of a small number of corresponding "aggregative" variables. The fitting, as a rule, is accomplished by means of a "least squares" or another similar curve-fitting procedure.[153] While the labels attached to symbolic variables and parameters of the theoretical equations tend to suggest that they could be identified with those directly observable in the real world, any attempt to do so is bound to fail: the problem of "identification" of aggregative equations after they have been reduced…was raised many years ago but still has not found a satisfactory solution.[154]

Leontief describes how the disengagement from economic reality has become increasingly entrenched with the rising sophistication of mathematical models:

> Year after year economic theorists continue to produce scores of mathematical models and to explore in great detail their formal properties; and the econometricians fit algebraic functions of all possible shapes to essentially the same sets of data without being able to advance, in any perceptible way, a systematic understanding of the structure and the operations of a real economic system.[155]

It is possible that the persistence of these mathematical models despite their detachment from reality arises from the fact that they serve as justifications for actual policies, and in particular for advocating less government intervention in the belief that the "invisible hand" will iron out the kinks of an imaginary self-serving and coldly rational homo economicus, as Leontief points out:

> Many opponents of government intervention in the operations of the economic system agree with the characterization of the theory of rational expectations as a "most powerful" and "widely applicable methodological generalization," while their more skeptical colleagues…cite that theory as an example of a development "in which theory proceeds with impeccable logic from unrealistic assumptions to conclusions that contradict historical record."[156]

The doctrine of self-interest

Analyzing the origins of economic thought, Jed Stephens points to some of the discipline's prevailing absurdities and their origins:

---

[153] Leontief, Ibid, p. 104.

[154] Leontief, Ibid, p. 104.

[155] Leontief, W. (1982). Academic Economics. *Science*, Vol. 217, Issue 4555, pp. 104-107, p.107.

[156] Leontief, W. (1983). Academic Economics Continued. *Science*, Vol. 219, Issue 4587, p.904.

> It came into the head of certain economists that they wanted to be the Newtons and Copernicuses of economics… they wanted to formalize it. It begins with a thought experiment in regard to the concept of value... Economists had an "objective" theory of value related to "scarcity".[157] According to Adam Smith, air was cheap because it was plentiful while diamonds were rare and therefore expensive. The value of an object was objectively defined by its scarcity – people were purported to make an objective assumption as to rarity.[158]

Obviously, all of these "objective" assumptions, based on a strange differentiation between air and diamonds, completely miss the point in ascribing value to "things" while disregarding the intersubjective origin of all values. Diamonds have no inherent value and air's value has little to do with its purchase price.

Not everything that is rare is valuable. A preliminary sketch can be one-of-a-kind yet no one ascribes value it, even if a great deal of 'labor' had been invested in it.

As Stephens points out:

> Ricardo's theory on skilled labor falls into… problems of circularity: The factor by which skilled labor is more skilled than unskilled labor is determined by the market… but the market determines the price, which also then determines the factor… which means we can't say objectively that skilled labor is 2.2 times as powerful as unskilled labor.[159] The utilitarian point of view attempts to solve these problems by adopting a subjective theory of value: "Jevons," says Stephens, "postulated that the amount of pleasure I get from the second good is not as much as the first. The amount of pleasure I get changes."[160]

Obviously, the worldview underlying this assumption is one focused on "pleasure" and "self-interest". In addition, the assumption that pleasure decreases is based on certain biological drives wherein satiation decreases value: if you've just eaten heartily, you can't look another condiment in the eye.

However, this assumption quickly becomes irrelevant when one looks at other things that bring pleasure without satiation or matters that go against self-interest, which are among the most profound pleasures of human existence – from a song that one can't stop listening to, a book re-read once and again, a mother's love, or even the avarice of a miser.

The very idea of decreasing pleasure as an economic factor is surprisingly unreal even if we were to take it at face-value, for even satiated appetites eventually reset themselves. And what of the appetites of others? Would not demand increase if one wished to appease the appetite of others, especially if it was mediated by the symbolic forms of money, for there is no limit to human avarice when its object are symbolic forms that can be collected without end, even if there is no immediate tangible pleasure involved.

---

[157] Jed Stephens https://youtu.be/PwdjmgG7gok?t=602

[158] Jed Stephens https://youtu.be/PwdjmgG7gok?t=711

[159] https://youtu.be/PwdjmgG7gok?t=1027

[160] https://youtu.be/PwdjmgG7gok?t=1388

Moreover, the focus on individual "pleasure" ignores many aspects of social life, the most salient of which being the value of things for others – such as a mother valuing extra food to give her children.

Were it not for the "envy of mathematics" as Stephens describes it, and the need to find some "converging" factor that would serve as the nail-head for his calculus hammer, Jevons would not have come up with this ridiculous idea, which was to feed so well into "self-interest" assumptions, with all their ancient theological underpinnings assuming evil and selfishness as the worldly side of the Manichean divide.

Eventually, the use of mathematics in economics spread widely for it was the ultimate in scientific posturing and could hide the inanity and irrelevance of any theory and the arbitrariness of any dogmatic supposition under a pile of convoluted calculations and intersecting graph lines.

There is no invisible hand. There are only believers in an invisible hand who promote very specific types of markets based on their belief. The market is created by intentional policies. It was not an invisible hand that created the enormous mortgage market in the US, but an orderly economic policy implemented by the US government, including the tax deductibility of the interest on mortgages, just as it was government policy that brought the market crashing down in 2008. As Fergusson writes:

> The same governments that avowed their faith in the 'property-owning democracy' also turned out to believe in price stability, or at least lower inflation. Achieving that meant higher interest rates. The unintended consequence was one of the most spectacular booms and busts in the history of the property market.[161]

Thus, paradoxically, though economists talk in tangibles and in hard numbers, they are in fact purely in the business of faith – conducted with tangibles as idols.

Graeber writes about the way that the discipline of economics is intimately involved with the economy:

> Economics is all about prediction. It came into existence and continues to be maintained with all sorts of lavish funding, because people with money want to know what other people with money are likely to do. As a result, it is also a discipline that, more than any other, tends to participate in the world it describes.[162]

We have only to think of Bernanke steeped in Milton lore advocating for QE, and thereby tangibly impacting the economics of the entire world through the application of belief to life.

How deplorable the paradox that the advocates of non-intervention by the government have intervened in all governments with the aim of demolishing all obstacles in the way of greed; how atrocious that the devout believers in the "the invisible hand" have destroyed the human mechanisms that were achieved through blood sweat and tears on the basis of the bitter experience of people who aspired to

---

161 Ferguson, N. (2008). *The ascent of money: A financial history of the world.* Penguin, p. 253.

162 Graeber, D. (2001). *Toward an Anthropological Theory of Value: The False Coin of Our Own Dreams*. Palgrave, p.7.

right the wrongs of inequality and shape a government policy that would help the less fortunate. A good government welfare program can achieve many things that luck does not provide, even when such luck is portrayed as the providence of an "invisible hand".

The moral underpinnings of economic dogma purporting to be objective are often quite pernicious:

> Should we feel sorry for our fellow Americans in the Midwest (or elsewhere) who are, from time to time, flooded out of their homes by nearly forty days and nights of continuous rain and snow? Of course, we should…*to some reasonable extent*… Victims of major natural disasters—whether in the form of floods, earthquakes, or hurricanes—receive a great deal of attention… They are natural candidates for government largess. There are very good reasons for exercising considerable restraint, especially when many flood victims are fully capable of buying property outside of potential disaster zones, but choose not to do so.[163]

McKenzie's cold-hearted analysis is a typical example of economic superciliousness and a more-rational-than-thou attitude. Obviously, the proudly "reasonable" McKenzie has no conception of the vicissitudes of the non-affluent, and the fact that people are often constrained in their choices by tangible reality. Economic dogma is cold-bloodedly foisted regardless of the human situation.

It would not be surprising if it turned out that many flood-zone houses are owned by similarly bloody-minded people who are renting them out "on the cheap" to those who do not have the means to find a more secure place to live.

McKenzie is not alone in his pseudo-trendy presentation of classic economic cruelty – in fact he is emulating even more popular treatises of this kind, such as Freakonomics,[164] in which, according to Fine and Milonakis:

> economics imperialism reaches its most extreme version in the form of … the economic theory of everything on the basis of the shallowest principles.[165]

Graeber writes of the cruel underlying assumptions of these orthodox economic doctrines:

> All they really add to analysis is a set of assumptions about human nature. The assumption, most of all, that no one ever does anything primarily out of concern for others; that whatever one does, one is only trying to get something out of it for oneself. In common English, there is a word for this attitude. It's called "cynicism." Most of us try to avoid people who take it too much to heart. In economics, apparently, they call it "science." [166]

---

163 McKenzie, R. B. (2008). *Why Popcorn Costs so Much at the Movies.* Copernicus Books, pp.33-37.

164 Levitt, S. and Dubner, S.J. (2007) *Freakonomics: A Rogue Economist Explores the Hidden Side of Everything*. William Morrow.

165 Fine, B. and Milonakis, D. (2009). From Economics Imperialism to Freakonomics: The Shifting Boundaries between Economics and Other Social Sciences. *Economics As Social Theory*. Routledge, p. i.

166 Graeber, D. (2001). *Toward an Anthropological Theory of Value: The False Coin of Our Own Dreams*. Palgrave, p.7.

Even though some had argued more than twenty years ago that "economics is moving away from a strict adherence to the holy trinity of rationality, selfishness, and equilibrium, to a more eclectic position of purposeful behavior, enlightened self-interest, and sustainability,"[167] it is doubtful if this is more than wishful thinking, as we see the heavy handed policies of austere misanthropy everywhere.

Indeed, said "holy trinity" grows even more deeply entrenched as it becomes more mathematically obfuscated, notwithstanding evidence that undermines its applicability to reality. As Mallaby writes that as far back as:

> … the early 1960s, a maverick mathematician named Benoit Mandelbrot argued that the tails of the distribution might be fatter than the normal bell curve assumed; and Eugene Fama, the father of efficient-market theory conducted tests on stock-price changes that confirmed Mandelbrot's assertion. If price changes had been normally distributed, jumps greater than five standard deviations should have shown up in daily price data about once every seven thousand years. Instead, they cropped up about once every three to four years. Having made this discovery, Fama and his colleagues buried it. The trouble with Mandelbrot's insight was that it was too awkward to live with; it rendered the statistical tools of financial economics useless, since the modeling of abnormal distributions was a problem largely unsolved in mathematics… To prevent itself from toppling into this intellectual abyss, the economics profession kept its eyes trained the other way… Mandelbrot's objections were brushed off. "The normal distribution is a good working approximation," Fama now contended. The crash of 1987 forced the economics profession to reexamine that assertion. In terms of the normal probability distribution, a plunge of the size that befell the S&P 500 futures contracts on October 19 had a probability of 1 in 10^{160}.[168]

Rose[169] points out that the prevalent mode of unenlightened self-interest which permeates the standard "economic view" glosses over the actual underpinnings of this narrative of "self-interest", which is its cooperative obverse, since it is only when people mutually agree with each other that the doctrine of economic self-interest even becomes possible: its very existence depends on cooperation and understanding, and on "sharing the faith":

> A property ***regime*** generally, taken as an entire system, has the same structure as a common property… people have to cooperate to set up the system. They have to get themselves organized, go to the meetings, discuss the options, figure out who gets what and how the entitlements will be protected. … Participants have to cooperate to the extent of recognizing and abiding by the indicia of ownership that their customs set out…

---

[167] Colander, D., Holt, R. and Rosser, B. (2003). The Changing Face of Mainstream Economics. *Middlebury College Economics Discussion Paper* 3-27, p. 1.

[168] Mallaby, S. (2010). *More money than God: hedge funds and the making of a new elite.* Penguin Press, p. 104.

[169] For a brilliant exposition of the biased preferences underlying protestations of objectivity based on an averred proposition of "self- interest" which becomes the "economic point of view", see Rose's chapter on "Property as Storytelling" in Rose, C.M. (1994). *Property and Persuasion: Essays On The History, Theory, And Rhetoric Of Ownership*. Westview Press.

> people have to respect each other's individual entitlements out of cooperative impulses, because it is impossible to have a continuous system of policing and/or retaliation for cheating.
>
> Thus, a property system depends on people not stealing, cheating, and so forth, even when they have the chance. That is to say, all the participants, or at least a substantial number of them, have to cooperate to make a property regime work. **A property regime, in short, presupposes a kind of character who is *not* predicted in the standard story about property**. And that, I suggest, is why the classic theories of property turned to narrative at crucial moments, particularly in explaining the origin of property regimes, where the need for cooperation is most obvious. Their narrative stories allowed them to slide smoothly over the cooperative gap in their systematic analyses of self-interest.[170]

This gap between the imaginings of economists regarding self-interest and the reality of the extensive cooperation between people, even if such cooperation is only in support of such imaginings, is also expressed in:

> …a gap between the kind of self-interested individual who needs exclusive property to induce him to labor and the kind of individual who has to be there to create, maintain, and protect a property regime. The existence of a property regime is not in the least predictable from a starting point of rational self-interest; and consequently, from that perspective, property needs a tale, a story, a post hoc explanation. [171]

Many have pointed out that self-interest may in fact not be the most prevalent human motivation, as humans tend to be social creatures that often care and cater to each other, not to mention cooperate in team spirit.

Thus, while the assumption of "self-interest" has become the main driving vision of economic theorists who help create the policies that fuel the flames of a rather bigoted egoism, findings from a wide range of disciplines point to the magnanimous social nature of human beings who often make great efforts and considerable sacrifices for the good of others.

In her analysis of the "self-interest" doctrine Rose points out 4 distinct "types" that deviate from the dogma:

> ***Malice Aforethought (MA)*** would rather lose a great deal than have the other guy win. He is not looking very self-interested any more, at least in the usual sense. The reason is that he is "distracted" by interpersonal matters.
>
> ***Mom (or Good Citizen)*** too is out of line for a prediction based on self-interest-interest… She puts the other person first. Why would a self-interested utility maximizer do that? She wouldn't. Again, Mom seems to be distracted by interpersonal matters.
>
> ***Portnoy's Mom (PM)*** will be the first to tell you that her order of preference is: "I get zip, you get a lot". PM is even more out of line with a

[170] Rose, C.M. (1994). *Property and Persuasion: Essays On The History, Theory, And Rhetoric Of Ownership.* Westview Press. p. 37.

[171] Rose, Ibid, p. 38.

predicted preference ordering of self-interested maximization. She would rather have the other person come in first.

Hit Me. This is a kind of natural victim: This character is out of the economic predictor's ballpark. She is a mirror image of Malice Aforethought: She wants to lose; she wants to be beaten...[172]

These characters show up constantly in actual narratives, both historical and fictional. In Shakespeare's Iago or Gibbon's Commodus, to take just two illustrious examples, we see full-blown examples of Malice Aforethought in all his vengeance and spite; more recently, we have been seeing computer hackers who implant viruses for no apparent reasons other than pride and meanness.

Mom and the Good Citizen might be less dramatic, but they too are all over the place in heroic novels and tales; indeed, according to feminist literature, the cooperative, helpful character is really quite common.

Phillip Roth of course told the story of Portnoy's Mother in a way that is readily recognizable by a substantial segment of the population, and feminist literature has a good deal to say about Hit Me and about victimization generally.

Those other characters certainly make themselves felt in the law as well. Here as in literature and history, some of the most interesting examples revolve about the Malice Aforethought character.

In property law there is a whole category of cases about people who build the so-called spite fence; their story revolves about some character who goes to very considerable expense to wall in a neighbor's windows or put up some repulsive object to ruin the neighbor's view of the sunset...

Much sadder are the cases of Hit Me's, the victims. The criminal law is now seeing persons who give away all they have, even their lives, and appear consistently to defer to some others in what seems to be a kind of pathology of other-regarding behavior...

The Good Citizen or Mom is another category that shows up constantly in law, and, generally speaking, the law tries to encourage her cooperative behavior. The law allows people to set up all kinds of cooperative arrangements; people can form contracts and partnerships, hold joint bank accounts, and own property in various forms of common tenure...

The point of all this is that legal doctrines reflect the knowledge that these other preference orderings exist; certainly there is no monolithic legal expectation that everyone will behave as an individual self-interested utility maximizer. The further point is that all these off-beat preference orderings suggest an element of indeterminacy in the ways that people use property, trade it, and transfer it. There is no single ordering of preferences in the real world, and everyone knows it.[173]

[172] Rose, Ibid, pp. 31-33.

[173] Rose, Ibid, pp. 33-34.

Self-Interest and the Invisible Hand

Hard headed economists backed by short-sighted (and therefore easily assimilable) economic dogmas have had a tremendous impact on economic development and have contributed to a great deal of human misery.

The prevalent doctrine of self-interest justifies destructive behavior and uncompassionate positions: essentially a nihilistic and pessimistic vision of human nature that celebrates the most extreme egoism purporting that it would somehow find that sweet-spot so celebrated by Adam Smith who was the originator of this paradoxical and quite unempirical vision that: "the individual who intends only his own gain is led by the institutions of the market to promote the public interest: he is 'led by an invisible hand to promote an end which was no part of his intention'."[174]

And yet this beautification of uncaring self-interest relying on the baseless axiom that an 'invisible hand' will ultimately make everything "better", is no more than a theological doctrine greedily grasped by precisely those who "intended only their own gain", and who could now hold up an article of faith to all those who cry in anguish over the despoiling of cooperation, trust and goodness.

The unrealistic part of Smith's philosophy is the idea that people are motivated by unadulterated self-interest, an idea that goes against the grain of the truly social nature of human beings and the fact that humans cooperate for a variety of reasons, of which self-interest is but one. Smith's distorted formulation of human motivation[175] has provided a perverse dogma that has been poisoning economics and hobbling the great blessings of money for hundreds of years.

Let us take a closer look at the famous passage in which Adam Smith explains the existence of the invisible hand:

> The annual revenue of every society is always precisely equal to the exchangeable value of the whole annual produce of its industry,[176] or rather is precisely the same thing with that exchangeable value. As every individual, therefore, endeavors as much as he can both to employ his capital in the support of domestic industry,[177] and so to direct that industry that its produce may be of the greatest value; every individual necessarily labors to render the annual revenue of the society as great as he can. He generally, indeed, neither intends to promote the public interest, nor knows how much he is promoting it. By preferring the support of domes-

---

[174] Sugden, R. (2005). *The economics of rights, co-operation, and welfare*. Palgrave, p.2

[175] This is not the place to expand on the reasons that may have led him to these strange conclusions, but one can certainly point to the prevalent doctrine of "original sin" (the template for unadulterated self interest), which is at odds with the obviously wondrous cooperation that we find in the economic sphere, so that Smith found a way to settle the contradiction via Providence, which he euphemizes as an 'invisible hand', for God always harbors the solution for all theological paradoxes: Credo quia absurdum est.

[176] This is a false assumption, for during Smith's life, England enjoyed an entire empire of plunder that yielded far more than the "produce" of its industry.

[177] Here are many false assumptions about the (unselfish) productiveness of the endeavors of industrialists for industry and society as a whole, but such endeavors may just as easily be directed towards undermining rivals and conspicuous consumption.

tic to that of foreign industry,[178] he intends only his own security; and by directing that industry in such a manner as its produce may be of the greatest value, he intends only his own gain, and he is in this, as in many other cases, led by an invisible hand to promote an end which was not part of his intention. Nor is it always the worse for the society that it was no part of it.[179] By pursuing his own interest he frequently promotes that of the society more effectually than when he really intends to promote it. I have never known much good done by those who affected to trade for the public good.[180] It is an affectation, indeed, not very common among merchants, and very few words need be employed in dissuading them from it. [181]

It is difficult the plumb the depth of the misleading course of Smith's argument, riddled as it is with so many hidden assumptions and so many specific conditions on which the "success" of the hidden hand is contingent – chief among them England's geopolitical dominance in Smith's time and the enormous market based on exploitation of colonial conquests, slave trade and slave labor, and the outright plunder of the "Wealth of Nations".

England in Smith's time had beachheads of pillage all over the world, including Australia, Canada, India, vast expanses of Africa and the 13 colonies of North America, who rebelled against the heavy taxation of the English "crown" just the year before the publication of Smith's book on the Wealth of Nations.

Obviously, God-fearing Englishmen in Smith's time could ostensibly feel an invisible hand bringing England a great wave of bounties from its many conquests and the three-way Atlantic trade: buying people on the cheap in Africa, selling them to plantations in the Caribbean, then buying the produce of the slave labor and selling it in England. This was Smith's invisible hand. The bounty was so great that even England's poor could proudly enjoy a cup of tea with a lump of sugar – both prizes of empire – completely unobtainable by any "domestic industry".

Behind the scenes, unheeded by Smith (keen on invisibility as he was) the proliferation of monetary forms in Smith's day and their dissemination among ever expanding circles of British society, gave rise to a reality that was the obverse of the

---

[178] Why would he have such a preference? Did England not heavily support the non-domestic trans-Atlantic slave trade and the non-domestic lucrative commerce based on the sugar production of the selfsame slaves? Did England not enjoy the benefits of the great plunder of the world encompassing British empire?

[179] This was to become the great battle cry of "free market" advocates, who are in fact championing a distorted reading of this false proposition, so where Smith tentatively states that the purported invisible hand is not "always the worse for the society", and that it "frequently" does good, they positively claim that "By pursuing his own interest he promotes that of the society more effectually," thereby turning speculation into principle.

[180] Freakonomics type literature frequently emphasizes the false conclusion that can be drawn from this utterance: If those affecting to trade for the public good do not get "much good done", then let us support those who have no such affectation, who do not work for the public good, and even blatantly undermine the public good, for it they who will get "much good done".

[181] Smith, A. (1776) (1977). *An inquiry into the nature and causes of the wealth of Nations.* University of Chicago Press, pp. 594–595.

selfishness that rankled Smith to such an extent that he was obliged to invent an invisible hand to secure a happy end. It was the plentiful distribution of money that brought about a reality of wondrous cooperation made possible by a common faith in the value of symbolic monetary forms.

Smith simply got it backwards: it was not that self-interest was leading to the great benefit of a harmonious market, but rather the benefit of a money-based market was so great that it could even sustain those terrible marauding privateers and slave merchants who constantly undermined it.

Unfortunately, the false belief in universal self-interest, led to a false vision of money itself, since it was conjectured that money had originated with just such individuals striving to maximize self-interest. As shown by Ingham however, this is not only a distorted picture but actually quite impossible: It is only 'advantageous' for any given agent to mediate his transactions by money *provided that all other agents do likewise*. To state the sociologically obvious: the advantages of money for the individual presuppose the existence of money as an *institution* in which its 'moneyness' is established.[182]

The main historical abuse of Smith's distorted vision was that wherever people would point out the excesses and abuses that unbridled self-interest brings about, they were shown the great benefits produced by the boons of the market and the capital economy, and told that their suffering was for their own ultimate good.

There is no escaping the recognition that while money is the great boon of mankind, unbridled self-interest, especially that supported by cruel economic policies based on this pernicious dogma, are the bane of mankind.

On a psychological level, the prevailing economic dogmas provide the metaphysical system required in order to exploit those who are not affluent enough to transcend reality. The assurance that a free market is "good" and will eventually benefit everyone is no different from the assurance that an "indulgence" from the church will secure your salvation after your demise.

The beating heart of the economy are the beliefs that guide its actors and the belief in selfishness is the central doctrine that guides the captains of economy in the modern state, as beautifully summed up by Paul Oster who describes "liberty and justice" according to mainstream economic dogma.

> We had been taught to believe in "liberty and justice for all," but the fact was that liberty and justice were often at odds with one another. The pursuit of money had nothing to do with fairness; its driving engine was the social principle of "every man for himself." As if to prove the essential inhumanity of the marketplace, nearly all of its metaphors had been taken from the animal kingdom: dog eat dog, bulls and bears, the rat race, survival of the fittest. Money divided the world into winners and losers, haves and have-nots. That was an excellent arrangement for the winners, but what about the people who lost? Based on the evidence available to me, I gathered that they were to be cast aside and forgotten. Too bad, of course, but those were the breaks. If you construct a world so primitive as

---

182 Ingham, G. (2004). *The Nature of Money*. Polity Press, p.23.

to make Darwin your leading philosopher and Aesop your leading poet, what else can you expect? It's a jungle out there, isn't it? [183]

And all this is anointed with the perfumed oil of the great vision of the great prophet worshipped by the free-market faithful, who prophesied that an invisible hand will restore justice and compensate the dispossessed! All will be well at the end of times, and the Messiah will be riding down Wall Street on a snow-white donkey.

The cynicism goes very deep as the incessant calls for the non-intervention of government demand that the government intervene to remove any blocks to unbridled selfishness, and the government, guided by its misguided economists constantly intervenes to safeguard free capitalist space and truncate any initiative that would curtail that space in order to prevent harm to the non-affluent.

The Distortions of Game Theory

Games theory models purport to provide empirical models that "prove" the doctrine of self-interest. They do so by providing participants with various either-or scenarios that take most of reality, and certainly the most important aspects of human behavior, off the table.

These games, usually one form or another of a prisoner's dilemma, first remove or severely constrain the main element distinguishing mankind, i.e., communication, and impose a set of arbitrary rules without this essential element which is the very foundation of all social life, not to mention economic life.

Once communication has been removed from the table, they offer all kinds of unpleasant and unrealistic situations where people are manipulated to display self-interest, cheat or betray one another. Here is an example taken from Sugden:

> Two people, A and B, are taken to different rooms… The organizer of the game then tells each player: 'I have donated a £5 note and a £10 note to enable this game to be played. You must say which of the two notes you want to claim. If you claim the same note as the other player, neither of you will get anything; but if you claim different notes, you will each get the note you claim.[184]
>
> In the banknote game the players are not allowed to communicate with one another. This makes it impossible for them to co-operate when choosing their strategies… But in many game-like situations, deals between players are both possible and mutually beneficial… This is most obviously true of market transactions: I want to buy, you want to sell, and the problem is to settle on a price. But deals, agreements, treaties or contracts feature in just about every aspect of social life. Even in war – perhaps the closest analogue to the game in which each player's sole object is to beat the other – there is always room for mutually beneficial arrangements, for example over the treatment of prisoners. [185]

Sugden also points to the unreal assumption underling the games:

---

[183] Auster, P. (1997). *Hand to Mouth*. Faber and Faber, p. 12.
[184] Sugden, R. (2005). *The economics of rights, co-operation, and welfare*. Palgrave, p.10
[185] Sugden, Ibid, p.12

> It is a fundamental assumption of the theory of games that players are concerned only with outcomes. Strategies have no value in themselves: they are the means, and outcomes are the ends. [186]

Thus the well-known statement of immorality that "the end justifies the means", becomes the bedrock of economic game-play which will be subsequently applied as a Procrustean bed to reality – forcing the economy into twisted and terrible shapes.

The fundamentalist assumption of rationality too is common to both economics and game-theory, as described by Sugden:

> Economists and game theorists have usually defined utility in ways that presuppose that individuals have 'consistent' preferences and choose 'rationally'… this has proved to be a rather shaky foundation… reality… deviates from the axioms… there are some quite systematic patterns in human behavior that cannot be reconciled with the theory of expected utility. [187]

The silliness of making up various constraints to bind people to arbitrary rules is overlaid with the serious academic mien of these games that present a pose of "empiricism" as real people sit in actual rooms to play these games, but in fact brings the discipline of economics to its ultimate absurdity through reductionist moves, which would have been ludicrous, were not the conclusions of these forced choreographies subsequently used to shape cruel and tragic policies.

In a world where human cooperation and shared faith in value is the very foundation of our economic existence and well-being, these ideas of self-interest, scarcity and an all or-nothing mentality are destructive of the very economy that they purport to administer.

How can one possibly think that such a game as the "banknote" game above, both limited to a binary amount and devoid of communication, can in any way reflect a reality in which banks can create money, governments can print as many banknotes as they want, and people can communicate and share their expectations and desires?

Game Theory often attempts to create limiting conditions of pure self-interest, from which the doctrine of the "tragedy of the commons" is derived on the basis of the axiom of self-interest, in the form of a claim that "unless restrained by some outside compulsion, each actor tries to get the most for himself, and in the ensuing race, a resource that could be renewable is driven instead toward ruination."[188]

The theory claims that:

> When things are left open to the public they are wasted, either by overuse or underinvestment. No one wishes to care for things that may be taken away tomorrow, and no one knows whom to approach to make exchanges. All resort to snatching up what is available for "capture" today, leaving behind a wasteland - thus the tragedy. From this perspective.

---

[186] Sugden, Ibid, p.14.

[187] Sugden, Ibid, p.16.

[188] Rose, C.M. (1994). *Property And Persuasion: Essays On The History, Theory, And Rhetoric Of Ownership.* Westview Press. p. 37

> "public property" is an oxymoron: things left open to the public are not property at all but rather its antithesis. [189]

When one examines actual situations of contentions over limited resources, i.e., when the real "commons" are examined, it quickly becomes evident that the entire doctrine of "the tragedy of the commons" is a fabrication that simply ramps up the usual "scarcity" argument of mainstream economics as it is coupled with the doctrine of "self-interest". Mildenberger points out that in reality:

> Early pastures were well regulated by local institutions. They were not free-for-all grazing sites where people took and took at the expense of everyone else.
>
> Many global commons have been similarly sustained through community institutions. This striking finding was the life's work of Elinor Ostrom, who… showed the diversity of institutions humans have created to manage our shared environment.[190]

Rose explicates how a "shared environment" in fact underlies all ownership regimes, whether private property or common property:

> While our normal means of staving off the tragedy of the commons is a regime of private property, even private property is frequently governed only by custom. We see this, for example, in the prosaic example of the custom that permits us to stake a claim of first possession by leaving a coat on a seat in a movie theater or a towel at a spot on the beach. Indeed, an entire private property regime - whether governmental or customary - may be understood as a managed commons: a private property regime is itself a meta-property, held in common by those who understand and follow its precepts. In a sense, when we decide to divide up the commons into private property, we are only moving from a commons in a physical resource to a commons in the social structure that safeguards individualized resource management.[191]

Ostrom points out how the mean conviction of self-interest can spread to policies that become monolithic and blind to the actual solutions of cooperation possible:

> Many policy prescriptions are themselves no more than metaphors. Both the centralizers and the privatizers frequently advocate oversimplified, idealized institutions…[192] Nationalizing the ownership of forests in Third World countries, for example, has been advocated on the grounds that local villagers cannot manage forests so as to sustain their productivity and their value in reducing soil erosion. In countries where small villages had owned and regulated their local communal forests for generations, nationalization meant expropriation.

---

[189] Rose, Ibid, p. 111

[190] Mildenberger, M. (2019). The Tragedy of the Tragedy of the Commons, *Scientific American*.
https://blogs.scientificamerican.com/voices/the-tragedy-of-the-tragedy-of-the-commons/

[191] Rose, C.M. (1994). *Property And Persuasion: Essays On The History, Theory, And Rhetoric Of Ownership.* Westview Press. p.127

[192] Ostrom, E. (2015). Governing the Commons: *The Evolution of Institutions for Collective Action.* Cambridge University Press, p. 22.

> In such localities, villagers had earlier exercised considerable restraint over the rate and manner of harvesting forest products. In some of these countries, national agencies issued elaborate regulations concerning the use of forests, but were unable to employ sufficient numbers of foresters to enforce those regulations. The foresters who were employed were paid such low salaries that accepting bribes became a common means of supplementing their income. The consequence was that nationalization created open-access resources where limited-access common-property resources had previously existed. The disastrous effects of nationalizing formerly communal forests have been well documented.[193]

Ostrom calls for a turn to the empirical – to the reality of things rather than reliance on dogma that imposes short-sighted and often disastrous constraints on reality:

> ...policy scientists were... using the commons-dilemma model without serious attention to whether or not the variables in the empirical world conformed to the theoretical model. Many theoretical and empirical findings have been reported that should have made policy scientists even more skeptical about relying on a limited set of models to analyze the diversity of situations... Unfortunately, many analysts – in academia, special-interest groups, governments, and the press – still presume that common-pool problems are all dilemmas in which the participants themselves cannot avoid producing suboptimal results... [194]

Money is often used to solve the tragedy of the commons, by paying the losing parties the balance of their losses, thus using the symbolic to balance out scarce resources at a specific point by access to resources at other points of the human world.

Marginalism and ungenerosity

Marginalism possibly constitutes the ultimate idolatry of economist orthodoxy in ascribing ontological value to matters purely subjective. The most ludicrous example at the heart of marginalism is the example of diamonds and water:

> Marginal utility is used to explain the discrepancy between products that should be considered valuable but are not and products that are rare and expensive. For example, water is essential to human existence and, as such, should be considered more precious than a diamond. However, an average human being is willing to pay more for an additional diamond than a glass of water. The theory of marginal utility claims that this is so because we derive more satisfaction from owning an additional diamond than another glass of water.[195]

Beyond the hopeless mix-up of assigning inherent value to diamonds, it turns the actual state of affairs on its head, for the satisfaction to be received from an ever

[193] c Ibid.
[194] Fine, B. & Milonakis, D. (2009). *From Economics Imperialism to Freakonomics: the Shifting Boundaries between Economics and Other Social Sciences. Economics As Social Theory*. Routledge, p.23.
[195] https://www.investopedia.com/terms/m/marginalism.asp

increasing amount of diamonds lies in the potential power over others that an accumulation of wealth can provide, based on our mutual intersubjective belief in their function as monetary forms, and has nothing to do with any "utility" inherent in diamonds as raw materials.

This is part of the enduring misanthropy of mainstream economic doctrine, which views scarcity as the basis of the market. Yet, it must be remembered that the actual financial market is not a product of scarcity but of abundance, for it is only when people have more than they need that they begin to trade that surplus to others. It is only when one transcends poverty and achieves affluence beyond hand-to-mouth existence that a market is born.

As always where dogma is concerned, we have to ask who stands to gain. Faith is sustained by the followers who share it, some of whom may be naïve and find solace in the dogma, and some of whom may be quite canny, knowing that all types of dogmas are a means to refute the protestations of the masses.[196]

Ingham points to the explicit Aristotelian provenance of ideas at the root of prevailing economic doctrines:

> Many of the most influential… political economists… subscribed to the essentials of Aristotle's explanation of the evolution and functions of money… his conception of an idealized 'natural' economy that was neither capitalist nor market-based. It is therefore not surprising that theories implicitly based on his analysis have proved to be a very poor guide to the money of the modern capitalist world. [197]

Ingham is at a loss to explain the persistence of these unrealistic assumptions:

> How can such inadequate intellectual underpinnings remain the basis for conduct of monetary affairs?... academic entrenchment can be only part of the explanation for the persistence of this intellectually inadequate meta-theory. [198]
>
> The analytical reduction of money to a natural commodity, to the mere symbol of a commodity, or to nothing more than the neutral representation of existing values, is a powerful ideological tool. However, money is not merely a useful technique, comparable to weights and measures; it also consists in social relations that are inherently relations of inequality and power… in the actual process of the social production of money, promises to pay are ranked hierarchically in a way that expresses and reproduces these inequalities.[199]

Once one realizes that the economy is a belief system in which reality itself is subsumed, the role of economic theories comes to the fore as direct influences on market fortunes.

---

[196] Just as religion is often useful in providing the oppressed with acceptable justifications for their oppression, so one can frequently find dynamic theological thinking in the minds of people who have to make sense of social unfairness and financial inequity. Invisible-hand-based-marginalism is just as good a dogma as the afterlife: believe in the free market for it shall ultimately be your salvation even if at the moment you are but an unrecompensed drudge trying to make the rent.

[197] Ingham, G. (2004). *The Nature of Money*. Polity Press, pp.15-16

[198] Ingham, G. (2004). *The Nature of Money*. Polity Press, p.36.

[199] Ingham, G. (2004). *The Nature of Money*. Polity Press, pp.37-38.

In particular, the "orthodox assumptions of scarcity and competition",[200] have had the most destructive impact on economies as they often lead to great cruelty and indifference towards those who do not have sufficient assets, treating a free market economy in a Spencerian-Darwinist framework that accepts tragedy (of the non-fit) as the price of progress (by the fit, who are retrospectively proven to be the fit by their power). In many ways, economic thought is the last bastion of social Darwinism. The precepts of survival of the "fittest" are woven into the notions of "supply and demand" and of course into "scarcity", for only the fittest are presumed to be able to secure goods in the face of scarcity, and they become the very apex, the balance point of the market, and the convergence nexus of the differential equations so dear to the heart of economists.

Thus, within the web of faith that constitutes the economic life of humanity, economic doctrine is a driving and shaping force that assuages guilt and justifies injustice in strictly deterministic and jaundiced terms: self-interest is the fundamental nature of man and everyone gets their just deserts. No mercy or grace here... but certainly justification by faith...

---

[200] Heinsohn, G., Steiger, O. & Decker, F. (2013). *Ownership Economics: On the Foundations of Interest, Money, Markets, Business Cycles and Economic Development.* Routledge, p. 25.

CHAPTER 7: INFLATION AND FAITH

The concept of "inflation" is used quite loosely to describe a number of different phenomena such as a rise in prices or a decline in the value of the currency forms that are used by a given community. Inflation may be considered negative or positive depending on where it happens. In the vegetable markets frequented by the non-affluent, the significance of inflation is that fewer cucumbers can be bought for the same number of monetary forms, while an increase in prices in capital markets is not even called inflation, but appreciation, and the market is then described as a hot one in which everyone is eagerly in pursuit of inflated prices that are perceived as indicators of greater value and as a favorable portent for future inflation.

Economic literature dealing with inflation evinces a conceptual obliviousness that skirts over the quite glaring question of the precise mechanism by which inflation occurs. One tends to find extensive descriptive narratives of inflationary episodes and their accompanying statistics, without ever explaining how inflation develops at the level of the individual.

Something happens when a lot of people suddenly have a lot of money: It quickly loses its value. If they are suddenly plentiful, symbolic forms are depleted of their value so that you need more and more of them to buy the same commodity.

Yet why should a symbolic form be slowly leached of its value just because it is plentiful?

If you have more money, why should prices rise?

Why do countries have different rates of inflation? Even if prices are sky high in one place in the world, and inflation is rampant, in another place the same commodities maintain stable prices. National borders become a container of inflationary activity so that it remains localized. Why does it not spread? What isolates one county from its neighbors, when commodity supply chains spread into so many countries?

How is it that there are different levels of inflation even within each national boundary, as is clearly seen when one compares the prices of commodities in the richer and poorer sections of even a single city, not to mention urban and rural regions within a country.

How does such focused inflation occur?

Inflation mainly damages the storage of stable values in monetary forms. Under high inflation, the money form lying folded in your pocket loses value as you breathe. Forms become leaky, and their value seeps away.

The constant reality that has dogged human existence is one in which scarcity or plentitude of currency forms determined the rate of inflation, but also the willingness of people to pay others. When there is not enough money in an economy, everything shrinks, and when there is a lot of money, everything expands and prices inflate.

If you have 100 units of monetary forms in your pocket, the value of those units depends on the general consensus that sets the prices. If we measure the efficacy of those units in the number of eggs that you are able to buy with them, then when you go out to apply your symbolic trove to reality, your 100 will buy fewer eggs under conditions of inflation and more when deflation prevails.

Bothersome as it is for those eking a living on a fixed nominal stipend, inflation is also a universal phenomenon of a boom economy, and periods of deflation are the darkest periods of economic austerity.

Historically, inflation may be said to be the natural state of economic development.

Figure 1: Historical Inflation[201]

Inflation is a consequence of the dynamic balance between the quantity of monetary forms entering a market and the quantity of forms that people have to exchange for monetary forms. The balance is under constant flux: When there are more monetary forms than non-monetary forms, i.e., more money than merchandise – inflation results. When there are more non-monetary forms than monetary forms, i.e., more merchandise than money to buy it – deflation results. The perfect state and sweet dream of every government is a perfect balance between money and merchandise: lots of merchandise and just enough money to buy it with.

> We know that general but limited price increases occurred several times in antiquity because captured foreign treasures were put into circulation. It seems that a doubling of prices took place after Alexander the Great had coined the treasures won after the defeat of Persia. It appears that the price level rose less after the booty from Gaul and Egypt reached Rome… Another example of an increase of the price level… was brought about by the great inflow of gold and especially silver, stemming in a smaller part from the booty the Spaniards took when they destroyed the Aztec and Inca empires, and in a greater part from the newly established silver mines in Mexico and Peru. Even this is not a very impressive inflation, for it amounts to an average annual rate of about 1.5 percent. [202]
>
> A substantive inflow of gold as a monetary metal occurred several times in the 19th century. We recall the Californian Gold Rush from 1848 and the Alaskan Gold Rush and the discovery of large gold deposits in South Africa in the 1890s. But it has already been shown that this additional supply did not exert a permanent influence on the price level… Probably the growth of money demand has indeed helped to prevent a long-term increase of the price level. This especially in view of the fact that the supply of what we nowadays call money has also risen because of the ev-

[201] https://www.in2013dollars.com/us/inflation/1900?amount=1

[202] Bernholz, P. (2003). *Monetary regimes and inflation: History, economic and political relationships*. Edward Elgar Publishing, p. 7. pp. 21–22.

> er- widening use of banknotes and checking accounts as means of payment.[203]

Sometimes the extra money arrives just in time. New gold and silver deposits are discovered just as and industrial revolution surges ahead – hallelujah!

The important point is that in the 19th century, fractional reserve banking was already in full swing and gold, however much of it, was only the imaginary anchor used by the banking system to instill confidence in the monetary forms it was producing on demand in far greater quantities than the precious metals in its vaults. In this situation, even large incoming quantities of gold made no difference to the fractional reserve system, for no one was using the "actual" gold, but only the colored bits of paper referring to it… the assurance that it would be possible to convert the abstract monetary form of a banknote into solid gold or silver provided confidence in the banknote and psychological well-being, but the actual quantity of money in the economy was the paper, not the metal.

And it is that quantity of money, the one that can be generated by a bank at any time and in any amount, which has consequences for the level of inflation.

> All administrative measures by rulers or governments to stem the inflation arising from the increase of the money supply or debasement proved to be in vain, even if their violation was threatened with the death penalty.[204]

It turns out that people will naturally leave a monetary form when faith is lost in its value, in favor of another monetary form that still retains trust. People don't really have a problem because they can shift from one value holding form to another. It is the government that has a problem because it loses control of the money forms in the hands of the people. Therefore, the bottom line of inflationary troubles in the age of fiat money is that they are political.

> The stabilization of currency was necessary in Germany [in the 1920s] rather because of a crisis of the state than of the economy. The economy had widely changed to a foreign currency standard, with which it could have lived. The crisis originated since the Reich would and could not tolerate the use of foreign currency for domestic transactions wanted by the economy because of reasons of national self-preservation and especially as long as the inflation was needed as a source of revenues.[205]

Historically, there has been a wide variety of sources for the forms adopted by people to hold value by common consensus: gold was quarried, loot was plundered, shells were gathered, promissory notes were issued, banknotes were printed, loans were made by central banks and quantitative easing was delivered to too-big-to-fail institutions: In all cases, monetary forms entered the system at some point and began to be used as containers of value.

The point of entry is crucial in regard to the amount of money that will make it into the hands of the non-affluent. It is not enough to pour money into an economy. It has to get into the hands of the people before it will have an effect on the economy. Even the most ludicrously plentiful amounts of quantitative easing will not

---

[203] Bernholz, Ibid, p. 23.
[204] Bernholz, Ibid, pp. 37.
[205] Bernholz, Ibid, p. 79.

cause inflation if they just remain on the books of a bank that makes no loans. The symbolic must move into the hands of people for the economy to flourish, and it is these people who also create inflation.

Therefore, one of the best ways to combat inflation is to ensure that the pockets of the non-affluent remain empty. It is for this reason that despite the billions poured by QE into the system, inflation was avoided because most of the money did not flow into tangible reality.

Inflation undermines the usual public misconception regarding the tangibility of money and exposes money's fundamental existence as a symbol in the minds of men.

When the value that a symbolic form is capable of holding diminishes, and it suddenly becomes difficult to purchase stuff, the intangibility of money becomes very much in evidence, and public anxiety grows considerably.

When money breaks down, the "Matrix" suddenly becomes visible. The same money forms that seemed completely dependable and tangible one moment become intangible and unreliable in the next. Inflation rends the fabric of money faith to expose the void beyond.

Within the domain of the affluent inflation attacks existing accounts receivables quoted in nominal values, so that the passive income streams of the affluent are eroded. Incoming rent payments lose their buying power, and the repayment schedules of large loans become a joke.

Inflation undermines the good social order as legal fines intended to deter people from misbehaving lose their power. A fine of 10 dollars on illegal parking established in the 1980s will have little impact when its value has eroded many years later.

As inflation erodes the income streams of the non-affluent, they may slide into default because whatever they earn is spent on the basic necessities of life, food and shelter. They cease to be good consumers, sending retail stores into recession. Then, if inflation gets ahead of income to the point where the non-affluent can no longer afford the rent, they are evicted, and landlords lose their sources of income, or if the non-affluent had a mortgage, the bank now has a bad debt on its hands.

Ultimately, if the non-affluent no longer have enough for food, as has happened in several historical episodes of hyperinflation, they may starve, even though they are still employed and receiving the same wages that they did before the escalation of inflation.

It is the vulnerability of the non-affluent that poses the greatest threat to the market. It is their consumption that drives growth, since they are constantly swapping currency forms for all other forms. When they lose their buying power, their plight will eventually impact great tranches of the economy, as retail slows down, and people get laid off, and ultimately production too falters.

Even though the affluent may also be infuriated by such a contraction of the market, they do not contribute to it since they have enough surplus to continue buying all tangibles offered on the market, even though their prices may skyrocket.

These are the two extremes that faith in money must navigate: on the one hand a deep trust in the value of money that always drives people to want more and more of it, and on the other hand an eventual deep distrust following the great exuberance of faith, which may lead to such deep devaluation of the currency that it liable to derail the entire economy.

With the advent of fiat money, there can *always* be more money than goods. The symbolic can always engulf the tangible. One does not have to wait for a gold rush to obtain more monetary forms, so inflation is always a risk in our present economy.

Current inflation goals are usually set at 2%; a "creepy" enough rate as to be invisible. If prices keep visibly rising, a population may become restive, but if they rise very slowly, people may accept this as "the way things are". This is a form of political "stealth". If the rate of inflation is very low and only leaches purchase power slowly, most people tend not to notice it, while sophisticated economic players hedge their wealth.

But why not set the goal at 5% for a much more robust economy? Why not set an even higher inflation rate and reset it periodically every time it reaches 100%, just as governments restore balance and trust after hyper-inflationary episodes, and just as economies have inflated by thousands of percents over the last 100 years, e.g., the US economy, which has inflated around 3,000% since 1900, and all is well.

Inflation and national currencies

When inflation is examined from the point of view of the value-holding forms that are used as money, i.e., the currencies of different nations, a number of aspects that are usually invisible become evident.

In dealing with the interactions of different currencies it is useful to arbitrarily distinguish between the buyer-side form or "quote" form and the seller-side form, or "base" form. In any transaction where one currency is exchanged for another, the quoting form is the monetary form while the base form, even though it is a currency in its own right, becomes a "commodity" that is purchased with the monetary form.

If one currency is losing its value, a larger number of buyer-side forms are required relative to the seller-side, i.e. more "quote" forms for each "base" form to be acquired. It is always possible to switch the direction of trade by re-assigning the roles of "base" or "quote".

One central feature of modern economic life is that currencies function as money forms domestically but as commodities outside the country. The people living within the national area in which a certain currency is in circulation, use that currency as their monetary form, while people outside that national area buy that currency as a commodity by using their own national currency form as the monetary form.

Both these aspects of currency, the double aspect of "money" and "commodity", are responsible for a considerable measure of instability in the prices of currency. If a multitude of people are selling large volumes of money forms, they are indicating that they prefer other currencies as holders of value, and can cause a reduction in the price and a diminishment of the value that these monetary forms can hold, so that a greater number will be needed in order to capture the value of other forms, i.e. inflation will ensue.

Interest rates also have an impact on the difference between the "inside" and "outside" of a country, but in the opposite direction. The higher the domestic interest rates of a nation – the more attractive they will be for affluent parties outside the nation who are looking for places where they can receive higher returns, so the financial instruments of the high-interest-rate nation will become sought-after commodities and their value will increase, leading to deflation. At the same time the "inside" significance of high interest rates is that many potential domestic borrowers will not be able to afford loans and many people who have already accumulated debts may become insolvent, so again, deflation.

The obverse process takes place when the interest rates are low, so that foreign currency stays out of the country, and a great deal of domestic currency may be exchanged for foreign currency in order to achieve higher returns. At the same time, the low domestic interest rates may motivate people to borrow money, thereby leading to the flow of more domestic currency into the economy, decreasing the capacity of the domestic money forms to hold value and increasing inflation.[206]

Inflation is held in check when a currency is "strong", i.e., sought after by other nations. The US economy has benefited greatly by the widespread international demand for its currency – which curbs inflation domestically, but its own government has created deflationary havoc by raising the interest rates.

Even as governments take steps such as QE, they are still focused on the outmoded austere vision according to which one should not provide the masses with too much money, so they attempt to provide liquidity in a way that undermines the creativity of money. Analyzing the current state of affairs in which inflation rates remain low despite massive infusions of money into the economy, Koo writes:

> U.S. inflation has slowed even after three rounds of quantitative easing by the Fed…That we have not seen a more pronounced economic recovery and an acceleration of inflation is attributable to the absence of growth in private credit and the money supply. The same phenomenon can be observed in Europe [where] growth in both private credit and the money supply has been modest at best in spite of massive base money expansion and repeated interest rate cuts.[207]

Koo ascribes the cause of this state of affairs to a "balance-sheet recession", in which so long as private individuals and businesses are saving and paying debts – the economy remains in a slump.

The continuing stagnation in Japan may be attributed to the double impact of a nation with a strong mentality of thrift, and the double shyness consequent to the bite of the collapse of Japan's "golden era". This has led to enormous "idle balances" and continuing stagnation, as North comments:

There is no automatic relationship between the amount of money and economic activity. The Japanese found this out to their detriment when they issued bonds to all citizens to promote spending in an effort to overcome the deflation of the 1990s: they were just added to savings accounts. [208]

However, considerable risk of rampant inflation may now be hovering over all the nations that had pumped QE into their banking system:

---

[206] This scenario only applies when people are spending the extra money. When they prefer to save the money or use it to repay their debts, they will not take loans even when the interest rate is zero.

[207] Koo, R.C. (2015). *The Escape from Balance Sheet Recession and the QE Trap: A Hazardous Road for the World Economy*. Wiley, p. 9.

[208] North, Ibid, p. 4.

Historically, all countries that created liquidity on this scale ultimately faced hyperinflation and a redenomination of the currency, wiping out the wealth of hard-working savers. This time, however, the money supply has not increased much and inflation has not emerged so far because there has been no private loan demand.[209]

This may be an inflation bomb waiting to explode. As Koo explains:

A central bank that has undertaken QE has already supplied huge amounts of liquidity to the markets during the recession. These funds are harmless during a balance sheet recession… But once the private sector completes its balance sheet repairs and resumes borrowing, they have the potential to generate tremendous inflation. Thus, the central bank that supplied the funds, and the markets that received them, become increasingly nervous and vigilant as the economy starts to pick up. This is the new normal.[210]

The threat is imminent for it only takes a few rich apples to inflate the entire barrel. Without a concerted communal effort to have food that is affordable to everyone, most people will end up just wandering in an out of supermarkets with little to buy. So long as there are enough affluent people to pay the exorbitant prices, they keep the grocery stores afloat and the whole system continues to function smoothly.

The people starving on the street are simply outside the system. The food producers have their clients – those who can afford good prices – and there is nothing that farmers hate more than an abundant harvest that brings prices down.

This is an essential paradox within capitalism that can't be solved by a free market ideology. Farmers will destroy food outright if they can't get the right price, and governments too have intervened in order to "free" the market from low prices, such as the Agricultural Adjustment Act (AAA) of 1933 that was designed to raise prices by reducing surpluses using such tactics as the mass slaughter of millions of "unripe" little pigs or the dousing of oranges with kerosene while people all over the country were starving to death.[211] Faith in economic dogma is a force to be reckoned with!

As poignantly stated by Steinback:

The men of knowledge have worked, have considered, and the fruit is rotting on the ground… This little orchard will be a part of a great holding next year, for the debt will have choked the owner. This vineyard will belong to the bank. Only the great owners can survive, for they own the canneries too…

The works of the roots of the vines, of the trees, must be destroyed to keep up the price, and this is the saddest, bitterest thing of all. Carloads of oranges dumped on the ground. The people came for miles to take the… fruit, but this could not be. How would they buy oranges at twenty

[209] Koo, Ibid, pp. 101-102.

[210] Koo, Ibid, p. 102.

[211] Poppendieck, Janet (1986). *Breadlines Knee Deep in Wheat: Food Assistance in the Great Depression.* Brunswick, New Jersey: Rutgers University Press.

> cents a dozen if they could drive out and pick them up? And men with hoses squirt kerosene on the oranges, and they are angry at the crime, angry at the people who have come to take the fruit. A million people hungry, needing the fruit—and kerosene sprayed over the golden mountains.
>
> And the smell of rot fills the country.
>
> There is a crime here that goes beyond denunciation. There is a sorrow here that weeping cannot symbolize. There is a failure here that topples all our success. The fertile earth, the straight tree rows, the sturdy trunks, and the ripe fruit. And children dying of pellagra must die because a profit cannot be taken from an orange... [212]

The society of the affluent within the general population continues to prosper through thick and thin, and it will soon be seen to be a roboticized society enjoying all the fruit of a global supply chain, embedded within the masses who will have no way to obtain lodging or food but through government largesse.

Hyperinflation

Since money in abundance is ultimately a boon to all, it is important to take a close look at those historical episodes in which that abundance became a bane as inflation ran wild and became hyperinflation.

A close examination of the end of hyperinflationary episodes shows that in all cases inflation ended when people were brought to believe in the stability of a new currency after the quantity of monetary forms available to the public was drastically curtailed, and monetary forms external to the blighted economy were used as an anchor. Here are some examples of how hyperinflation was stopped:

> **Hungary:** The government adopted a radical stabilization program that included drastic tax reform, the recovery of gold assets taken abroad, and the introduction of a new currency, the forint, backed by gold reserves and world currencies. **Zimbabwe:** The US dollar and the South African rand became de facto currencies. In 2009, the Reserve Bank of Zimbabwe abandoned its currency and adopted the US dollar and the South African rand as the main means of exchange.
>
> **Yoguslavia:** the Serbian leader... agreed to adopt a new currency - the "new dinar" - backed by gold and hard currency reserves.
>
> **Germany:** The government introduced a new currency, the rentenmark, backed by agricultural land.[213]

Inflation is a direct consequence of the nature of the belief in monetary forms and can even arise from a belief in inflation itself. If people believe that inflation is increasing and that their money is going to lose its value, they hasten to spend their money, thereby bringing about that very eventuality.

It can be seen that the phenomenon of "self-fulfilling prophecy" is quite prominent in economic life: It is enough to believe in things for them to happen, not because of some inexplicable magic, but by dint of the fact that the entire system is

---

[212] Steinbeck, J. (1939) *The Grapes of Wrath.* Viking Press, *p. 349-350.*

[213] https://www.bbc.com/news/business-45523636

sustained by faith, so that belief in stability creates stability and belief in inflation breeds inflation.

The rise of MMO (Massively Multi-Player Online) games where many people interact with each other in a virtual reality, offers unique opportunities to learn about the phenomenon of hyper-inflation.

Game producers are the governments of the domains they operate, and they are often just as helpless and inventive as real-life governments when faced with the tremendous amounts of hyperinflation that arise when people mine for "gold", which is given them without limit by game fiat like any other fiat currency. James Portnow describes what happens in MMOs:

> Every time you kill a monster in an MMO, it drops money or a piece of loot that a vendor can conveniently covert to money for you... This money is magically created every time you win a fight, and with hundreds of thousands of players killing monsters 24 hours a day, 365 days a year, that's a lot of money being constantly added to the economy.[214]

These virtual economies quickly reach hyperinflation to the extent that people begin seeking to anchor their values to more stable forms – just as hyper-inflated economies ultimately shift to dollarization or some other external anchor of value.

> In Asheron's Call, the in-game currency became so inflated that shards were used as money. In Diabolo 2, Stones of Jordan rapidly replaced gold, and in Gaia Online the currency became so worthless that the company started offering to donate 250 dollars to charity every time the players threw away 15 trillion gold. Players just abandoned the designated currency and chose a different more restricted currency, because they could no longer trust the initial game currency to retain any value at all. [215]

Both features described by Portnow can be seen in non-virtual economies; both the edict from on-high to relinquish the denominations of the old currency for one of lower denominations, e.g. the monetary stabilization in Hungary, in which "when it came into force, one forint was worth 400 octillion (a billion billion billion) of the old currency"[216], and the choosing of a more restricted currency by the populace itself.

Game designers, just like any government, attempted to curb the amount of money circulating in their game by various means:

> We put money sinks in the game. Things like auction house fees, vendor-only consumable items that were practically necessary to play; Guild dues or even property tax for owning in-game real-estate. These sinks were designed to remove currency from the game.[217]

---

[214] Portnow, J. (2016). *MMO Economies - Hyperinflation, Reserve Currencies & You!* Extra-Credits. https://youtu.be/sumZLwFXJqE?t=29

[215] Portnow, Ibid, https://youtu.be/sumZLwFXJqE?t=86

[216] https://www.bbc.com/news/business-45523636

[217] Portnow, Ibid, https://youtu.be/sumZLwFXJqE?t=138

All these means eventually failed because it turned out that "there is practically no money sink you can build that's going to exceed how much people are willing to grind."[218]

As in the real world, people try to maneuver around the many restrictions, taxes and dues imposed on them by governments seeking to induce austerity in a booming market. And as in the real world, such measures are often both unpopular and damaging: "It might make your game less engaging to play if the player feels like they're spending all of their time just paying fees."[219]

As in the real world, games too have initiated the use of a "foreign" reserve currency in order to anchor values:

> In the real world, almost every nation holds onto a bunch of currencies from other countries to serve as a reserve currency. This reserve currency… is used to anchor the local currency… if you have 500 billion dollars in the bank and you tell everybody that they can trade 50 of your currency for one U.S. dollar, then the least your currency is worth is 2 cents. It can't go below that so long as you have some of your reserve currency left. If your currency starts to inflate, then people start to trade in your local money for the reserve currency, effectively creating a floor for what your currency is worth.[220]

In real world situations, when collapse of faith threatens, as it did in the Great Recession, the leading nations step in and bolster faith for each other by printing a great deal of money for each other's reserves – thereby easing the situation by providing mutual external anchors of trust to each other.

The outside anchor of value serving as a "bastion" of faith is crucial to the perseverance of belief – perhaps no less than a belief in some transcendental deity or justice is crucial in the world's religions – some outside value that is not subject to the vicissitudes of reality and can be adhered to as a pristine point of "saving grace". In games, this outside anchoring took a number of forms:

> Many MMOs started to allow players to buy things of real-world value with in-game currency, like Plex in EVE Online. Many of the Free-To-Play MMOs have gone one step further and let players buy their micro-transaction currency, the currency that has to be bought with real money, from other players for currency earned in game. By tying the in-game currency to real world currency, which has real value, the in-game currency now can't lose all of its value.[221]

Obviously, there is no "real" value anywhere, except that the limited number of believers enmeshed in the game economy now rely on the far greater network of believers who believe in the value of the symbolic in the non-virtual world. Money itself is never "real', neither in a game world nor in the actual world.

It does seem, however, that this form of 'faith within faith' helps to stabilize money: If there is a second layer of faith in more remote wealth, people are content to keep what they have. Just as in Ponzi schemes, so long as they can rest assured in

---

218 Portnow, Ibid, https://youtu.be/sumZLwFXJqE?t=162
219 Portnow, Ibid, https://youtu.be/sumZLwFXJqE?t=171
220 Portnow, Ibid, https://youtu.be/sumZLwFXJqE?t=184
221 Portnow, Ibid, https://youtu.be/sumZLwFXJqE?t=229

"future" profits, people play along, so, if there are dollars or gold or some index "behind" the currency – which promises "future" coverage – people are content to hold the less preferable currency.

The phenomenon of "gold farming" provides an interesting anecdote that sheds light on the way in which various types of intangible forms freely intermix, so that any form is a good form and may be traded with any other, and any over-abundant form can lead to inflation.

As fantasy MMOs expanded in the affluent West, they became an important source of revenue for the citizens of poorer countries.

For example, as the RuneScape MMO universe expanded, its role in the real lives of players was increasingly impinging on the game. Players found devices in the real world to "get ahead" in the world of the game:

> A gold-farmer group is an organized group of people who are paid to just get gold from a game and then sell that gold for real world cash… quite often, these people would be running hundreds of accounts… and getting … RuneScape gold, and then actually creating websites, very official looking websites, where you could enter your credit card details and then organize to buy that gold from one of these gold farmers in the game…[222]
>
> They are working in a virtual world, but this is a real-life sweatshop.[223]

Just as in the real world the enormously grown financial sector has swallowed up other sectors of the economy, so in the virtual world, the drive to accumulate more power and wealth became a factor that slowly swallowed up the game itself:

> It was really obvious to everybody that was playing the game that these accounts weren't real and they… really started to upset the fundamental balance of the game. You know, when you walk up to four or five people and no one is saying anything, and it's very obvious that they are just doing the same pattern over and over again…[224]

This "ill-gotten gold", purchased by players for cash in order to "unfairly" advance within the game, was in fact produced by hard working 3rd-world gold-diggers, just as bent on extricating some value from the game as the prospectors of the California gold rush laboriously sifted through riverbeds. Inflation quickly followed, and like many actual governments facing inflationary conditions, which immediately resort to austerity and draconic measures, so the authors of RuneScape took steps that included prohibition, restriction and austerity:

> We had one idea of how we could completely break it by restricting trades...we made a decision, which we didn't take lightly, to remove free trade from the game, which meant a lot of players couldn't pass items to each other, they couldn't give gifts or presents to each other. That was pretty huge.[225]

---

[222] *The RuneScape Documentary - 15 Years of Adventure*. Official RuneScape YouTube Channel. https://youtu.be/7RNK0YBdwko?t=2781

[223] *The RuneScape Documentary,* Ibid, https://youtu.be/7RNK0YBdwko?t=2823

[224] *The RuneScape Documentary* Ibid, https://youtu.be/7RNK0YBdwko?t=2876

[225] *The RuneScape Documentary - 15 Years of Adventure*. Official RuneScape YouTube Channel, https://youtu.be/7RNK0YBdwko?t=3015

Indeed, the action was so "huge" that it actually destroyed the entire RuneScape economy:

> People were going into the wilderness to gain each other's weapons or gain each other's gold. This was done in the wilderness and that obviously mad e the wilderness a vastly different place. Before the change, the Wilderness was probably the busiest place in RuneScape, and then overnight that just changed and all of a sudden no one was going there. There was no point. You could go into the Wilderness, but it was dead.[226]

The RuneScape creators had literally "killed the economy", and just as similar draconic measures in the real world immediately give rise to "social unrest", so did the "community" now rebel:

> The removal of the wilderness was the single most dramatic event in the history of RuneScape, and it was unique in that it unified the community against Jagex.... I remember those riots that were going on for an entire week or so after the update happened. The relationship between the players and Jagex was never quite the same again after that.[227]

Indeed, as the founder confesses: "if there's one thing I could change going back now, it'll be that decision in 2007 when we decided to get rid of the real-world trading".[228]

The principle of limitation seems to be one of the core means for regulating inflation, as Hayek writes of the gold "standard" that once imposed a limit on the amount of money that governments could create:

> As soon as it was widely understood... that the convertibility into gold was merely a method of controlling the amount of a currency, which was the real factor determining its value, governments became only too anxious to escape that discipline, and money became more than ever before the plaything of politics.[229]

As in so many things in modernity, we again encounter the specter of "choice". While the various external limitations of gold production make it a restricted commodity and therefore suitable for hoarding as a commodity asset to link to other forms holding value (i.e. "the gold standard"), this was no more than a chance historical occurrence, which ultimately gave way to the freedom of fiat money, representing a higher, more transcendent level of faith, and governments are still struggling to perfect methods for organizing its tremendous power in productive ways.

Adolf Wagner, a German economics professor writing in 1868 explained the difficulties involved in a monetary regiment where nothing can limit the powers of the sovereign:

> One would have to introduce the most reliable guarantees to prevent that paper money would ever be used for financial purposes to create artificial purchasing power for the issuing agency without labor out of nothing;

---

[226] *The RuneScape Documentary,* Ibid, https://youtu.be/7RNK0YBdwko?t=3036

[227] *The RuneScape Documentary,* Ibid, https://youtu.be/7RNK0YBdwko?t=3088

[228] *The RuneScape Documentary,* Ibid, https://youtu.be/7RNK0YBdwko?t=3136

[229] Hayek, F.A. (1976, 2007). *Denationalization of Money*. Institute of Economic Affairs, p.35-36.

> and to secure that it would be increased only according to the true necessity of the economy... Men would first have to be capable of unlimited self-discipline to resist any temptation to increase money arbitrarily, even if their very existence, or that of the state, were at stake.[230]

In the absence of inflation, the abstract and universal nature of monetary forms, which are capable of representing and absorbing the value of any one of the endless forms generated by human creativity, gives the party who acquires the monetary form in a transaction the advantage. The payer is at a disadvantage because he has traded a universal form for a specific form, even though the value of the two forms is identical. This is why stinginess is powerful in keeping its hands on the universals, while profligacy is weak as it converts a universal power into point-of-sale consumerism and forms with terminal value.

Faith supports economies like a huge featherbed cushioning and separating the princely existence in the stratosphere of affluence from the hard dried peas of reality. The accumulation of ephemeral surpluses of value, which is but reification of the public faith in value, creates a quantum effect in which people live on the clouds of faith in the value they own, as measured by the number of money faith-forms.

A person holding a million dollars in the bank, or rather, owed a million dollars by the bank, is called a millionaire, but all he has is the public faith in the numbers ascribed to him, the numbers that the government, the legal system and the enforcement agencies secure his ownership of, the numbers for which others would be willing to give him other forms that contain value.

The vast reservoirs of capital awaiting to be spent in tangible reality are but figments of the public consciousness that establish them, and this faith is subject to frequent fluctuations in the value ascribed to money: How many monetary forms equal how many tangible forms? How much does a banana cost?

When faith in the value of a monetary form is strong, a few units are enough to transfer ownership to a banana. Everything is "cheap" compared to the money available to the people. When faith in value weakens, it takes a lot more units to transfer banana ownership, so everything becomes "expensive" as people no longer have enough money to cover their tangible needs.

The Rhetorics of the Real

While the prices that surround us are but numerals representing symbolic values, economists intimate that they are capable of discerning the real value of things, and they call those particular values that they calculate "real" values, thereby endowing them with the status of criteria for the truth so that they can use them as an impressive argument in demands for various "corrections" needed in order to adapt reality to the "real"

The "real" holds a place of honor in the great struggle with inflation. It is important, though, to distinguish between what is termed "real" in economics and the "real" of the empirical kind, as studied by scientists and experienced by ordinary folk; for the "real" of economists is no more than another form of the symbolic.

---

[230] Quoted in Bernholz, P. (2003). *Monetary regimes and inflation: History, economic and political relationships*. Edward Elgar Publishing, p. 7.

What economists call "real" is one of the tools used in a fiat regime to shift values in the obverse direction from the visible denominations of monetary forms in a response to counter-faith pressures that depreciate them.

The human need for calories is an example of the "real" of empirical reality. A potato can tangibly satisfy this need in empirical reality, but the price of the potato is always set in the symbolic, even when an economic text refers to the "real" price of a potato.

The "real" price of a potato, in the sense that "real" is used in economics, is an agreement over price. Contracts quoting "real" sums stipulate some symbolic point in time that the parties agree to "freeze" so as to protect against changes in the value of the currency. The calculation of a "real" value fixes a currency to its value at a certain given point in time relative to various "commodity" forms, thereby establishing a kind of "tradition" to be upheld.[231]

The linkage of numbers to past values is an argument aimed at convincing that the price is "true" by means of a narrative that sets up the fiction of a past price in order to pacify the faithful. If it is possible to convince you that this is the "real" value, you may be more willing to pay an additional fee to offset inflationary depreciation of the currency.

Linking prices to an index is quite ineffectual. When governments enforce the doctrine of "real" wages in an inflationary market, employers simply sack some employees and pay the new bloated salaries dictated from on high to those that remain. Another common reaction is to raise the price of products so that the purportedly anti-inflationary mechanism of linkage contributes to inflation.

In any event, only parties that have the power to enforce the dogma of linkage to some "real" prices are able to do so. All the rest continue to lurch up and down on the waves of the symbolic, without the benefit of these sticking points masquerading as "real". Those who are forced to cope with the rise in prices perpetrated by linkage are such parties as business owners who do not have the power to enforce price linkage and simply raise their prices to offset the "linked" increase, thereby contributing to further inflation, and of course, all those who do not derive income from an officially "linked" source cannot benefit from the dogma of the "real", and are obliged to suffer the consequences of continued increases in inflation.

As Ayres et al., write about the attempts to stop Brazilian hyper-inflation, the process itself is inflationary:

> The highly indexed economy was the essence of the inflationary process… Since inflation was supposed to decrease substantially after the plan, the differences in real wages at the moment of the plan would prompt losers to claim rights to be compensated, while the winners would not complain. If the losers were compensated, that would reignite the inflation spiral.[232]

Even as we read through such seemingly straightforward historical descriptions it becomes obvious that they are skewed by a distorted conceptualization of the nature of money. The problematic use of the term "real" creates an illusion that there is

---

[231] Indeed, they could have just as easily agreed on entirely new prices.

[232] Ayres, J., Garcia, M. Guillén, D.A. & Kehoe, P.J. (2019). *The Monetary and Fiscal History of Brazil* 1960-2016. NBER Working Paper No. 25421, pp. 10-11.

some empirical tangible value that can be used as reference, whereas there is, in fact, none.

The motivation of the market is not targeted at the value held by forms but at their prices, with an incentive to always push prices up in order to increase profits, so that greater efficiency is not passed on to the end consumer, but rather serves to garner more profits, and calculation of the "real" only serves to justify increased prices. As adroitly analyzed by Joseph:

> A company that sells a good for $5 that costs $3 to make, finding that it can reduce that production cost to $2, does not lower its original selling price if it can avoid doing so. The whole point is to increase profits, not equalize them based on production savings. No company is going to make itself obsolete by reducing its costs to near zero, selling at near zero value.[233]

Another interesting adjunct of indexing is to establish inflation more firmly, as the index is always more trusted than the current pricing of currency, so that belief in the central currency is never properly restored.

The economy is maintained by dint of contracts signed in regard to a great many aspects of the market which are constantly inflated by the selfsame contracts. The purported cure is in fact coordinated inflation, and those who find themselves outside "the contract" are obliged to flee to other currencies in order to preserve their values.

In its attempt to combat inflation, the Brazilian "Real" plan was based on the ingenious idea of shifting the waning trust of the people to a currency that they would believe in, which was in fact pegged to the mighty Yankee dollar. Ayres et al. report how:

> The creation of a new unit of account, the URV - *Unidade Real de Valor* (unit of real value) aimed at establishing a parallel unit of value to the Cruzeiro Real, the inflated currency. … Prices were quoted in both URVs and Cruzeiro Reals, but payments had to be made exclusively in Cruzeiro Reals. The URV worked like a shadow currency that had its parity to the Cruzeiro Real constantly adjusted, since it was one-to-one with the dollar… That would allow agents to observe the low inflation of the parallel currency, therefore breaking the expectations of high inflation once the currency was changed…. the URV was extinguished on July 1, 1994, when it was converted to the new currency, the Real, with the parity being 1 dollar = 1 Real = 1 URV = 2,750 Cruzeiro Reals.[234]

Brazil, not wishing to relinquish its sovereign power to print its own money found a way to create the crucial external link by inventing a unit of economic propaganda[235], which was actually linked to the dollar.

The plan thereby managed to gain the "trust" of the people over a few months until the currency was actually changed. The entire campaign took place in the

---

233 Joseph, P. (2017). The new human rights movement: reinventing the economy to end oppression. BenBella Books. p. 290.

234 Ayres, J., Garcia, M. Guillén, D.A. & Kehoe, P.J. (2019). The Monetary and Fiscal History of Brazil 1960-2016. *NBER Working Paper No. 25421*, p.17.

235 It was called "Unit of Real Value" for goodness' sake!

minds the people up until the point that the "propaganda currency" was converted into the tangible banknotes and coins of the new "Real". From its initiation to its termination the URV remained wholly virtual – an exercise in pure faith.

The inventive Brazilian manipulation of faith, the brilliance of reverting to the old currency name "Real" in the sense of "royal", but imbuing it with meaning of "true", illuminates the way that consensual public faith is always the driving force at the bottom of things, and is often manipulated by political forces. This plan was brilliant in that it addressed the very core of the money system: faith and doubt:

> Facing the Brazilian citizens' deep skepticism about stabilization programs, the implementation of the Real Plan demanded unique coordination and innovation efforts from the policy makers. First of all, the government announced previously every step of the Plan, denying surprises, breach of contracts and the freeze of prices, wages or assets—recurrent elements of the unsuccessful stabilization programs previously implemented.[236]

The plan's first step was to fully embrace the actual belief of the people, which, following many years of inflation, was a deeply entrenched faith in the validity of various means of linkage that purported to index payments to the "real economy".

The entire Brazilian economy had for many years used these means to carry out adjustments vis a vis what was perceived as the "real" value. This belief in the efficacy of linkage was not just a widely adopted mechanism for coping with inflation, but a major causal factor in its perpetuation:

> One of the causes of inflation in Brazil was the inertial inflation phenomenon. Prices were adjusted on a daily basis according to changes in price indices and to the exchange rate of the local currency to the U.S. dollar.[237]

The economic "real" does not represent any reality outside the collected minds of human beings, and the "real GDP", one of the main misleading uses made of the term "real", cannot really (!) be compared across eras. The reason for this is that the GDP itself is but an arbitrary collection of products and services. As Gleeson-White writes:

> The accuracy and usefulness of national income measures have been questioned from the beginning, by Keynes and others, including Simon Kuznets himself. For example, Kuznets believed the national accounts should include the value of unpaid housework, despite the fact that including this vast contribution to the national economy would present statisticians with the difficult task of making monetary estimates of this valuable work. The US Commerce Department refused to calculate these estimates—and as a result Kuznets broke his association with the department in the late 1940s.[238]

---

[236] https://www.bcb.gov.br/en/monetarypolicy/realplan

[237] https://en.wikipedia.org/wiki/Plano_Real

[238] Gleeson-White, J. (2011). *Double Entry: How the Merchants of Venice Shaped the Modern World – and how their invention could make or break the planet.* Allen & Unwin, p. 72.

Moreover, even if taken at face value, everything included in the GDP is constantly changing in all respects, thereby emptying any vaunted comparisons of all sense.

Can one compare an egg collected from a coop at the beginning of the 20th century with one so collected in the 21st century? Seemingly a coop is a coop and an egg is an egg, but actually the coop is not the same (think technology, engineering, mass production) the egg is not the same (think genetics, hormones, veterinary medicine, agricultural innovation) and the supply chain is very different (think refrigeration, transportation, globalization), not to mention the market itself (where eggs are now but a single source of protein among hundreds in the same supermarket aisles).

When even such a seemingly stable basic commodity as an egg cannot be compared across time, any attempt to compare other aspects of the economy is certainly futile, since everything is being constantly transformed.

Attempts to evaluate the "real GDP" usually take the form of "before and after" comparisons, as in the table below, which compares the Great Depression with the Great Recession:

Table 1.1. The Great Depression vs. Great Recession in the advanced countries

	Real GDP	Price level	Unemployment (%)	Trade volume
1929	100.0	100.0	7.2	100.0
1930	95.2	90.8	14.1	94.8
1931	89.2	79.9	22.8	89.5
1932	83.3	73.1	31.4	76.5
1933	84.3	71.7	29.8	78.4
1934	89.0	75.3	23.9	79.6
1935	94.0	77.6	21.9	81.8
1936	100.6	81.4	18.0	85.7
1937	105.3	91.5	14.3	97.4
1938	105.4	90.4	16.5	87.0
2007	100.0	100.0	5.4	100.0
2008	100.0	102.0	5.8	101.9
2009	96.4	102.8	8.0	90.2
2010	99.5	103.8	8.3	101.2
2011	101.1	105.3	7.9	106.5

Source: Crafts & Fearon (2013).[239]
Table 5: Purported Real GDP over time

The above table purports to compare the "real GDP" of 1929 with that of 2011. How is this even remotely possible? In 2011 we were already using smartphones, not so in 1929, so obviously this GDP comparison cannot include the price of a smartphone. So, what is being compared? What does this "real GDP" actually include? Supposedly, it includes things that were around in 1929 and are still around.

We saw how problematic this was for eggs, but what about cars? How about Ford Model Ts? No. They stopped production of those in 1927, even before the comparison begins. How about all the huge multi-billion industries (Pharma, IT, etc.) that were not even dreamed of in 1929?

As shown by Mazzucato, GDP beliefs are theoretical dogmas that only reflect the worldviews of economists who ascribe value to certain life-efforts but not to others, and thereby support certain beliefs regarding market behavior that carefully avoid certain aspects of reality while prominently embracing others. Mazzucato writes the following on the accounting biases that create the fictions of GDP:

> National accounts exclude all housework, and therefore a large part of women's work, from production. The architect of the first and second

[239] Crafts, N. and Fearon, P. (2013). *The Great Depression of the 1930s Lessons for Today*. Oxford University Press, p. 1.

editions of the System of National Accounts ("SNA") (1953 and 1968), the Nobel Prize-winning British economist Sir Richard Stone (1913–91) – sometimes called 'the father of national income accounting'... simply thought it was impossible to know how to do it – and even if a solution could be devised, doing so would be socially awkward... Now, seventy years later, since there is still no theory – beyond ignorance or shame – that explains why housewives (and house husbands) should not be included in GDP, the SNA architects have come up with a different defense. They have expressed a 'reluctance' to include such work because, although it is equivalent to work done by servants, 'By convention ... only the wages of the domestic staff are treated as the value of output... the convention has been cherry-picked because it is convenient for the current system.[240]

Fullbrook says it even more forcefully:

> If rich households pay servants to do their cooking and housework and child care and gardening and bookkeeping, these services are counted as economic output. Why not when household members do the work for themselves and one another? If Australian mothers stopped breastfeeding their babies, economists would increase national income by \$2.2 billion for producing the equivalent artificial milk and another billion or so for doctoring more sick infants. Extra costs and worse health care would count as economic growth.[241]

Moreover, the more expansive capital aspects of the economy are not included in consumer price indexes. The reason that the consumer price index did not rise in an exorbitant fashion despite the tremendous uptick in capital markets and real estate in recent years is quite simple: houses and stocks are not included in the GDP, nor in the consumer price index.

The big money is hidden from the national accounts. It is invisible.

The skewed nature of GDP rhetorics has far-reaching implications for political maneuvering and policymaking. As Gleeson-White writes:

> GDP measures not only record the economic life of a nation but help to determine it. They are used by governments to calculate budgets and to assess the impact of fiscal and monetary policy on an economy. They are used by politicians in campaign strategies, and by corporations for investment decisions and Wall Street takeovers. As former chairman of the US Federal Reserve Alan Greenspan acknowledges, GDP figures have 'a profound influence on markets' and 'are the basis for Federal budget projections and political rhetoric'.[242]
>
> The GDP measures only those things that have monetary value, only those things that are legally bought and sold. Or, in the officialese of the

[240] Mazzucato, M. (2018).*The Value of Everything. Making and Taking in the Global Economy*. Penguin, p.91.

[241] Fullbrook, E. (Ed.). (2004). *A guide to what's wrong with economics*. Anthem Press., p.11.

[242] Gleeson-White, J. (2011). *Double Entry: How the Merchants of Venice Shaped the Modern World – and how their invention could make or break the planet.* Allen&Unwin, p. 84.

> Australian Bureau of Statistics (ABS): 'The national accounts are a macroeconomic data set revolving around the central economic concepts of production, income, expenditure and wealth. They also comprise a monetary system, and therefore rely substantially on being able to measure the money transactions taking place between the various economic agents in a market economy.' As mentioned, they do not include unpaid work, natural resources or wilderness areas. A tree in a forest is not counted as a national asset. But when that tree is cut down and sold as timber it is measured in GDP—and only then does it contribute to economic growth as officially measured[243]

There is no way to estimate the "Gross Domestic Scandal" of assigning economic credit and support to the exploitation of natural resources, without assigning any value to their preservation in their natural state, and anyone appalled by the sale of large swathes of beach and forest and other natural resources, will do well to remember that these sales are considered to be the hallmarks of blessed economic growth.

Here and there, in dribs and drabs, awareness of the evil perpetrated by the conception of GDP has begun percolating into various fora:

> The UN began to develop its environmental accounting guidelines in 1992, when it recommended that the GDP and other traditional systems of national income measurement should include supplementary environmental and social information. Most countries have since attempted to expand their national accounts to include such satellite accounts. The United States published its first environmental satellite accounts in 1994, which adjusted the GDP for the depletion of oil and other non-renewable resources. But the figures with their downgraded view of US wealth proved so controversial and so politically explosive that Congress shut down the program almost the moment the revised numbers were published[244]

Fullbrook explains that the bottom-line vis a vis the strange dogmas of modern economic doctrine is a choice between two options:

> 1. You can decide that economics is really too difficult a matter to understand ('because of maths') or
> 2. You can accept the quite evident fact that all these models with a 'representative agent' (called Robinson Crusoe or not) are nonsense.
>
> Obviously, the second possibility is the right one. But it is difficult for a mere, poor student to accept the idea that all these professors and doctors - some of them Nobel Prize laureates - have built their careers on such nonsense. [245]
>
> I hope also that environmental organizations and civil society organizations will increasingly come to understand the role of neoclassical economics as a barrier to new thinking in the development dialogue. Be-

[243] Gleeson-White, Ibid, p. 85.

[244] Gleeson-White, Ibid, p. 87.

[245] Fullbrook, E. (Ed.). (2004). *A* guide *to what's wrong with economics*. Anthem Press, p. 123.

> hind the present activities of criticized institutions, such as the World Trade Organization, the World Bank, the IMF and even in some respects the European Union, is a 'mental map' held by influential actors which is very much connected with neoclassical economics.[246]

Once accepted, these arbitrary conventions create the dogma under which economic life labors, as Mazzucato writes:

> The marginalist theory of value underlying contemporary national accounting systems leads to an indiscriminate attribution of productivity to anyone grabbing a large income, and downplays the productivity of the less fortunate.[247]
>
> National accounts now state that we are better off when more of our income flows to people who 'manage' our money…[248]

The seemingly ontological existence of the symbolic arises from its firm integration and full interchangeability with tangible forms. The same embodied value can be exchanged for intangible forms or more tangible commodity forms with equal ease: the same money buys other money or derivatives or bonds, just as it buys bananas or the hourly billables of a lawyer.

In this way, the financial sector has expanded amazingly, thanks, quite simply to its phenomenal ability to gather huge amounts of symbolic forms that no "working person" could even imagine. Since reality is left outside – prices and profits spire to dizzying heights – then crash to heart-wrenching depths – all contingent on the faith and loss of faith of people shunting virtual forms back and forth among themselves – in magnitudes that far exceed the capital used in the part of the economy that also has tangible forms.

The dogma of economic equilibrium become far less relevant where pure financial markets are concerned as supply and demand become wholly contingent on faith in prices, both as the bubble "inflates" and more and more people jump on the bandwagon, and as it "bursts" and the deep-pocketed affluent, who have been lurking in wait begin scooping up the "bargains".

Ultimately, the symbolic bubble bursts when the tangible part of the economy ceases to support it. When the Fed raised interest rates before the great crash of 2008, it pushed into insolvency thousands of mortgagees who were working in the real world to pay their debts.

Paradoxically, the powerful producers of money are not free in the "free market". The central banks of capitalist countries are subject to the bureaucratic control of the state and behave accordingly as a command-economy quite capable of arbitrarily increasing the interest rates for the "good" of the people but to the detriment of the actual people.

The power of the Federal Bank made it possible for a single short-sighted move to shift the balance of reality. The shocks then reverberated through the entire system, until they reached the stratospheric levels of the symbolic and burst the "bubble".

---

[246] Fullbrook Ibid, p.167.

[247] Mazzucato, M. (2018).The Value of Everything. Making and Taking in the Global Economy. Penguin, p.98-99.

[248] Mazzucato, Ibid, p.107.

Despite the many economic theories that espouse market equilibrium as their dogma and therefore tend to construe "booms" and "busts" as cyclical, this is not a cyclical thing but a development with clear directionality. The rich now are far richer than ever in the past for there is a lot more money in the system than there ever was, and wealth constantly accumulates.

In many senses the distinction between empirical reality and the symbolic is a developmental one. The empirical is only real in the sense that it has value even when that value remains unarticulated[249], but it gradually becomes enveloped in the symbolic as a person matures, just as all of empirical reality is enveloped in language, understanding and knowledge, not to mention faith.

Once economic reality is embedded in the symbolic, it becomes quite chimeral. Once the equivalence of value between the real necessities of life and intangible forms has become deeply entrenched, i.e., when one finds equal value in a piece of paper and a piece of cake, then reality itself becomes as distinctly dependent on the symbolic as any other aspect of the human world.

Inflation and interest

The decrease in the value of money as its quantity increases, i.e., inflation, is also driven by the fact that the monetary system is forward-looking, and expecting greater returns on every penny loaned. Since most of the money in circulation is a product of loans, earmarked for repayment at a higher cost than the principal, it is obvious that within a market that is fed by these loans, more and more money will become necessary to repay them.

Beyond the interest on common consumer loans, from credit cards to mortgages, there are also many industrial sectors in which people take loans to cover periods when their produce is not ready for sale yet, such as farmers who need loans to tide them over until their crops can be harvested, contractors who must complete a building before they can sell it, or any other industry that requires time until a product matures.

Interest, however, always requires an expansion of the amounts of monetary forms available in the economy in order to pay it. Where will all those credit card holders, mortgagees, farmers and builders find all that additional money? Who will produce it for them?

How would the interest on loans be paid without additional "growth"? If such growth is not forthcoming or slower in developing than the interest due, then the only option is an increase the prices of existing products and services. This increase in prices necessitates the generation of more and more currency forms to cover the new prices, so new loans are made in order to generate more money to cover the existing loans.

The same process that sends people out to obtain additional monetary forms in order to pay their loans ultimately leads to a decrease in the value of these forms, and thence also a decrease in the value of the loan itself, so that even if payment of the symbolic forms is made in full qua forms, the "value" of the forms used for repayment decreases with inflation, at which point, hasting to "link" the value only

249 The "real" is ontologically present: It's falling makes a sound even if your hearing isn't too good.

accelerates inflation even more because it once more demands the production of additional monetary forms.

Interest itself represents unrealistic future expectations. What kind of future is embodied in the "interest", in this additional debt beyond debt?

Additional debt requires inflation in order to pay it. There is no way to collect interest without someone injecting more money into the economy so that the borrower can have it to cover that interest.

As Kennedy writes: "the continual payment of interest and compound interest is arithmetically, as well as practically, impossible. The economic necessity and the mathematical impossibility create a contradiction which - in order to be resolved - has led to innumerable feuds, wars and revolutions."[250]

---

[250] Kennedy, M. (1995). *Interest and inflation free money: Creating an exchange medium that works for everybody and protects the earth*. Stranger Journalism, p. 7.

CHAPTER 8: FREE VS. LABOR - A SPLIT WORLD

Throughout history, a small number of affluent people held most of the wealth, while the rest of humanity lived its life at some level or other of enslavement. The powerful men in each society appropriated its resources in order to support themselves and their wars. In addition, whenever they were able to overcome the men of other societies, they assimilated the wealth of other nations as loot. These men at the top of the social hierarchy formed groups of equals with special privileges who ruled society and had rights of ownership.

Thanks to the spread of money forms in the past few centuries, a dramatic transformation has taken place in human hierarchies as increasingly wider social strata were not only officially released from slavery, but also acquired property rights and franchise, thereby expanding the inner circle of "equals" within each society.

For the first time in history, instead of the classic dominance and patronization hierarchies, there developed societies with beliefs that resonated with the phrasing of the American Declaration of Independence: "We hold these truths to be self-evident, that all men are created equal, that they are endowed by their Creator with certain unalienable Rights, that among these are Life, Liberty and the pursuit of Happiness."[251] Though not stated explicitly, many Americans have come to equate the "pursuit of happiness" with the "acquisition of possessions". The unalienable right to own.

This seems indeed to have been the original intention as Thomas Jefferson, who formulated this paragraph in the Declaration of Independence, was actually paraphrasing one of the Locke's well-known assertions that: "Being all equal and independent, no one ought to harm another in his life, health, liberty, or possessions," (wherein possessions were replaced by "pursuit of happiness"). John Locke also explicitly stated that: "The great and chief end therefore, of Mens uniting into Commonwealths, and putting themselves under Government, is the Preservation of their Property."[252]

Although the liberty part was bit of wishful thinking as many of the signatories were slave owners, the sentiment of liberty slowly spread through the beneficial influence of monetary forms which made it possible to pay employees instead of coercing slaves, and to invest in a great many endeavors that are not possible in a slave economy.

Throughout the twentieth century, these liberties expanded as the right to vote and the right to own property spread through the population, until they became the given ideal of Western civilization and many world cultures.

The deepest transformation took place in the self-perception of people who gradually forsook the ideal of the "good slave" and of "acceptance of one's station in the world" with consent and obedience, and transitioned into a belief in self-worth, in equality and in universal property rights regulated by law.

---

[251] *Declaration of Independence*. 4 July, 1776.

[252] Locke, J. (1689). *Second Treatise of Government.*

During a brief golden period immediately following WWII, in parallel with the increasing spread of respect for human rights, money allowed significant numbers of people to attain the financial independence necessary for supporting the principles of liberty and equality.

This golden period seems to be drawing to a close. Inequality in ownership has been constantly rising over the past few decades, as summarized by the world inequality report for 2018:

> Top 10% income shares increased… between 1980 and 2016, but with large variations in magnitude. In Europe, the rise was moderate, with the top 10% share increasing to about 35–40% by 2016. However, in North America, China, India, and even more so in Russia (where the change in policy regime was particularly dramatic), the rise was much more pronounced. In all these regions, the top 10% share rose to about 45–50% of total income in 2016.[253]

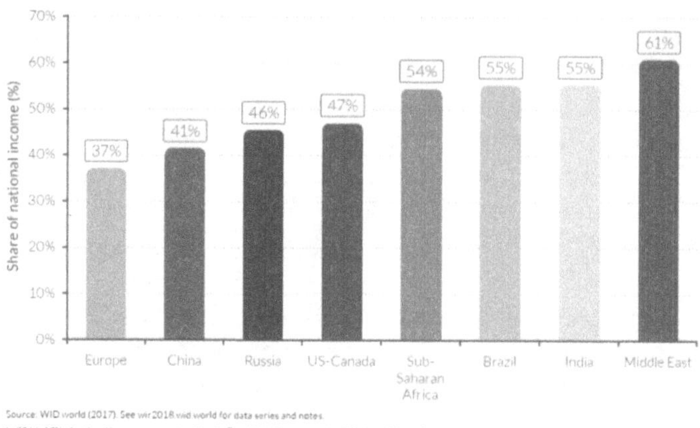

Figure 2: Worldwide Rise in Inequality[254]

This blatant increase in inequality may tempt us to think of the ancient stratifications of class, which had impacted so much economic thinking over the years, but this new "inequality" is different, not just because some of the richest people in the world are computer programmers and writers rather than kings and nobles, but also because many low-income persons are highly-educated and skilled, and could have easily been classed as "middle class" or "nobility" in previous eras.

Moreover, even if we were to distinguish firmly between the rich and the poor on the basis of their very different life agendas, and in particular the freedom of the affluent from the obligation to labor, and the need of the less-affluent to run very hard in order to stay in place, still they are all part of the same ecosystem: All so-called classes are different patterns of the way that the human talent for faith has created a shared belief in the value of money; a universal faith that has allowed human beings to combine their efforts across an entire planet.

---

[253] Alvaredo, F. Chancel, L., Piketty, T., Saez, E. and Zucman, G. (2018). *World Inequality Report 2018*. World Inequality Lab, p. 42.

[254] Alvaredo, et al., Ibid, p. 43.

Can we even draw a line separating the rich from the poor? The upper percentile from the rest? The leisure class from the laboring classes? Can we distinguish between the "haves" and the "have-nots" of this modern era?

Obviously, it is possible to distinguish between a Free zone and a Labor zone, where Free zone and Labor zone people live in very different worlds even though they share a belief in the same symbolic forms. The main distinction is between those who have surplus value stored in various forms that allow them to purchase pieces of reality, be it commodities or the life-efforts of others at will; and those who have no such surplus and are obliged to labor unceasingly, or become dependent on the charity of others, in order to subsist.

This distinction obliterates the differentiation between "toil" and "freedom from toil", as distinguishing the poor from the rich. Many single-parents, widows, children, pensioners and other beneficiaries of sundry annuities are freed from the need to labor, but cannot be rightly classed in the Free zone, since they have no surplus value stored for a rainy day, and are wholly dependent on government magnanimity.

This unique stratum of people who are considered incapable of securing symbolic forms through their efforts, is not part of the Free zone because the moment that welfare beneficiaries shift from the category that provided eligibility, government support is withdrawn and they are obliged to cope once more with the difficulties of empirical reality like all other Labor zoners.

The two zones are in constant interference with each other as people move between them. People high in the Labor zone may accumulate enough symbolic surplus to finally cross over to the Free zone, while Free zoners are liable to lose their fortunes and thenceforth be mired permanently in the Labor zone.

The main line drawn between the two zones is that in the Free zone people own sufficient embodied value to enable them to wholly live off the value held in symbolic financial forms without having to ever actually resort to empirical reality. They have enough money to acquire all necessary commodities (and then some), but are never required to exert any life efforts.

In the Labor zone people have to exert life efforts in order to obtain money, and they almost never accumulate enough to cross into the Free zone. They have no surplus and no security.

The interface between the Free and Labor zones is not a static one, as the two zones interpenetrate each other. Particularly in the current age of financial capitalism, in which the investment of monetary forms in the more sophisticated symbolic forms of capital instruments makes it possible to amass a great deal of wealth without mixing in too much labor on the part of the investor. This more sophisticated usage of value-holding forms often constitutes a siren call to gambling where Labor zone people are concerned.

A poor man may be willing to squander the little he has for the chance of getting out of the mire he is stuck in, even if it means digging an even deeper hole for himself. The investment tempest that destroyed the Albanian market came from this place: from the desperate hope of Labor zone dwellers who thought they had an opportunity to give their bodies a rest and let their money make money.

In contradistinction to the residents of the Free zone, Labor zone people do not have any unneeded surplus that can be placidly invested in order to make more surplus. Rather, they are obliged to skip a meal in order to invest, or get the money by some other means through which people obtain money, ergo loans, debts, mortgages, etc., so that that money too is swallowed up in the world of financial capital, and the poor grow poorer while the holders of surplus will hardly feel the difference.

When Free zoners lose money, even a lot of money, it rarely impacts their lifestyle, while when Labor zoners lose even a little, it can destroy their lives.

Is it at all possible to protect people who are barely subsisting from the folly of investments that will ruin them? The question is one of demarcation: How would you draw a line that would separate the Free zone from the Labor zone so as to protect "small" investors from being swallowed up by the machinations of the "whales"? Is it even possible to demarcate a boundary that only lets through Free zoners whose fate does not depend on any particular investment?

This is obviously impossible. Everything is linked together: the person who needs money to raise a crop or to manufacture something ingenious and innovative lives within the same matrix as the person who needs money to play the stock market. They live in the same world and are swallowed up in the same conceptual universe. One cannot just tell people that they can't join the game because they don't have enough money.

It is true that there are many places from which the poor are excluded from the outset simply because the investment bar is very high: Poker games that demand five-thousand dollars for a seat at the table, investments with an entry level of thousands of dollars, or the Euro-Dollar markets in which the minimum tranche is a hundred thousand dollars. This probably excludes some of the more vulnerable players from the game, but there are many other places where you can lose any surplus you have, followed by everything that was not really surplus. This is part of the freedom of people to make truly reckless moves when they are at their most desperate. When one has little to lose, one is ready to lose even that little for the hope of getting something.

Money and Liberty: Patterns of Ownership and Dependency

A majority of people still live precarious livelihoods. Construction workers can be replaced with robots, a translator can be replaced by AI, and travelling salesmen have been made redundant by internet sales. Most people who are dependent on other people may lose their jobs at any time.

Only full members of the Free zone, whose dependence on others is decentralized and spread over society at large thanks to the broad social willingness to provide favors for money, are actually free to do as they like. Ultimately, it is Free zoners who fully benefit from the symbolic system of embodied values that is money.

Free zoners and Labor zoners live within the same symbolic world and share the same beliefs about the value of symbolic forms. However, their existential positions, as determined by their access to these forms of value vary considerably.

As a concrete example, let's examine a fictitious group of people inhabiting a single building whose different life-stories are expressed in their divergent access to value held in symbolic forms.

The tenants of this building are:

John, the landlord, owns most of the building and lives in the penthouse which is accessed directly by a private elevator from the lobby. He has a magnificent vista of the city skyline through floor-to-ceiling windows in his spacious living room.

The landlord's wife, **Kendra**, thirty years his junior.

The couple's two children – **Linus**, a 14-year-old boy and **Marcy**, a 4-year-old girl.

Also living in the building is the building caretaker, **Raul** who lives in a basement apartment, ventilated through small windows at ground level.

The building caretaker's wife **Olivia**,

The couple's two children – **Adam**, a 14-year-old boy and **Eve**, a 4-year-old girl.

A tenant – **Rosie**, who is a widow.

A tenant – **Stan**, who is employed by the IRS.

A tenant – **Paul**, who is a self-employed translator.

A tenant – **Andrew**, who trades stocks on the internet.

Two tenants – **Josephine**, who works as a private nurse, and her husband **Moshe** – a travelling salesman who is often away on business trips.

Four tenants sharing an apartment – **Romiko**, **Yaji**, **Juan** and **Christos** – who are construction workers.

One apartment owned by John's sister **Anne**, is occupied just two weeks every year when she comes to visit, but is regularly cleaned by Olivia and maintained by Raul.

These tenants are all living together within the same building, yet, they are separated from each other by the extent of the constraints and obligations regulating their life efforts, which are directly tied to the measure of ownership they have over value held in symbolic forms.

John inherited the building from his father, along with a dozen other buildings in the city. John spends most of his time collecting works of fine contemporary art, and is considered quite a maven among collectors. He has a great deal of value held in such forms as real estate and artwork, and also has a steady income stream from rents.

John has access to additional symbolic forms: he can easily get loans from banks by using his property as collateral, and he can always sell some of his more tangible forms.

Even if John should do nothing at all, and live a life of complete indolence, his circumstances would remain the same as his access to symbolic forms does not require any obligatory life-effort on his part.

His affluence depends on the social consensus that supports his legal ownership of his assets. This is expressed in many dimensions including general social consent and a regulatory regime that supports legal ownership.

The risks to his affluence are war and revolution, or changes in law such as deeper taxation of the affluent, though he mitigates these risks by means of offshore tax havens and properties he has in various places in the world – which considerably hedge his risk.

In fact, short of a global catastrophe and the actual destruction of planet earth, his wealth is secure. His affluence is such that he is not concerned for an economic downturn, since even in such downturns his assets remain his own and his earnings remain on par with the market. When the market is up, he can charge more rent, if it is down, he can charge less, but his expenses also decline in a recession. He does not directly depend on people or mutual obligations and does not have to appease anyone to get the forms he needs to sustain himself.

The landlord's wife, **Kendra** has signed a prenuptial agreement which leaves her with about 10,000 symbolic forms to her name in the event of a divorce. She has her own checking account to which John transfers a monthly stipend of 10,000 symbolic forms.

She does not work outside the home, though she puts some effort into instructing the house manager who manages the cleaner, the cook, the nanny and various tutors. Her main effort is invested in preserving her marriage through intensive self-maintenance and a cheery and supportive demeanor aimed at appeasing John.

Thus, although her husband is certainly a well-entrenched Free zoner, Kendra herself may be said to live in a precarious Labor zone since she does not **own** any wealth and is dependent on the goodwill of another for her livelihood.

Although accountants may not carry the value of her labors on their books, she is certainly making a great deal of personal effort to sustain herself and is deeply obligated to John.

Unlike John, whose livelihood is sustained by universal recognition of his ownership rights, by social consensus and by law, Kendra has no recognized rights of this kind and therefore little security.

Linus, John's 14-year-old boy from a previous marriage has been raised by Kendra since he was 4 years old, but his biological mother, whom he visits once every fortnight, disparages Kendra's authority and there have been times that John had sided with her against Kendra on issues of education. This has led Kendra to tread very lightly around Linus and refer to John in every decision. Linus receives a monthly allowance of 200 monetary forms from both his father and his mother and spends most of it on expensive Belgian bonbons and comic books.

Marcy, John and Kendra's 4-year-old girl is very close to both Kendra and her nanny. She gets no embodied value. All her needs are met.

Unlike Kendra, both children have independent trust funds that will be fully owned by them once they reach the age of 21. The trusts are of sufficient value to place them firmly in the Free zone.

The building caretaker, **Raul** is a skilled Jack of all Trades capable of fixing anything from rusty hinges to burnt-out thermostats. He takes pride in maintaining the building at a high level so that everything is clean and functional. John pays him a monthly salary of 2500 monetary forms, of which 600 monetary forms are withheld at source for rent, a 50% discount relative to other apartments in the building. This is a unique perk that has motivated Raul to stick to his job, even when rising costs eroded the purchasing power of his remaining wages (1480 monetary forms after various taxes and provisions). Raul is beholden to John who is both his employer and landlord, and who has been quite generous towards him, awarding him with nice bonuses (200 monetary forms) on the holidays.

Raul is deeply mired in the Labor zone. His access to symbolic forms depends on his efforts in providing good service, and on maintaining good relations with John. Raul is concerned over what will happen if he should fall ill or simply grow too old to maintain the building – but puts these concerns aside. The future will take care of itself.

Olivia, who works part time as a cleaning woman in order to supplement the family income, is also dependent on Raul's job and the discount they get on the rent. She too has little surplus to put aside, and her savings are earmarked for emergencies rather than the building of affluence.

Adam, Raul and Olivia's 14-year-old son is already feeling the pinch. He gets an allowance of 5 monetary forms a week, which he spends on cheap chocolate bars at discount rates. He had a paper route but lost the position to another boy because he had overslept once.

Most of his needs are taken care of by his parents – and he has little access to embodied value. He frequently accompanies his father on jobs and is picking up the skills.

Eve, Adam's sister, is an ebullient and brilliantly intelligent four-year-old that brings much joy to her family. Her parents and brother dote on her. She is their princess. She is already aware that many good things require monetary forms, which are often insufficiently available.

Rosie is a tenant who has had the misfortune of losing her husband at an early age, but the good fortune of receiving a steady pension. She spends most of her days watching daytime TV, with an occasional happy visit from her children. She gives her children regular stipends amounting to about 20% of her income.

Despite having no surplus and therefore not belonging to the Free zone, she is not dependent on any single individual for her livelihood. She relies directly on the public consensus that sustains pensions and annuities. In the age of fiat money, Rosie is not worried. She believes in the power of the government to continue supporting her.

Because she does not have to make a personal life effort to sustain herself, Rosie is living her life in a way that is not very different from how Free zoners can spend their lives, although she cannot afford few of the luxuries of leisure.

Stan is employed by the IRS in the archives department and is worried that as paperwork becomes increasingly digitized, his position will become redundant. He spends most of his money on books and live theater shows and has accumulated a great deal of consumer debt. Should he lose his job, he will be hard put to find another.

Stan has no job security because he works in a department slated for eventual computerization: All one needs is to scan and digitize the archives. The only thing that prevented his dismissal years ago is the general procrastination of a large bureaucratic organization.

Nevertheless, since he is a government employee, Stan has some provident funds and a pension fund that will allow him to subsist if he is fired but not to continue renting his current domicile or cover all his debts. He is considering bankruptcy and a move to a cheaper apartment but presently carries on as usual.

Stan is clearly a member of the Labor zone, but should he be terminated, his situation will be more similar to Rosie's, with the government stepping in to provide him with embodied value according to the social benefits to which he would be eligible.

Paul, a self-employed translator, freelances with large companies that subcontract projects to him. He has never met his employers or the final recipients of his labors. He is part of a supply chain entirely mediated by the internet. He is feeling the pinch of market forces as competition in the translation industry grows. He loves to travel and learn new languages and is deep in consumer debt – mostly incurred in his frequent travels.

Despite the fact that Paul's formal education is far higher than that of Stan, his situation is worse than Stan's because he has no salary and has not accumulated any social benefits. Should Paul lose his ability to compete in the translation market – he will become destitute and be forced to live in the lower regions of the Labor zone.

Andrew, who trades stocks on the internet, wishes he had a paid position with a financial institution, in order to rid himself of the tensions of his current work. However, Andrew leads an ostentatious lifestyle and is deeply in debt, so he can't quit.

Andrew's economic status is higher than Paul's but his situation is very similar because should he be tempted to develop an overly leveraged position and fail to skillfully navigate his investments in falling markets, he is liable to lose all liquidity and not be able to continue trading, thereby passing immediately to the lowest area of the Labor zone alongside other debtors who have nowhere to obtain additional symbolic forms.

Josephine works as a private nurse for minimum wages. She is emotionally attached to her employer, a ninety-year-old former-actress with independent means. Josephine is worried about the future, should her employer die. She fastidiously scrimped and saved for many years in the hope of buying an apartment one day, but the sharp increase in house prices has dashed her hopes.

Her husband, **Moshe**, a travelling salesman who is rarely at home, has suffered a sharp decline in income in recent years, as most of his products are more easily accessible on the internet, and at better prices than he could possibly hope to offer.

He now tends to approach smaller towns in more traditional areas, where a segment of the population is not yet completely on board with the internet. He is rather morose and worried about the rent.

Romiko, Yaji, Juan, and Christos are all foreign workers who are deeply in debt to the middlemen who brokered the work for them. They earn less than the minimum wage per hour and most of their money goes to their families and to repaying their debts.

All four of them find themselves in the paradoxical situation of being deep in the Labor zone in the country where they live and work, but the money that they send home embodies significant value in their country of origin, to the point that they have a tangible hope that within a few years they can return home, buy a house and live well within the Free zone.

Their position demonstrates the deep dependency of symbolic forms on social conventions. The consensus regarding the value of forms and prices in their home countries is very different from where they currently work, and they can leverage the difference to their benefit. Different places on earth are assigned different values by the people living there, and people deeply mired in the Labor zone of one country can float up to the Free zone of another country.

John's sister, Anne, is a woman of independent means who has inherited many apartments from her father and lives entirely on the rent produced. She has never married, raises two small pedigreed dogs and is frequently involved in charity events.

It can be seen from the above example that certain people are situated in similar positions in respect to the extent of their dependency or ownership.

The position of children and wives is structurally similar and relegated to the Labor zone despite the fact that their spouses or parents may live in a different zone.

It can also be seen that the life patterns of the affluent and the pensioned are very similar. The state, capable of generating wealth at will, becomes the patron of people found eligible to receive its annuities.

However, the relationship between the state and its dependents is more akin to that of a parent and children, since it is considered the duty of the state to support its citizens, and should the state remove its benefaction, the citizens would be as helpless as orphaned children.

Patterns of dependency and ownership distinguish the life-positions of different people: The greater the ownership the less the dependency. Free zoners depend on the functioning of the entire economy to provide them with rents and sustain their rights of ownership, while Labor zoners depend on individual benefactors to whom they give their life efforts in exchange for symbolic forms of value.

How does each one of the people in the building access money? What effort does it entail? How does money enter their lives? Does it magically appear in one's account because one is entitled to a government subsidy? Because one's investments have borne fruit? Because one has slaved over an 80-hour work-week to construct a new high riser in the city? Or is one using a credit card issued in the name of one's husband, or the pocket money handed one by a parent?

Everyone depends on the human environment to provide the symbolic forms of value that will make it possible to secure one's needs from other people.

These are all measures of freedom: the higher you are in the Free zone, the more freedom you have to determine your fate. Pensioners are almost as good as Free zoners, if they can live within their means like the widow Rosie. Pensions are a form of dependency that give a sense of freedom by shifting the relationship of dependency to the government.

One cannot compare dependency on individuals to dependency on society in general. The redistribution and anonymization of dependency create a situation that mitigates the shame. It becomes a "right" akin to the rights enjoyed by owners of property, rather than a "boon".

The Person	Source of value	Labor?	Effort required for "living wage"	Dependency on others
John- landlord	Affluence	No	None	Independent
Kendra	Husband	No	Appeasement	Yes
Linus - son	Parents	No	None	Yes
Marcy - daughter	Parents	No	None	Yes
Raul - caretaker	Work	Yes	Labor	On employer
Olivia - caretaker's wife	Husband and work	Yes	Appeasement, non-paid work	Yes
Adam - son	Parents	No	None	Yes
Eve - daughter	Parents	No	None	Yes
Rosie - a widow	Pension	No	None	Independent
Stan - employee	Work & Debt	Yes	Labor	On employer
Paul - self-employed	Work & Debt	Yes	Labor	On market
Andrew - stock trader	Work & Debt	Yes	Labor	On market

Josephine - nurse	Work	Yes	Labor	On employer
Moshe - salesman	Work & Debt	Yes	Labor	On market
Romiko - laborer	Work & Debt	Yes	Labor	On employer
Yaji - laborer	Work & Debt	Yes	Labor	On employer
Juan - laborer	Work & Debt	Yes	Labor	On employer
Christos - laborer	Work & Debt	Yes	Labor	On employer
John's sister – visiting owner	Affluence	No	None	Independent

Table 6: Ownership and Dependence

The booming credit market, too, dilutes patterns of dependency and turns them into anonymized ones. You do not have to kiss the ring of the credit card company (though you had better make the minimum payments).

In traditional societies, the giver and the recipient are known to each other so that one cannot avoid such issues as expectations and obligations, disappointments and defaults, borrower self-sacrifice[255] and righteous harassment by lenders.[256]

The following table illustrates how shame has been leached out of human dependence relationships with the rise of money.

	Obligation	Further action	Shame on default
Buyer	Fulfilled	No	No
Seller	Received payment in full	No	No
Lending bank	Yes	Yes	No
Borrower	Yes	Yes	No
Credit cards	Yes	Yes	No
Landlord	Yes	Yes	Yes
Tenant	Yes	Yes	Yes
Gift giver	Owed	Expects reciprocation	Yes
Gift receiver	Owes	Must reciprocate	Yes

Table 7: Financial reciprocity and shame

The Very Poor: No skin in the game

The oft-hungry poorest people on earth populate the lowest levels of the Labor zone in their multitudes and rarely have access to enough money to accumulate any surplus whatsoever. As Weatherford writes:

> In studying the poor Indian immigrants from the countryside into Mexico City, Oscar Lewis found that they rarely bought in bulk but instead bought minute quantities. Rather than shopping in a large grocery store, the Indians more frequently bought small meals or snacks such as tacos, ice cream, pineapple, or a plate of beans and rice from a local vendor.

---

[255] As so artfully depicted in Guy De Maupassant's heart-rending short story "the necklace" published 1884. https://www.owleyes.org/text/necklace

[256] For a modern example of such inevitable sense of obligation, see my study of Chabad Mission in Bulgaria, *Priest of Exile*. Clients make donations to the establishment, defraying operating costs, but the proprietor still feels a sense of ownership, and deserving of gratitude, since they were dining at **his** table.

> They bought cigarettes one at a time from a local vendor even though they cost twice as much as cigarettes bought by the pack or carton in a store.[257]
> Similarly, people in the poorest parts of contemporary American cities buy hamburgers or fried chicken for cash and for one meal at a time. Even in the grocery store, they buy many snack foods already packaged in small, and therefore more expensive, amounts.[258]

The poor do not have enough skin in the game to get the lower prices achievable by buying cigarettes by the packet, so they buy a cigarette at a time. Just as all Labor zoners never acquire sufficient symbolic forms to cover the value of a house, and are obliged to run, run, run, just to pay the rent, the very poor never have enough surplus to buy an entire carton of cigarettes, and the surplus is scalped by those who have enough currency forms to capture an entire pack of cigarettes and sell them piecemeal.

Not having enough symbolic value to buy anything but the smallest quantities, the poor are of course distrusted by the purveyors of credit[259] and are obliged to transact in cash. In fact, as Weatherford writes:

> The economy of the ghetto, the barrio, and other poor neighborhoods from Mexico City to Milwaukee and from Seattle to Istanbul functions around cash, but this same cash that keeps the poor people's economy operating also puts up barriers against their participation in the general economy that bases its operations on checks, plastic cards, and electronic impulses.[260]

Smith describes the ultimate vulnerability of all Labor zoners:

> A landlord, a farmer, a master manufacturer, or merchant, though they did not employ a single workman, could generally live a year or two upon the stocks which they have already acquired. Many workmen could not subsist a week, few could subsist a month, and scarce any a year without employment.[261]

Labor zoners are always circling the drain of subsistence – the minimum needed for survival – and this is usually where the minimum wage ultimately finds them, as prices rise just enough to absorb the minimum wage into subsistence. No large clothing, car or dentist bills for these fellows. Marion Nestle describes this delicate balance in the U.S.:

> SNAP (Supplemental Nutrition Assistance Program) is a program aimed at promoting human welfare and nutrition. In 2013, it provided an average of $133 per month to an astounding
> 47 million down-and-out Americans, one out of seven, who, because of low-wage jobs, job losses, illness, lack of education, or plain bad luck,

---

[257] Weatherford, J.M. (1997). *The History of Money.* Crown Publications, pp. 210-211.

[258] Weatherford, Ibid, p. 211.

[259] Even when they get credit through micro-loans or from various oppressive black market parties who are always ready to provide the poor with extremely expensive credit, they do not get a credit card. Their credit is based on cash too.

[260] Weatherford, J.M. (1997). *The History of Money.* Crown *Publications*, p. 214.

[261] Smith A. [1776] (1981). *An Inquiry into the Nature and Causes of the Wealth of Nations,* Volumes I and II. Indianapolis: Library Fund, pp.83-84.

> had so little income that they qualified for this form of food aid… Today's Republican critique of SNAP. that it is not an appropriate role of government, is too expensive, induces dependency, and encourages fraud, is old news… These laws aimed to relieve hunger and misery, of course, but also to preserve the social order and maintain a workforce willing to work for very low wages. The laws managed these multiple objectives by giving the poor barely enough food and other necessities to prevent people from starving on the streets or rioting.[262]

> The American economy regularly has the capacity to produce goods and services that poor people cannot afford to buy but need or would like to own. Goods are distributed on the basis of purchasing power, not on the basis of need, and many human needs and desires go unfulfilled not because society is unable to produce the goods and services to satisfy them, but because the distribution of income does not permit those in need to purchase what they could use. [263]

There are many obstacles to talent, many barriers, and the absence of surplus money has become one of the most significant. Contrary to money's essential ability to cut across all boundaries, surplus is hard to come by in a market that is constantly adjusting itself to take up any surplus made available to Labor zone residents.

The increasing chasm between the Free zone and the Labor zone is evident in many countries where rent-receiving landlords are living off the rent-paying homeless. Thus, paradoxically, the very ability of money to cross all boundaries becomes the means to convey the values produced by Labor zoners into the Free zone.

Split world: Between the tangible and the financial

The abstraction that is money has given birth to an increasing trend whereby the human world is split into the tangible world in which people labor for their wages and spend most of the money on subsistence, and the abstract world of finance.

One world is the empirical reality mediated and enveloped by symbolic monetary forms, a world in which people are still busy with the things that they had always been busy with: survival, livelihood, food and a roof over their heads; and a second world, in which money, like pure mathematics, does not envelop anything but other monetary forms, and the symbolic does not represent anything but other symbols, a world in which wealth breeds wealth.

The complex interaction between the Free zone and tangible reality is the source of all our economic woes. Menkhoff and Tolksdorf call it "Financial Market Drift" or "Decoupling of the Financial Sector from the Real Economy":[264]

---

[262] Nestle, M. (2014). Preface. In Poppendieck, J. (2014). *Breadlines knee-deep in wheat: Food assistance in the great depression* (Vol. 53). University of California Press. pp. x-xi.

[263] Nestle, M. (2014). Preface. In Poppendieck, J. (2014). *Breadlines knee-deep in wheat: Food assistance in the great depression* (Vol. 53). University of California Press. p. xvii.

[264] Menkhoff, L., & Tolksdorf, N. (2000). *Financial market drift: Decoupling of the financial sector from the real economy?* Springer Science & Business Media.

There can be no doubt that financial aggregates have grown at a faster pace than real aggregates in the past ten or twenty years. The relative importance of stock markets, capital flows and international financial transactions has grown in comparison with companies' capital stock or the real national product. Some analysts believe that this development has resulted in a shift in quality, as it were - a de-coupling, detachment or move towards autonomy: traditionally, the productive real economy was in center stage, and the role of the financial sector was to support its growth. Now, however, this position of dominance sometimes seems to have been turned on its head. Events on the financial markets correspondingly follow their own logic, and the real economy has to adapt itself to the consequences of this. This is the "pessimistic view" or - as it represents the core theme of this study - the "decoupling hypothesis."[265] Perhaps the most frequently debated issue associated with high-growth financial markets is the tremendously strong growth in the volume of foreign exchange (market) transactions, which is now about 25 times higher than the volume of foreign trade. Many observers see this ratio as exemplifying the core problem: financial markets have grown so strongly that they now have little in common with the real economy. In the present example, this means that the currency conversions accompanying real foreign trade are of marginal importance compared with foreign exchange transactions, which are evidently driven by other, meaning purely financial, motives.[266]

The forex transactions in which one currency buys another take up an enormous volume relative to the more tangible parts of the economy. This is a prominent symptom of the way in which the most central monetary transactions, those between one nation and another, are swallowed up in a virtual world in which one symbolic monetary form buys another symbolic monetary form without ever touching the ground of reality.

Capital markets are an engrossing world in which numbers fluctuate constantly. People buy and sell strings of letters that symbolize currencies, such EUR and USD, ILS and BGN, or commodities, such as EMA (corn) and EBL (wheat), or stocks, such as AAPL (Apple) MSFT (Microsoft) or GOOG (Google), and of course, all the mind-boggling diversity of imaginary financial goods on offer, the derivatives and convertibles, futures and swaps, and, in general, the entire stratosphere of abstract transactions involving abstract symbolic forms that hold their values nicely but never touch the good earth.

The financial crisis of 2008 illuminated the deep rift between the two worlds and their financial fate. While the tangible world sustained terrible blows, the financial world just kept floating higher and higher. Price wrote about events following the injection of Quantitative Easing into the financial world:

> Wall Street giants and their major corporate clients hoarded money and used significant portions of it to buy back their own shares, elevating their stock price and providing the illusion of financially healthier com-

---

[265] Menkhoff, & Tolksdorf, Ibid, p. 1.

[266] Menkhoff & Tolksdorf, Ibid, p. 1.

> panies. This had the effect of pumping up stock and executive bonuses linked to the price of stock.
>
> These firms effectively manipulated their stock prices with central bank support and paid themselves bonuses for doing so—as a result of a financial crisis… Nobody went to jail. No one was subject to real, long-term consequences. In contrast, people the world over were subject to austerity measures that hurt students, the vulnerable, and lower-income earners the most. [267]

The mindset of austerity places a stranglehold on both the economy and human creativity in general. People who are being frugal in a recession are not going to pay for creativity. They'll stick to the basics and make their own art. They'll do a free sing-along and save on the concert ticket. Everything crashes down to the level of bare necessities. Yet, even as the tangible world suffered stagnation and a decline in the standard of living, the financial world continued to flourish and expand after the crisis.

> The annualized growth of the stock market from its twenty-first-century low point in March 2009 through March 2020, the onset of the COVID-19 pandemic, was on average 12% per year. The average annual growth in US GDP over that same timeframe was about 2%.[268]
>
> The dark secret revealed by the war between supposed "smart money" and small retail investors is that the stock market has relatively little to do with productive investment. It was the Federal Reserve that ultimately killed the notion that fundamentals, or objective metrics related to the value of a company, drive stock prices. [269]

Naomi Prins describes the differential concerns of the two worlds in the crisis of 2008:

> In the upper echelons of society, the concern was that banks weren't functioning reliably, stock and bond markets were in free fall, and scores of investment bankers could see their bonuses evaporating. On the lower rungs of the economic ladder, there was a more visceral fear—of not being able to pay rent, losing jobs, being kicked out of homes, and having a less stable future.[270]
>
> Despite the premise that emergency central bank action would save the Main Street economy, the unprecedented monetary support from the world's main central banks to the banks and markets increased inequality, magnified debt, ushered in isolationism, and elevated the wealthy and powerful.[271] All the easy monetary policy had not fostered sustained economic growth, but it had rejuvenated stock markets. The US economy grew just 2.2% in 2012, while the S&P 500 index grew 13.4%. China's economy was wobbling, too. As of July 2012, its second-quarter GDP

---

[267] Prins, N. (2022). *Permanent distortion : how the financial markets abandoned the real economy.* Hachette Book Group, p. 14.

[268] Prins, Ibid, p. 18.

[269] Prins, Ibid, p. 140.

[270] Prins, Ibid, p. 21.

[271] Prins, Ibid, p. 21.

growth had slowed to 7.6%, while the Hang Seng Composite stock market index finished the year up 22.9% over 2011.[272]

The lines differentiating the affluent from the non-affluent are more prominent now as the affluent have come to dominate the world in an unprecedented fashion. As a class, the affluent are a pretty varied bunch thanks to the social mobility that allows anyone to cross from the Labor zone to the Free zone and vice versa – but the thralldom of those who have no hope of ever making such a crossing is only deepening. As Prins writes:

> The idea that someday things could be even better under the right leader, despite the continual flow of money to the top no matter who is in charge, is the tragedy of the era.[273]
>
> The part of the global economy that relied upon consumer spending was broken. Around the world, many consumers were simply too poor and stretched too thin. Meanwhile, the wealthy did not need to worry about cost, but they didn't buy enough to make a difference in overall global economic growth. If people are impoverished, disenfranchised, and angry, consumption is less important than survival. The middle class was feeling increasingly depleted, which only further diminished demand for goods and services.
>
> The problem was not new, but the outsized effect of central banks' policies on the world was… Megabanks and massive global corporations would continue to receive epic subsidies in times of turmoil, while ordinary working people got no such financial cushioning. This was anything but a temporary phenomenon.[274]
>
> The link between abundant monetary aid and a robust economy remained the prevailing narrative, mostly on the notion that big banks were able to take more risks from an economic lending perspective because they had been able to fortify their capital levels… None of that changed conditions for workers.[275]
>
> The pandemic widened the resilience discrepancy between the Main Street economy and the markets. Though the Fed injected funds into the big banks and corporations, the real economy sank like a rock. US GDP tanked 9.5% in the second quarter of 2020, for an annualized drop of 32.9%—its sharpest contraction ever. In contrast, the Dow went on to recover all of its February–March losses by November 2020. Globally, people were subject to restrictions and economic instability, while markets hit new records—without restrictions.[276]
>
> If the 2008 financial crisis had exposed the biggest banks on Wall Street as entities that were "too big to fail," during the pandemic the policies of the Fed and other key central banks had been exposed as "too big to correct." Ultimately, the failure of these monetary policies occurs because

---

[272] Prins, Ibid, p. 30.
[273] Prins, Ibid, p. 36.
[274] Prins, Ibid, p. 42.
[275] Prins, Ibid, p. 42.
[276] Prins, Ibid, p. 102.

> the stock market of the modern era has relatively little to do with long-term, productive, economy-fortifying investment. [277]

Most of the symbolic monetary value circulating in the world economy today is some form or other of financial gambling that has nothing to do with tangible reality. as Maverick summarizes:

> The derivatives market is, in a word, gigantic – often estimated at more than $1.2 quadrillion on the high end. How can that be? Largely because there are numerous derivatives in existence, available on virtually every possible type of investment asset, including equities, commodities, bonds and foreign currency exchange. Some market analysts even place the size of the market at more than 10 times that of the total world gross domestic product (GDP).[278]

How tiny the economy of tangible forms, including all conspicuous consumption, when compared to the mammoth edifice of the speculative symbolic. How tiny the worth of the Labor zone: A drop in the bucket? A few trillions?

It must be remembered that all this frantic speculative activity, this 1.2 quadrillion dollars of symbolic frenzy, obviously now glutted and eased with a great deal of "quantitative easing", is all happening in the Free zone.

The people who "short" or "hedge" the market, have the symbolic means to do it. This is a wholly intra-Free zone affair on both sides of the "market": The only chumps are the Labor zoners who tried to jump into the Free zone, or those innocent Labor zone bystanders who paid their rent but the owner defaulted on the mortgage, like Tracy Munch who: "watches as an eviction team removes furniture from her foreclosed house… She and her husband had been renting from an owner, who collected the monthly payments but had stopped paying his mortgage." [279]

As Mian and Sufi point out – things could have been done differently – and have been done differently historically:

> In contrast to the Great Recession, governments in 1819 at the state and national level responded aggressively to the needs of indebted individuals, in particular farmers. Many state governments immediately imposed moratoria on debt payments and foreclosures. [280]

Hoarding and Sterilization

At the Free zone's stratospheric layers, money never touches the ground. A Japanese businessman bought Van Gogh's portrait of Dr. Gachet[281] for more than 80 million dollars. This exorbitant value many have been culled from different sources, but was now replicated simultaneously in the Van Gogh painting and Sotheby's bank balances. It is doubtful if any significant part of this sum (on the Sotheby's

---

[277] Prins, Ibid, p. 102.

[278] Maverick, J.B. (2018). How Big is the Derivatives Market? *Investopedia.* www.investopedia.com/ask/answers/052715/how-big-derivatives-market.asp

[279] Amadeo, K. (2020). 2007 Financial Crisis. Explanation, Causes and Timeline. *The Balance.* https://www.thebalance.com/2007-financial-crisis-overview-3306138

[280] Mian, A. and Sufi, A. (2014). *House of debt: how they (and you) caused the Great Recession, and how we can prevent it from happening again.* University of Chicago Press, p. 143.

[281] https://en.wikipedia.org/wiki/Portrait_of_Dr._Gachet

side of course, for the value replicated in the painting is now simply affixed to some wall somewhere, or perhaps it's not even on a wall but in some dark vault with carefully controlled humidity) was used to buy groceries. Most of the money in existence is far removed from the reality where people use their symbolic forms to purchase such things as food or pay rent. Nevertheless, the Van Gogh buyer at Sotheby's and the buyer of half a loaf of remaindered rye bread at a local grocery belong to the same conceptual value system and believe in the same symbolic forms.

The ability to store exorbitant value in artistic objects is one of the main consequences of the fundamental capacity of any form so designated by the human mind to hold value.

In a world of constantly accumulating wealth, the problem becomes what to do with a glut of embodied value, which creates an incessant search for "collectible" forms, in which a limited number of rich mavens create their own market for forms which can be as ephemeral as domain names or as concretized as an Old Master. The art market is a fine example of the way in which value depends on agreement on the symbolic.

> As art prices soared... speculators added fuel to an art market that was already becoming overheated. The art market bubble at the end of the 1980s was particularly exacerbated by strong Japanese buying, mainly in the Impressionist and Post-Impressionist sectors... Surplus cash, combined with a lack of discrimination on the part of new purchasers, caused prices to rise sharply, often with huge sums paid for mediocre works. That art boom ended abruptly in 1990 as a sharp rise in interest rates by the Bank of Japan[282] forced many speculative collectors to go under... Many collections still remain in bank vaults, previously secured as collateral against corporate loans that failed during the Japanese recession that followed.[283]

Art is the perfect form for the ostentation of the affluent. It has no use value. Dr. Gachet would not save you from hunger and is solely the province of deep pocketed individuals. It is strictly a Free zoner's game.

Since such artistic forms have no price outside the circles of the very rich, their value is measured directly by the extent to which they aggregate large volumes of symbolic values, the bigger the better. Such forms are a good hedge against inflation as they are capable of absorbing all the QE that governments are pouring into the world economy. The art market is a true inner-circuit of the Free zone: the rich trading expensive forms with the rich and getting to show off in the bargain.

Sterilization of money undermines the Cantillon effect and inflation too, since it maintains ownership of money without exchanging it to obtain ownership of other commodities and services, as nicely summed up by North:

> While quantity theorists argued that the supply of money is a function of the amount of money in circulation and its velocity (how many times a given note lubricates transactions) in relation to the volume of goods and

[282] Yes, in Japan too, the sanctimonious economists who raised the interest rates perpetrated the market collapse.

[283] McAndrew, C. (2010). *Fine art and high finance: expert advice on the economics of ownership.* Bloomberg Press p. 4

> services, Keynes argued that this ignores whether people choose to spend money or hold onto it in what he called "idle balances." Having money does not mean that one spends it, so printing more money can be like "pushing on a piece of string."[284]

These are the deeper shapes that value holding forms take in the different zones: Labor zoners put all of their symbolic forms into play. They are "all-in" in the market, for every crumb of symbolic value is critical for their survival, while Free zoners constantly drain most of their wealth out of the active market. Free zoners wait for a "rainy day", while Labor zoners are constantly dancing in the pelting rain.

The Free zone art-market game is completely cut off from the feeding frenzy of the financial markets. The art market is not looking for profits or rents, it is investing for the long-term. They have no need to transfer the embodied value into other forms in order to have enough money for subsistence.

This is the perfect sanitization of wealth, and so long as more and more come-uppers are emerging from the turbulence of the markets with awesome profits, the status of these artistic forms only grows.

Often, on their demise, Free zoners bequeath these behemoth containers of symbolic value to the public sphere, to museums that will subsequently enshrine their names. The art market is a place where rich people trade prestige, and there is little room there for the actual producers of the stuff, the artists. The progenitors of the more expensive art works are mostly dead. As described by McAndrew:

> The much larger secondary market is where dealers and auction houses offer works of art for subsequent resale. One of the distinctive features of the art market is the predominance of trade on this secondary tier, with by far the bulk of value in trading taking place here between former and future consumers. In the primary marketplace, prices tend to be lower than on the secondary market, as it can take considerable time before a work is recognized for its artistic value, rarity, historical importance, or notoriety. By the time a work is resold, these second sales tend to be higher priced...and purchases tend to be less risky. The fall in risk is connected to a distinct feature of works of art, that is, their value tends to appreciate rather than depreciate over time. This is quite different from other goods commonly traded on secondary markets...[such as] the second-hand car market... Art collectors... will often be more wary and pay less for new and contemporary artists' works, whose value may not be as well established as older, more renowned works sold on secondary markets.[285]

Rarity is a central driving force in the prices of art

> The fixed supply of most paintings can cause prices to catapult, as buyers attempt to grasp increasingly limited opportunities to buy high-quality works that often have a lengthy market cycle.[286]

---

[284] North, P. (2007). *Money and Liberation: Micropolitics of Alternative Currency Movements.* University of Minnesota Press, p. 13.

[285] McAndrew, C. (2010). *Fine art and high finance: expert advice on the economics of ownership.* Bloomberg Press, pp. 8-9.

[286] McAndrew, Ibid, p. 19-20.

McAndrew sums up the availability of commodities in the art market as follows:

> A a typical cycle to market can take about thirty to forty years. In other words, from the time the work is first sold, it will take several decades (on average) for buyers to get the opportunity to purchase that work again, which adds to the scarcity value of art.... A work of art often arrives on the market because of one of the famous "three Ds" (divorce, death, or debt).[287]

In contra-distinction to monetary forms that can be created without limitation, rare works of art are unique forms that are not made for "spending" but only for the hoarding and sterilization of value.

At a certain point in the modern age, in the course of an auction where certain persons of wealth traded the "values" contained in unique works of arts, one Free zoner by the name of Dimitris Daskalopoulos bought a limited-edition replica of Marcel Duchamp's famous "fountain",[288] a urinal signed with the name R. Mutt, for the sum of $1.76 million, thereby closing the magical circle of "only the valued has value", and providing a tangible social and interpersonal proof that Duchamp was right: Art is what the artist finds to be of artistic value, and collectible art is all that collectors find to be of financial value.

Urinals too are forms and they too have a value and a price.

---

[287] McAndrew, Ibid, Ibid.

[288] https://en.wikipedia.org/wiki/Fountain_(Duchamp)

CHAPTER 9: MONEY IN THE PRESENT AGE

A person who has acquired his wealth through trade in stock symbols with other Free zoners decides to give his money some tangible anchor and invests in a residential building as an income-producing property. Other Free zoners are also interested in tangible investments of this type, which are connected to the concrete need of human beings to occupy a place in reality, and therefore obliging said humans to produce the income that will cover the rent.

After a brisk bidding war that appreciates prices for beyond the value of the materials and work invested in creating the building, one of the Free zoners comes out on top and purchases the building. The financial symbolism enveloping the tangible existence of the building is now far greater than the ability of most Labor zoners to attain. In fact, over time, this process places most of the world's major cities beyond the reach of Labor zoners.[289]

When one acquires an "income-producing property", the connection with tangible reality is deeper than the property itself, since the factor producing the income of the property are people in the Labor zone who derive their monetary forms through endeavors such as selling tangible goods or services, who now have to become even more industrious in order to supply the income that these properties "produce".

This process has expanded exponentially since credit cards were invented at the beginning of the 1960s and made it possible for Labor zoners to behave like Free zoners for a while, until the accumulating burden of credit card debt throttled their financial position. The ability to receive new money on the strength of one's signature, without having to sell any goods or services, but on the mere promise of paying the money back in future, is truly intoxicating for those who live from hand to mouth.

Credit cards also made it possible to purchase tangible goods and services with far greater value than the amounts that are immediately available to a Labor zoner, as they are paid from the deep pockets of banks and credit-card companies. This, again, leads to a rise in prices, thereby pushing those still working for their livelihoods in the tangible world to the bottom of the financial hierarchy.

---

[289] In the margins of these processes, one may point to those individuals who generate their wealth through another aspect of the mind, i.e., intellectual property that is sold to a multitude of buyers, such as patent-holders, producers of visual and auditory media and best-selling authors who have created forms that many people find valuable. This is a unique and direct path for creating replicable value that emulates monetary forms in that one can print as many copies as one wants by publisher fiat, according to the spread of demand, just as governments produce money according to demand, and just like money, if too many copies are printed, the books lose value and are sold at bargain basement prices. Rolling, Grisham and King still made their fortunes in the Labor zone, with the sweat of their brows and the clicking of their keyboards, but they produced such successful symbolic content that it became a generator of monetary value in it is own right, as every copy of their books became a form holding value, to the extent that Grisham, for example, speaks of the publication of his books as a kind of sovereign event on which depend the livelihoods of thousands of distributors, marketers and booksellers who exchange the value held by his book form for the value held by monetary forms.

At this point in history, almost two decades after the global crisis of 2008, the world is saturated with enormous quantities of money supplied through quantitative easing. The Free zone is fully and pleasantly functional, while the middle classes have been erased, and the Labor zone is full of poorer people with declining self-sufficiency. All is engulphed within the symbolic, and the price of the symbolic, within the minds of Free zoners has long appreciated beyond the reach of Labor zoners. As Posner and Weyl describe:

> The financial crisis of 2008 and the subsequent recession were the first tremors. Yet even though the economic downturn was the worst since the Great Depression, for a time it seemed to be no different from most recessions. People lost their homes, jobs, and access to credit, but this had happened many times before and the economy had recovered. Only in 2016 did it become clear how dramatically things had changed... Ballooning inequality, stagnating living standards, and rising economic insecurity made a mockery of the old style of policy analysis... The public lost faith in the mainstream policy analysis of elites who had supported financial deregulation and then the unpopular bailouts. [290]

Fervent Faith

When faith in value is particularly fervent, the entire market can be swept up into ecstatic heights of abundance, buoyed on trust in appreciating value. In his critique of the prevailing economic dogma that attempts to apply a view of rational equilibrium to the market, Shiller describes the deep faith in the ever-upward rising of the stock market, a belief that is not only widespread in the market but also shared by hard-headed market mavens.

In the capital markets one can always transfer value from one vessel to another and create new forms into which the value from previous forms can be transferred.

> ... conventional wisdom holds that the stock market as a whole has always been the best investment, and always will be, even when the market is overpriced by historical standards... This attitude invites exploitation by companies who have an unlimited supply of equities to sell.[291] "You want stocks? We'll give you stocks!'"[292]

Like money itself, the abstract forms that are bought and sold in financial markets can also be infinitely reproduced, and so long as faith is maintained, the entire market can soar higher and higher, and in periods of abundance, this faith is shared across the board and is so strong that it becomes 'self evident', as Shiller describes:

> Most investors seem to view the stock market as a force of nature unto itself. They do not fully realize that they themselves, as a group, determine the level of the market, and they underestimate how similar to their own thinking is that of other investors. Many individual investors think that institutional investors dominate the market and that these "smart money"

[290] Posner, E. A. & Weyl, E. G. (2018). *Radical Markets*. Princeton University Press, p.12.
[291] In fact, shares and other financial instruments are symbolic forms created ex-nihilo in the very same way that fiat money is created or liquidity is born via loans made by commercial banks. All it needs is the will and the inscription to be absorbed into the general faith.
[292] Shiller, R. J. (2000). *Irrational exuberance*. Princeton University Press, p.xv.

investors have sophisticated models to understand prices—superior knowledge. Little do they know that most institutional investors are, by and large, equally clueless about the level of the market. In short, the price level is driven to a certain extent by a self-fulfilling prophecy based on similar hunches held by a vast cross section of large and small investors and reinforced by news media that are often content to ratify this investor-induced conventional wisdom."[293]

And why not? There is no reality beyond the reality thus created. And when the "bubble" bursts – it is another kind of "belief" that predominates, the belief in "real" prices and tangible forms, that is no less a "self-fulfilling" prophecy than the belief in eternal abundance. There is no equilibrium; it is either growth sustained by exuberant belief or decline caused by a no less forceful backsliding in heart.

Market beliefs are often directly produced by authority. When the Fed dictates dogma by raising the interest rate, this is immediately instituted as canon, and everyone believes now that money is more expensive, shifting calculations across the board.

An essentially pessimistic view of economics as always waiting to plunge into doom has led to the obverse illusion that when the market is flourishing it is either a delusion (bubble) or a cheat (Ponzi). Thus, Shiller writes:

> The amplification mechanisms work through a sort of feedback loop… a type of naturally occurring Ponzi process. Investors, their confidence and expectations buoyed by past price increases, bid up stock prices further, thereby enticing more investors to do the same, so that the cycle repeats again and again, resulting in an amplified response to the original precipitating factors.[294]

Shiller has to go so far as to postulate a "naturally occurring Ponzi scheme" in order to justify the way in which trust builds on trust, and faith begets faith. So that:

> We see the extraordinary public confidence in the stock market that underlies recent market valuations. People seem to think that they have discovered a safe and lucrative investment, one that cannot lose. They perceive no real downside risk, and this explains their willingness to buy stocks even when, by conventional measures such as price-earnings ratios, they are so greatly overvalued.[295]

Albania provides a forceful example of the power of shared human faith to create a market, as an entire country was enticed into a Ponzi scheme. A country deeply mired in poverty that harnessed its hopes to a rainbow:

> When Albania started the transition from central planning to a market economy, it was the poorest and most isolated and backward country in Europe… When the transition began in 1991, the country had been reduced to desperate poverty, and the vast majority of its population was unfamiliar with market institutions and practices.

---

[293] Shiller, R. J. (2000). *Irrational exuberance*. Princeton University Press, p.xv.
[294] Shiller, R. J. (2000). *Irrational exuberance*. Princeton University Press, p.44.
[295] Shiller, R. J. (2000). *Irrational exuberance*. Princeton University Press, p.46.

> In early 1996, two new pyramid schemes, *Xhafferi* and *Populli*, were created, and an already existing scheme that had no real investments, *Sude*, stepped up its activities, offering interest rates of 12-19 percent a month. The proliferation of schemes had baleful effects. First, more depositors were drawn in. *Xhafferi* and *Populli* between them attracted nearly *2 million* depositors, in a country with a population of 3.5 million, within a few months. The investment funds felt pressured to compete and began to offer higher interest rates on deposits... In September, *Populli* began offering more than 30 percent a month. In November, *Xhafferi* offered to treble depositors' money in three months; *Sude* responded with an offer to double the principal in two months. By November, the face value of the schemes' liabilities totaled $1.2 billion. Albanians sold their houses to invest in the schemes; farmers sold their livestock.[296]
>
> ... Despite repeated warnings from the IMF and the World Bank... Press and public reaction was mostly negative: the IMF was accused of trying to close down Albania's most successful firms.... On November 19, *Sude* defaulted on its payments, and the collapse began.
>
> *Sude*'s collapse shook the public's confidence in all of the companies and new deposits dried up... In January 1997, *Sude* declared bankruptcy, triggering riots... The government belatedly took some **useful** steps. First, it **refused to compensate depositors for their losses**, which made achieving economic stabilization after the crisis much easier than it would otherwise have been... By March 1997, Albania was in chaos. The government had lost control of the south. Many in the army and police force had deserted, and 1 million weapons had been looted from the armories. Evacuation of foreign nationals and mass emigration of Albanians began. The government was forced to resign...
>
> Some 2,000 people were killed in the violence that followed the pyramid schemes' collapse. Large parts of the country were no longer within the government's control. Government revenues collapsed as customs posts and tax offices were burned.
>
> Winding up the pyramid schemes proved to be more difficult. The government encountered resistance from both the operators and the outgoing parliamentarians, many of whom were reported to have invested in the schemes.[297]

Note that the IMF considers non-compensation of defrauded depositors a "useful step". Certainly, no one was offering them any "easing", quantitative or otherwise.

People sold off all possible surplus - homes, farmsteads, any property they could divest themselves of - in order to get onto the wagon. Who benefited? Who were the buyers? Who had the surplus cash to buy Albania?

---

[296] Jarvis, C. (2000). The Rise and Fall of Albania's Pyramid Schemes Finance and Development – *Quarterly Magazine of the IMF*. March 2000, Vol. 37, No. 1. https://www.imf.org/external/pubs/ft/fandd/2000/03/jarvis.htm

[297] Jarvis, Ibid.

One of the poorest nations in the world was tantalized by the sudden fierce hope of economic rejuvenation, spearheaded by their own government, whose members were leading proponents of the Ponzi scheme.

Messianic faith gripped the entire nation, and anyone who had even a modicum of surplus pitched in, not to mention those who assumed debt for the chance of participating.

This is always the main issue: who will have a seat at the table, and who will just longingly gaze on the action from outside. The Albanian people, long suffering under a tyrannical communist regime, were thrust headlong into the heady rhetoric of the free market and taken for a unique government-sanctioned Ponzi ride.

Ponzi schemes are eerily similar to "regular" bubbles, except perhaps for greater pre-meditation on the part of the schemers who create a reality of faith that refutes doubt by spreading monetary forms around, so that even if people hear mavens declaiming the "scheme", they see all the early joiners who "didn't listen to reason" and made a hefty profit, so they kick themselves for being so timid and jump onto the bandwagon too.

When the evidence of the senses conflicts with information received from others, empirical reality eventually leads people to correct their theories until they more closely coincide with actual evidence.

In Albania, the people were swayed by the clear evidence of people making a lot of money, by the blatant competition between a number of simultaneous Ponzi schemes that were making payouts to early joiners, and the clear evidence that many in government were joining and profiting.

The great frustration of Labor zoners is that they are forever outside the true money-making loop. All they have are their life-efforts which allow them a piece-meal share of the infinite abundance of value-forms, quickly consumed in the flow of their lives with no surplus left over.

The bitterness of seeing early joiners making big profits, while hesitators hung back, pushes the hesitators to "go all in" when they do decide to join, with all the grand fervor of the converted heretic who becomes the most zealous for the once rejected and now vindicated faith.

Credit ratings and exclusion

A significant point of inequality is that you can only borrow more money if you already have some. Risk rating agencies award their ratings on the basis of your current assets and your past reliability in repaying debts.

You'll never really know what "adverse" pattern you may fall into, that will lead wary bankers to refuse you: a suspicious zip code, a non-preferred skin color, a downgraded gender, an unsavory age, a suspect religious affiliation, or just because you fall into the category of over-thirty single mothers. Also, the bank will not give credit if a rating agency discredits you.

On the basis of such external categorizations, even if you are as diligent and hardworking as the legendary quakers of yore, you may be barred from getting a good education, opening up you own business or buying a home, and in the post-2008 slump, even though banks have considerable QE liquidity, they're not going to mess around with the likes of you[298], certainly not when the interest rates are so low. You won't even be able to get a sub-prime loan. Sorry.

The more the market battens down in order to avoid "risks", the more people are excluded from the blessing of money. Talented people with initiative and ambition who could have been a great blessing to the world are excluded for lack of "collateral" so that affiliation to the Free zone has now also become the threshold for entering the world of debt as well.

To a considerable extent, a "high risk rating" has become a category of exclusion similar to the pernicious discriminations based on race and gender. The criteria are "either or", and if you fall outside the acceptable boundary and have no good credit standing, your ability to leverage things in reality becomes significantly limited.[299]

Kyotaki and Moore describe the interpersonal nature of credit ratings:

> If I want to borrow today, potential lenders don't consider so much what I want to use the funds for. Nor do they even consider what collateral I have to offer. Mostly, they look at my credit history, and other aspects of my past life. The reason is that much more information can be stored about my past, which can be used to assess the likelihood of my defaulting.[300]

It ultimately boils down to trust in the person or institution based on their reputation, and reputation is of course directly contingent on consensus. It is defined by the Cambridge dictionary as: "the opinion that people in general have about someone or something, or how much respect or admiration someone or something receives based on past behavior or character."[301]

Faith and skepticism are packaged and quantified as credit ratings. The greater the faith, the better the rating, and the lower the interest rate, while when skepticism is high, it is called "risk" and the rating is reduced while the interest rate is increased.

Risk is a measure of distrust assuaged by promises of returns. The deeper the distrust the higher the promised returns… just as in other, grayer, parts of the market, the deeper the desperation, the higher the interest rates.

Everything is tied in with trust and distrust, confidence and fears, to the extent that there is an index called the implied volatility index (VIX) which is a "real-time market index that represents the market's expectation of 30-day forward-looking volatility… it provides a measure of market risk and investors' sentiments. It is also known by other names like "Fear Gauge" or "Fear Index."[302]

---

[298] As we have seen once and again, whenever an economy collapses, people who really need money are immediately excluded. There is no problem in continuing to pour money on those who already have it – it will not change the status quo.

[299] Jeffery Archer's classic financial thriller, Kane & Able, illustrates this point well: The conscientious banker who refuses an entrepreneur a vital loan because the bank's risk criteria do not allow it, even though he personally believes that the man is worthy, and ultimately finances him "in secret". See: Archer, J. (1979). *Kane & Abel*. St. Martin's Paperbacks.

[300] Kiyotaki, N. & Moore, J. (2001), *Evil is the Root of all Money* Clarendon Lectures - Lecture 1, p. 26

[301] https://dictionary.cambridge.org/dictionary/english/reputation

[302] https://www.investopedia.com/terms/v/vix.asp

However, in a modern market one obviously "feels the fear and does it anyway". This is what insurance is for! In exchange for an appropriate premium, insurance can cover all risks and set up that wondrous situation that prevailed before the crash of 2008, when everyone was making profits. Risk takers raked in high interest rates and insurance companies took a percentage of risk-taker earnings in order to cover the risk. The insurance companies shared the faith of the risk-takers that the risk event would not occur, so they were just happy to get paid for "free". When the risk event did come to pass, they had to turn to the government for their salvation.

How good things are when everyone believes! When ebullience is everywhere! As Casey writes about the pre-2008 boom:

> In Spain, the cheaper credit came with an easing of mortgage lending standards… Come the 2000s, home loans looked much more like the U.S. model: thirty-year terms and down payments as low as zero… Spaniards acted as if all their Christmases had come at once…. With a dearth of productive industries in which to invest this cheap capital, they plowed it into real estate, as housing developers tapped a network of underregulated savings banks to build vast new residential complexes.
>
> For a long time, this credit and property boom worked wonders. Spanish unemployment dropped from 20 percent in 1995 to below 8 percent in 2007… Investment in the residential sector rose by 150 percent over the same period, far outstripping growth in the economy itself…[303]

There is, however, no "real" value. The value is created by the trust of the many, and when the market crashes, it crashes down to the level of skeptical trust espoused by Free zoners. **It is the holders of the sanitized surplus who among them dictate the bottom of the market** – for they are always ready to unfreeze some assets to pick up bargains.

Free zoners stand above the market and can enter it and leave it at will. Buffet famously said that a good investor is "fearful when others are greedy and greedy when others are fearful", a statement that hinges on the ability to stand apart from "others" and have the ready cash and wherewithal to go against the market trend.

When one looks at great depressions and crashes, one is amazed by how they constitute but "froth" on the economy.

Even the greatest stock-market crashes ultimately led to general economic declines of 20-30%. No economy crumples down to zero. It only slides down to the purportedly "real" value, which is in fact the value dictated by Free zoners who, standing outside the market, are ready step in when fear has led most players to move their assets into cash, and others to lose their assets to foreclosure. It is at this point that Free zoners can start applying their greed to the forsaken assets.

When a breach of trust in money occurs, people think that the money system is broken, rather than understand that what caused the break is a breach of trust, and the only way to fix it is to drown it in the even-greater trust of infinite liquidity.

Indeed, it is only loss of trust that can prevent infinite liquidity and infinite asset inflation, for nothing real can break the cycle, no scarcity can shock the system, for "quantity" is infinitely easy.

---

[303] Casey, M. (2012). *The unfair trade : how our broken global financial system destroys the middle class*. Crown, p. 129.

Liquidity only dries up through loss of faith, usually on the part of "hard-headed" tangibilists who have an eye on past prices and judge what is sustainable and realistic and get their profits out when they have judged themselves to have profited enough, thereby raising doubts about sustainability that feed into the "bursting of the bubble" just as their obverse had fed the bubble.

The "slow slide" into distrust is a mystery. Where does it start? Is it a few "prudent" people who begin to spread their distrust? Inevitably, these prudential stalwarts can afford to secede from the market and "sit" on their assets.

The very people who are the foremost representatives of the "blessing of money", i.e. wealthy Free zoners, present a frugal front, and are the first to demand better collaterals, better safeguards. Safeguards that are also imaginary elements of the system, which "hard-headed" people demand as if they were more than consensual trust.

These "collaterals" and "reserves" always assume some embodied form that is not available in the system in wide circulation, some external sanitized form of wealth that can be pointed to in order to assuage any misgivings about value.

Even today, attempts to "heal" economic systems move in that direction. They are not directed at the mechanics of faith that generate the entire system, but rather at the objects of faith, the forms that represent value in people's minds. Governments are setting up clearing houses to assure collaterals, as they strive to provide more and more tangible "liquidity" to support the system of trust, as if there actually existed some kind of "core" value that exceeds the authority and trust of the nation itself, that transcends the full authority and confidence of the government.

Money between Present and Future

A central aspect of all forms of money is that they conserve values originating in transient, sometimes unique efforts, over time. Money creates a bridge between the efforts of the present and the consumption of the future. It allows even frivolous crickets to get paid for their enchanting music (on concert), not just industrious ants. It converts present effort into sustainable values, and the more of the value of your present efforts that you can convert into symbolic embodied value, the greater your surplus, and the greater your future security.[304]

By converting tangible life streams into the intangible forms of money, we receive a consensual other-based obligation to accept our embodied value in the future in exchange for other forms of equal value. Money is always forward-looking. It has no inherent value in itself except its convertibility to other things at some point in future selected by its owner.

By converting them into money, we relinquish ownership of our time, our efforts, our commodities, and accept instead an obligation to accept our stored value in the future in exchange for other things that we wish to possess.

It is the **future** that lies at the heart of all financial transactions, since people are willing to exchange some money they have in the present for more future money. The whole credit-debit system is contingent on deferring into the future the use of money to acquire possessions, in exchange for the acquisition of more money. It is

---

[304] The obverse is also true: the more future you can convert into present debt, the more of an enslaving lien you create, and the less secure your future.

embodied potential used to get more embodied potential, deferring the realization of that potential. Akin to physical potential energy, the greater the potential accumulated, the greater the ultimate power that can be exercised.

In all types of faith, the "future" has a central role to play in both individual and intersubjective minds. It is on the ability to foresee in advance the consequences of actions and events that the entirety of human life depends, from sowing to reaping, from the expectation of a redeemer or better incarnation yet to come, to the just deserts of the wicked, humanity is always forward looking. The entire basis of cause and effect is that occurrences separated by time are causally connected, wherein the effect is the future of the cause.

The future, whether scientifically postulated or dogmatically announced is at the core of all human action, and institutions make that future more easily foreseeable in that they provide clear consequences for actions, and rules within which everyone is expected to operate, thereby enhancing the ability to foresee things.

Value captured in a monetary form is always potential value, and will not be manifest until it is transferred to another in an exchange. As seen in the great capital markets of the present era, and as is evident in every Ponzi scheme, so long as it is not released, potential value can grow exponentially, for it represents pure faith in value. The potential value of money is actually stored in the collective consciousness of the community that believes in it.

The community inscribes its beliefs by assigning authority to certain contexts of numbers, which transforms those numbers into forms that can contain value. This is the crucial role of banks, accountants and other creators of context in the financial system: to inscribe, document and maintain through various means of "memory" the values ascribed to forms.[305]

This basic characteristic of the financial system makes it inherently divorced from reality and anti-consumption. Use of money in the real world is mainly restricted to consumers who actualize the potential of their monetary forms by giving them to others in exchange for other forms.

[305] Even though the face value of a monetary form may remain unchanged, values are always fluctuating for they are being constantly re-evaluated in comparison to other forms of value, exchange rates, indexing and the like, so that an entire mirror-hall of reflections in other symbolic forms surrounds every symbolic form, impacting the consensus of its perceived value.

CHAPTER 10: THE FUTURE OF MONEY

Economic freedom flows from on high.

Historically, it turns out that the powerful are often generous and award liberties to their inferiors: they have abolished slavery, they have enfranchised women, they have passed laws prohibiting the exploitation of children.

If one were to predict the future in a similarly optimistic vein, one can perhaps foresee that the abstract world of Free zoners of legendary wealth is ready to be bequeathed to the rest of humankind.

There are preliminary indications of this in various annuities and grants awarded by fiat. It is possible to provide quantitative easing for the less-affluent.

There is a chance, and there is hope, that "out of the strong shall come forth sweetness"[306] and the power of money to free will be granted to all of humanity rather than a narrow segment of it. The possibility of an "account of your own" may yet provide inspiration and incentive just as the idea of "a room of your own" fermented a demand for liberty and self-empowerment.

Humanity is up for anything and symbolic monetary forms can buy anything, and the combination has given rise to an entire new world that is being formed at this very moment. Money, when it is available in abundance, is the great empowerer, as it bestows freedom and provides people with the wherewithal to determine their own fates.

We have seen how the accumulation of a great amount of value-holding symbolic forms has allowed a few to act as if they were many. The "forces" of the market are but various owners of the value held in symbolic forms who are constantly competing with each other. The form owners look at the forms that others value in order to value them themselves. Value is the ultimate inter-personal creation. What others value is valuable, what others believe seems to us to be true, and we renounce our own opinions before theirs. This is how value is actually made.

There is no financial value that is not collective.

We now have hundreds of years of documented history of booms and busts across the entire spectrum of human civilization, and the pattern is clear: we are buoyed on shared belief in embodied value, and when the symbolic forms of money are available to greater numbers of human beings, we all thrive, and when doubts and fears set in and the forms lose their power to hold value, the whole market stagnates, and people are miserable.

The Covid19 pandemic has shown us a great deal about the basis of human life. Even as the ports were shut to human beings living their free lives out in the open, and all the venues of civilization, the museums and movie halls, the restaurants and cafés, the universities and offices, were emptied of humans; still the great food sourcing chains continued to churn out nourishment for the world.

Even when the roads emptied of commercial cars and the oil industry was stuck with a production glut of many millions of barrels per day, still the great cross-country trucks continued to thunder on the roads, and still the tiny percentage of

[306] Judges 14 14 KJV.

workers needed in a modern economy to keep everyone well-fed continued to toil in the fields, in the packaging plants, in the great warehouses and shops, and in home delivery.

While all "higher functions" were relegated to online platforms the food chain continued to function as if the plague had never happened. The just-in-time-based logistics networks of the "free-market" continued to place their orders and outsource their needs through the great world-wide chain of production. The human-life sustaining system on this planet continued its work even as the rest of the people went home.

In the future, a great deal of these life-sustaining chains will be automated, and will continue to work even as the people involved in them will also go home. Human life on this planet will become sustainable without human labor, and we will have to learn to live with the generous money-based freedom that we have created for ourselves.

Obviously, the access of only a few to the medium through which all human cooperation flows is blatantly "unfair", and any ultimate attempt at achieving a panacea for the world's economic woes must address it: How to introduce the monetary forms needed by the economy in such a way that they will not disrupt the market? In such a way that they will be available to all for accessing the abundance produced by the life efforts of humanity?

The capacity to collect surplus value is a deeply satisfying characteristic of monetary forms, which will always involve some measure of inequality as some will have more surplus than others. But if Quantitative Easing is infinitely available, why not put everyone at ease?

As ever, some hard-headed souls opposing universal income claim that such profligacy would be a disincentive to work. This may be true, but no different from the conditions that have always prevailed in the Free zone. Free zoners have always accumulated and dissipated wealth. Heirs are known to squander fortunes, which are no more than a quantitative easing for which they did not toil, and many hereditary holders of wealth are notorious for their lives of indolence, as described by Thorsten Veblen[307], who wrote a rather venomous little book and on the barbarism of the "Leisure Class". Other Free zoners, however, have been extremely creative and industrious. Why should the rest of humanity be deprived of the freedom to actually decide what to do with their lives?

Everyone should have access to the advantages of this universal belief system that currently functions differentially in the Free zone and the Labor zone.

It is not democracy that we need but an *accessocracy* or *availocracy*: a regime that will provide all people with access to everything human that humans can do for each other.

Money, like knowledge, should be available to all at all times, disseminating to the multitudes the wonders initiated by the few. Just as the dissemination of knowledge has empowered and enfranchised humanity, so the dissemination of money strengthens and fertilizes it.

---

[307] Veblen, T. (1899). *The Theory of the Leisure Class: An Economic Study of Institutions*. B.W. Huebsch.

The challenge facing governments at the present time is not how to torment its poorer populations through austerity, but rather to achieve a universal condition that emulates the functioning of the economy in the Free zone, where money is so plentiful that it is constantly being sanitized and kept out of the market.

What if everyone had access to sufficient currency forms? What if universal basic income could be linked to just the basic commodities, taking these markets "out of the game", i.e., provide everyone with enough money for rent and food, constantly linked to their prices. The rest of the market could fluctuate at will, but these commodities will be always affordable – something that is already happening among extensive strata of "eligible" persons in modern welfare states. Is it not possible to provide sufficient affordable housing that no matter how much the price of housing increases in 'prestigious' areas, there will still always be sufficient affordable housing available?

During the pandemic, it became glaringly obvious that symbolic surpluses and an influx of rather miserly stipends from governments kept everyone afloat, and with good aforethought they may do so indefinitely.

An abundance of money is conductive to human happiness and health. It is the great irrigator of potential. The core action needed in order to achieve this is to alleviate the enslaving burden of debt that mires entire societies in crippling obligations, from indebted individuals to companies tottering on the brink of insolvency, to governments deep in debt to other governments.

But how is it possible to skip the debt step in the generation of money? Can we retain just the step in which a government prints money or transfers money to an account, without the step at which it sells debt in order to distribute it.

A Labor zoner looking to spend would just as happily spend money provided by a no-strings-attached government subsidy as money provided through consumer debt.

The 'debt' element of a thriving economy is in fact an artifact, for it is the spending part that is the actual stimulus. The fact that money has been increasingly generated through debt is an unfortunate trend attributable to a miserly viewpoint that refuses to provide money users with their money for free, so the creators of money are always providing the money as loans that create onerous obligations.

But in a fiat economy, this is completely unnecessary. It is just as easy for a government to deposit money in a person's private account, like any subsidy or stipend, and once the money is there, it can be spent in the economy and help bring back the good times.

The creation of money through debt distorts the picture because it extracts payment in exchange for the creation of money, on the basis of the conception that the government or the bank "own" the money they create and should therefore not only receive "rent" for their willingness to create it, but also get it back!

Instead, the "ownership" of created fiat money should be transferred to the public, the true sovereign, which should not have to "pay" for it or "return" it to anyone.

Money should be sourced directly from the sovereign to the citizens, free and clear of debt, as has been done, albeit in an aggravating tight-fisted manner, since the advent of the welfare state.

If we look closely at the dynamics of recessions, we will see that debt, with the rigid demands that it be paid on the part of the lenders and the deep sense of obligation on the part of the borrowers, is a dark shadow cast on the economy, and is the source of a great number of adverse effects.

It is time to expand money's central function: the removal of debt, and generate enough money for the specific purpose of covering all debts. The ultimate bailout of humanity.

Imagine that all the money that poured into the economy before the crisis of 2008 through all those sub-prime mortgages had not been debt at all but government grants and that a collapse (if such a collapse would have occurred at all) would not have left people deep in debt, but merely with reduced asset prices, which is in fact the situation in the Free zone, where debt is small and surplus is large, so that the day after a collapse is bargain-hunting day rather than belt-tightening day.

In such a situation there would be no problem to rally on the day after and continue spending. The great challenge should not be how to convince people to assume debt once more so they can spend money in the economy, but how to provide them with no-strings-attached money in such a way that would not give rise to inflation.

The specter of hyper-inflation is the driving force behind the position of austerity adopted by many economists, but the cure, i.e., the minimization of the amount of money reaching Labor zoners, is worse than the illness. It is a short-sighted cure born of distorted narratives that miss the true nature of the economy as a system of beliefs, and it is time that QE for the Free zone be followed by QE for the Labor zone – so that the economy can flourish again.

Human talent will then be able to give rise to new and imaginative enterprises, and even those who are not inclined to enterprise will be able to enjoy the good life rather than the abject misery of an economic downturn.

Our civilization has known two great worldwide shocks that have clearly shown up the interconnected fate of people on earth. The Great Recession that began with a bang in 2008 and has been giving off a sustained whimper since then, and more than a decade later, the great Covid19 pandemic, which sent the last shreds of labor packing, but did not break the world.

Covid19 has exposed the intangibility of the economy, the ease with which millions withdraw from employment yet life goes on. This is the future made concrete in the present, the future in which those same millions would eventually have been made redundant by robotization and AI.

If only world governments were brave enough to come together and provide all the liquidity necessary to maintain the world's standard of living as it was before the outbreak of the pandemic (or better still, before the 2008 Recession), the transition to the future economy could have been greatly eased.

Governments could have simply transferred to people, by fiat, the same income they had before the crisis, thereby providing for the prosperity of all humans on this planet. If people wish to resume their labors they may do so at any time, but moneywise governments can take the subsidy path to give people their freedom.

As we have seen with pensioners and other recipients of subsidies, all that society needs is a good pretext for the public to support a Free zone lifestyle, in the sense of no need to work, even in the lowest strata of the Labor zone.

All that is required are just a few more criteria of subsidy-worthiness, such as "constrained by pandemic" or "job has been given to a robot", in addition to the already established criteria such as poverty, sickness, old age, spinsterhood, and a myriad of other exceptions to the rule of "labor begets value". All one needs is the justification. The fiat way is already in place.

The key to our money problems has already been found, all we need is to turn it in the lock. We now have the knowledge as well as the political infrastructure for finally cracking the great puzzle of economic life and offsetting the imbalances between forms by mitigating the divergence of national currencies that has been the cause of great misery, as the great captains of surplus entered into economies and withdrew from them with devastating flurries of consequence.

As the world tottered on the brink of financial disaster in 2008, the G20 came together to support each other and create new fiat flows that will sustain their financial institutions. They were successful in staving off the worst of a recession, but since they were battling against their own economic traditions of austerity and risk mitigation, they were unable to go "the whole way" and pour some quantitative easing into the Labor zone rather than just continue watering the ever absorbent Free zone.

Nevertheless, the Covid19 pandemic has forced governments to take that extra step and begin feeding currency forms into the accounts of many of the Labor zoners that were sent home. However, rather than the great flood of currency that we have seen in QE, governments have been quite timid in the steps they took, ever fearful that too much money in the hands of those who don't have any would lead to inflation.

The global map of financial cooperation has now changed sufficiently to prevent this eventuality. Governments can support each other in their fiat plans, so that countries evincing too many signs of an inflationary spiral can be quickly saved from their fate by the fiat currencies of their peers.

As we have seen, inflation in itself is the positive outcome of an expanding human world, and the thousands of percents of inflation that we have seen over the past century have only shadowed the great rise in prosperity.

The time is ripe now to take the reins of this surprisingly global horse and direct it gently in the direction that it has been going anyway: greater democratization of money, and a lot more money in the Labor zone.

For a start, a coordinated G20 can set a 15% inflationary target and allow their constituent governments to start transferring money into Labor zone accounts, so as to allow the world to return to the prosperity of a plentiful money supply.

Thanks to global coordination, speculators, suddenly starved of arbitrage, will find it difficult to utilize this sudden plentitude of international liquidity to speculate against the plentiful currencies. Where will the hot money flows go? Into gold? Into cryptocurrencies? Will they be able to circumvent a concentrated G20 effort in order to find some magic haven where their money continues to increase in value?

They may as well stay home, as increasing international currency flows will increase prosperity everywhere. A G20 or hopefully a G40 or G100 or perhaps even full global cooperation can offset the deleterious effect of currency expansion by coordinating a worldwide network of mutual fiat aid, where one government creates money for the other, thereby keeping the net fluctuations in exchange rates quite small.

If all the great currencies depreciate together, no change is felt, just as for more than a hundred years, inflation has soared by thousands of percents, but the exchange rates between the great currencies rarely deviate greatly from each other, as the inflation pace of different nations eventually synchronizes, thereby reducing the difference between their respective fiat currencies.[308]

All these aspects of a robust global economy are in place, and the governments of the world are experienced in handling them. All it will take is to continue the G20 coordination efforts on the level of the Labor zone, shifting from the tight-fisted attitude of such programs as SNAP to a much more open-handed approach that would keep the currency forms available to the Labor zone at a level that would allow people to pursue fully productive lives.

Money and enfranchisement

The development and spread of money tend to emulate the development and spread of democracy by flowing into a greater diversity of hands, like the extending of suffrage to ever-increasing circles.

It is even possible that money itself played a causal role in the increasing demand for universal suffrage and equality, as it percolated into all social strata and loosened feudal fealties. The clear direction of the historical flow of money is one of expansion in quantity as it moved from the few to the many.[309]

Similarly to the proliferation of life on earth, with its great extravagance of potential, which mostly falls on inhospitable soil and fades away, but of which some part ultimately blooms and flourishes, so money, born of debt, spreads wealth from its loci of accumulation in the hands of the few to the hands of the many, spreading over civilization and fructifying it as it percolates into all human endeavors.

Some flourish, pay off their debts and build reality with their unique talents; others flounder and fall into insolvency, and their share in the symbolic is taken from them along with great swathes of their more tangible forms, including the enslavement of their life-streams, but humanity as a whole seems to flourish when irrigated by capital and to wither under regimes of austerity.[310]

As nicely put by Marian Keyes in regard to a certain period of economic prosperity in Ireland:

> … the boom was still going strong. But if house prices were astronomical, so were wages. Jobs in PR were abundant, as you'd expect in an economy crammed with gleeful people only desperate to spend their new-found wealth. (Which wasn't real but none of us knew that at the time.)[311]

When they have money, people indeed become gleeful, and very generous to others, allowing everything to flourish. Throughout the history of money, we have

---

[308] Not to mention the fact that countries battling hyper-inflation often establish parity with the USD as a first step towards instituting a new fiat currency.

[309] Even though this trend has been reversed in recent decades as debt-generated money created new entanglements and more money became concentrated in the hands of its creators.

[310] Of course, there is never any austerity in the Free zone. So it is entirely possible for a thick enough Free zone to remain unimpacted by the plight of Labor zoners.

[311] Keyes, M. (2017). *The Break*. Penguin, p. 92.

seen increasing egalitarianism and generosity as money allowed people to break out of their traditional niches and become participants in the wider world of pan-human cooperation. Ultimately, the wilting during depressions, as the full symbolic irrigation of the fragile flowers of human initiative tapers off, arises from the same root as the years of plentitude.

It all depends on the amount of money in the hands of the public.

Governments have the ability to produce any amount of money that may be required to irrigate the economy and pollinate both the private and business sectors. Unfortunately, governments are prone to the same mentality of careful distrust that leads the entire market to withdraw, so that historically, they have often exacerbated crises by not taking firm action to provide the market directly with money through public spending. Koo writes with some bitterness that this:

> ...was proved beyond the shadow of a doubt by Herbert Hoover's Treasury secretary, Andrew Mellon, who endorsed such policies with the famous words, "Liquidate labor, liquidate stocks, liquidate the farmers, liquidate real estate... it will purge the rottenness out of the system... Values will be adjusted, and enterprising people will pick up the wrecks..." His approach caused U.S. GNP to plunge 46 percent from the 1929 peak and pushed urban unemployment up to 50 percent by 1933. Not even Roosevelt's New Deal was sufficient to drag the U.S. economy out of the resulting morass; it took the astronomical fiscal stimulus necessitated by World War II to do that.[312]

Once shattered, trust takes a long time to recover since disbelief and distrust are just as much articles of faith as their obverse. If one believes that prices will continue to rise and markets to expand, one may exuberantly seek to spend more money, and if one believes the opposite, one will tighten one's fist and stop spending.

Governments are the only market players who are in a position to generate whatever belief they wish to, resonating Dylan's poignant insight that: "the master makes the rules for the wise men and fools".[313]

Money's boon: The freedom to create

The freedom to create is a wondrous outcome of a system in which regular people are allowed to have private property, a system in which every person can become a node of creativity.

As we have seen, the universal human ability to "own" things in the world is the natural foundation of a free market, and attempts to construct societies without private property quickly lead to stagnation and to ancient systems of tit-for-tat patronage and clientelism.

At the same time, when the free market is based on the premise of selfish self-interest and governments are barred from helping their populations to become affluent, this too eventually leads to disenfranchisement and the inability of the poor to attain sufficient affluence for freedom and self-determination.

---

[312] Koo, R.C. (2015). *The Escape from Balance Sheet Recession and the QE Trap: A Hazardous Road for the World Economy*. Wiley, pp. 38-39.

[313] Dylan, B. (1965). It's Alright, Ma (I'm Only Bleeding). *Bringing It All Back Home.* Coloumbia records.

Austerity is the root of all misery. It is always directed at putting down the participation of the masses. It is sufficient to look at what happened to what was once "great" Britain. Because all of its economic pundits believe in austerity – it matters not who governs – they all listen to the same down-sizing, prosperity-slashing dogma that enriches the rich and impoverishes the poor, and ultimately, once you disenfranchise the masses, the cloud on which the rent-gatherers float also dissipates, because the connection of the Free zone with reality becomes untenable.

The method that has not yet been tried is a government focused on empowering the creative individual by creating the spaces of freedom and wealth required to support such creativity.

Imaging the great blessing that could have been achieved if all that quantitative easing that was invested in an attempt to sustain the formal existence of financial institutions that did not innovate anything and did not create anything, if all that money that was spent in an attempt to shore up trust in an ailing financial system, would have been applied towards fostering a regime that was focused on empowering an autonomous, democratic individual capable of investing in self-development. Such an orientation would have paved the way to independent initiatives that would no longer be blocked by regulatory forces, but quite the obverse, would find significant encouragement and support from governments that desired to promote such independence.[314]

Inventors and entrepreneurs have been cropping up throughout history in a random, organic and rather wondrous way, and one finds that they were always enveloped by bubbles of freedom and affluence that floated on the great ocean of enslavement, coercion and exploitation. The free citizen, Archimedes ran around slave-bound Greece and Galileo Galilei's rebellion created a new world within Inquisitorial Italy thanks to the financial freedom granted him by the Medicis.

In the United States, the number of patents registered in the anti-slavery north was a hundred-fold more than the number of patents registered by slave owners. Wherever a place was formed in which a person could navigate his own fate vis a vis the authorities – these wild shoots of initiative and innovation sprouted forth.

Three Approaches to a New Economy

In view of the insight that money's provenance in debt is the root cause of our economic diseases, the following are various suggestions for getting money into the hands of Labor zoners without incurring the burden of debt:

Approach One: Debtless Ex-Nihilo Fiat Generation

A simple solution, which would be "unthinkable" to most mainstream policy setters, but which accords well with the way that money actually functions in the

[314] And if you're thinking that all those agencies that promote small businesses and entrepreneurs are already doing this, then please read the fine print, for the main focus of such bodies is to entice the fledgling business or entrepreneur to take out hefty loans, with "government backing". The focus is on hoovering the future income of these businesses into the financial system. Getting deep into debt from the word go does not independence make.

economy, would be the addition of another "fiat" step to the creation of money: multiplication by some small decimal fraction.[315]

The scheme could be called the **Per Mille Loan Program**, and governments would make contributions to citizen accounts and offset them with a discounted debt.

For example, all citizens may be credited with a certain influx of money, while the mirror debt "asset" on the government's books would be reduced by fiat by a factor of one thousand, so that the "asset" side on the government books is multiplied by a tenth of a percent before being entered on the books.

Government fiat can decree the conversion of debt-based money into debt-free money, so that money enters the economy from the outset as no-strings-attached 3rd-round money.

Approach Two: Debt Forgiveness

A classic approach, actually a Biblical one, is that of debt forgiveness. The Old Testament was obviously well-aware of the debt-bondage that could deeply enslave men, and in support of its deeper agenda that only free men can properly worship God, created a complex system of debt forgiveness, which erased all debts once every seven years.

It seems almost inconceivable that a system should take away the interest payments due on loans and release the debtors, but imagine the relief of all debtors if once every seven years their debts were erased, and the relief of markets, if instead of the periodic downturns that destroy them, wiping away the fortunes of many and transferring wealth only to those who have deep enough pockets to weather anything, periods of wealth accumulation would be re-invigorated with a "clean slate" every seven years.

A critical feature of this approach is that the wiping of debts only wipes off future income, not present wealth, so that in fact, it would be as if the market is rebooted every seven years, removing the encumbrances that are suffocating it.

The obvious precedents of this method in modern economies are the many "bailout" plans that have been offered Free zone residents who became entangled in debt, effectively erasing the debt. It is only necessary to expand the method to Labor zoners too.

Approach Three: Lottery grants

Government may create a lottery, similar to the U.S. citizenship lottery, and give every citizen a certain amount of money on the basis of luck. The lotteries may be focused on certain areas into which the government wants to inject money, so that direct quantitative easing is transferred to people.

Such funds may be dedicated solely to the buying of real-estate so that the same people who may have been eligible in the past to receive subprime mortgages would be able to attain a home with money that does not embroil them in debt. In this way, the government would be able to ensure that its citizens did not remain homeless, while at the same time boosting the economy without debt.

---

[315] So as to refrain from overly rocking the foundations of the GAAP.

Economic Reform

Ultimately a corrective process must inevitably be one that accords with the market's creative trends rather than trying to block them, as was attempted under socialist regimes, and only ended up with oppressive patterns of patronage.

A truly creative approach would be to extricate those enslaved by rents by shifting the entire real-estate market from the tangible to the abstract through the provision of unique quantitative easing that would pay the landlords of all rent-paying tenants, in exchange for transferring ownership to the tenants.

There is no escaping the conclusion that coercive oppression is part and parcel of the present fabric of the economy, especially the real-estate markets that use the ownership of resources in order to artificially exploit the life stream of those who lack resources. Wherever markets collapsed, it was real-estate speculation that was the greatest contributor for the very reason that the need for a roof over one's head is the iron collar around the neck of most of humanity.

The key to all this is in the hands of governments, and the extent of their corruption or mere obtuseness negatively impacts their ability to provide solutions where housing is concerned. The economic interests of Free zoners hold the world of Labor zoners in a reduced and debilitated state, ensuring that any government stipends should remain minimal and that the supply of residential dwellings should always remain small enough to cause frequent appreciation in the prices of homes.

It seems as if there is no generosity to be had in governmental handling of economies, but in democracies this horizon does exist if the state can be administered justly. Does not all government property belong to the citizens in a democracy, and does not all private property belong to the citizens because the government supports such ownership? In this way, governments are poised to create a new future for their citizens, if they but knew how to take the right approach.

The challenges are great. Domestically, governments must face the powerful elites who benefit from the current situation, in order to facilitate a massive investment of funds in public construction, so as to ensure housing for all; and internationally, governments must band together in order to block the destructive impact of hot money flows seeking enrichment.

When one examines the regimes and doctrines proposed by economic schools and scholars, one sees how the need for ad-hoc justifications and the widespread and mean assumption of "self-interest" as descriptive of "human nature", have undermined our freedoms. This is of crucial importance: do not ask about the wealth that the dogma of self-interest bequeaths others, but about the liberty that it takes from you.

Contrary to the fantastic axioms that guide economists, a very large body of knowledge accumulated by other disciplines indicates that the basis of human behavior is not self-interest, but rather sociability and kindness. Even when "scarcity" raises its ugly head, it does not amplify self-interest, but rather the obverse, illustrating how human sociability is organized to solve this problem exactly, as mutual assistance helps tide over the bad times.

When money is plentiful, people share the fruits of their labor quite generously, as money allows one to be both generous and selfish at the same time, i.e., to provide others with beneficial forms, and receive in exchange another form of equal value but with universal applicability – the monetary form.

Money is not the destructive instrument of greedy capitalism, but the universal medium that makes it possible to share things in a manner that allows everyone to enjoy an abundance that no person alone could ever attain: an abundance that arises from the contributions of the entire world.

The old pejorative concept of "capitalism" arose from the misdeeds of a wealthy minority bolstered by governments and economic dogmas of selfishness, which abused the innocent universal faith in money and gave capital a bad name. Mean monetary regimes have deformed the pure human capacity for a common faith in abstract value-containing forms capable of organizing the discrete efforts of all people into a harmonious whole.

Let us forsake the various dogmatic systems elbowing each other under the umbrella of capitalism and the free market, and examine the actual freedom that money can give us in a web of mutual creativities that allows us to share the talents and toil of each and every other human being who shares our world and who creates the world along with us.

Once forms holding value accumulate in the hands of Free zoners, their value continues to appreciate and rarely declines. This means that most governments, controlled as they are by Free zoners, keep their construction programs in check, so as not to depress the prices of existing houses.

Only a bold plan that will add millions of residential units within cities, while at the same time compensating (via quantitative easing) current home owners for any depreciation in prices, would be capable of finally abolishing the state of homelessness – just as only a compensation amounting to about 40% of the British GDP at the time could convince slave owners to relinquish their ownership, so that slavery may be abolished.

This is the place to stress the need for the democratization of money production. If the pre-2008 sub-prime borrowers had been given a "voice" in the production of money, would the federal government have been able to raise the interest rates in such a callous fashion?

Is it not preposterous that under a regime purporting to be "by the people for the people"[316], the public using money has no influence on its production?!

In a computerized and roboticized economy where all resources are in the hands of the rich, who pay the rest of humanity only for those services that have not been roboticized yet, most of humanity becomes redundant from the point of view of the Free zone. The trickle-down effect is rapidly diminishing: If robots are sowing and reaping, the money for the produce will be transferred to their owners, who are most probably Free zoners. In this way, as all menial work and starting level jobs are transferred from the human to the robotic, all wealth will circulate in a closed system within the Free zone.

This is why there is no choice but to liberate money from the curse of labor by the "sweat of one's brow" and all doctrines of toil. It is time to dedicate money to humanness: To all entities capable of holding this wondrous faith in the value of

---

[316] As famously stated by Lincoln: "that these dead shall not have died in vain– that this nation, under God, shall have a new birth of freedom and that government of the people, by the people, for the people, shall not perish from the earth". Lincoln, A. (1863). *The Gettysburg Address*.

abstract forms in their minds. It is for them that money is intended and for them one must generate, by firm fiat, sufficient symbolic monetary forms for their livelihood.

APPENDIXES:

Appendix 1: Labor and Post-Labor Economies

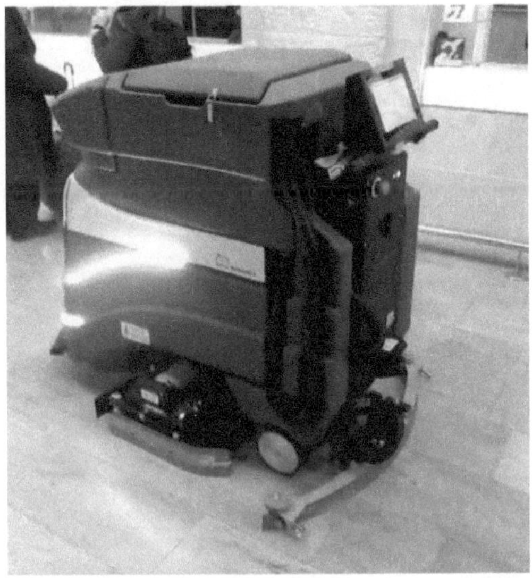

A robot cleaner at the Ben-Gurion Airport in Tel-Aviv

Last of the laborers (soon to be replaced) at that same airport

The human cleaner has already been dehumanized through commoditization. He is wearing a shirt branding him as "Cleaning". The cleaning department outlasts the redundancy of all human cleaners. [317]

[317] For a brief glimpse of these two in motion, see YouTube: https://youtu.be/hdJIjOyYL5g

Let us imagine the world ahead, when all Labor zoners are out of work, when labor has been removed from the economy, and no one can get money for "labor", not even through debt – because there are no longer any needed life-efforts to capitalize on, no longer any menial jobs available, they have all been roboticized, and all professional "positions" have been taken by AI.

Yet everything can continue as is for the great flow of ex-nihilo money created by commercial banks in exchange for a promise of garnishment of a sizable portion of future income will no longer be tied to life-efforts, but merely to income.

Were we to remove the Labor zone from the system entirely and imagine a world made up entirely of Free zoners, a world in which robots and computers now carry out all "labor" in the classical sense, so that only elective "work" is done by people, would the economy not function well then, and with much greater happiness?

Appendix 2: Epistemology of Money and Mind

The unique phenomenon of the ascription of value to form takes place in the context of the ever-changing interaction between individuals and a "reality"[318] mediated by the social fabric.

The fundamental ignorance of the individual in regard to reality must be acknowledged. Ultimately, we cannot know because of the limitations of our senses and the untrustworthiness of our consciousness.[319]

The root of all wisdom is the acknowledgement of these limitations:[320] Acknowledging that our direct empirical experience of the world is not enough in order to "know" the world.

We simply cannot know the nature of things without the input of other people. This is beautifully illustrated by the parable of the elephant and the blind men, in which each member of a group of blind men, limited to his own perceptions, reports some other aspect of the elephant, as if it were "reality", while in fact it is but a partial perception of an underlying phenomenon. One takes hold of the elephant's tail and talks about a rope, another touches the trunk and talks of snakes, yet another embraces a foot and talks of trees.

Since each of these blind men is limited to his own personal experience, none of them is capable of perceiving the elephant in its entirety.

The elephant of reality.

Reality is always a bigger picture than the ability of an individual to perceive. In the original story a seeing person eventually comes along and has a schadenfreude-ish ableist laugh at the expense of the blind men, but we do not have the luxury of having someone stand outside reality and tell us the "truth", so we are all doomed to partial and frequently conflicting perceptions.

How then, when fundamental ignorance is a given, can we possibly be sure of anything?

Well, we can't really be sure, but we can have increasingly converging approximations of certainty if we rely on the reports of a multitude of blind men who by virtue of their great numbers slowly increase the resolution of the reports until the figure of an elephant slowly appears.

We learn about reality through our interface with other people, or more precisely, by relying on the intersubjective world of others as represented in our own minds. This is the key to all knowledge and the actual bedrock of our lives.

Each individual is enmeshed within the world of others who speak the same language, share the vision, and accord with the beliefs, and this intersubjective "communal consciousness" is represented in every individual mind.

---

[318] The tangibility given to the direct sensory experience of every individual.

[319] This fundamental ignorance has many philosophical and theological implications that have been the subject of much debate: all the deep questions of epistemology and ontology circle around this point.

[320] As so succinctly put by Tolstoy in War and Peace: "We can know only that we know nothing, And that is the highest degree of human wisdom." This is the fundamental position of all humans: That they simply cannot encompass the sheer magnitude of available knowledge about the world, so their position is always akin to that of an infant who comes into the world knowing nothing and subsequently slowly internalizes the wisdom of others through belief in its veracity.

This representation of the minds of others in our own mind is the most fundamental aspect of being human: the ability to position ourselves within the intersubjective world of others.

This representation labels the tangible and defines reality in consciousness. Language, serving us for both inner thought and outward speech, is entirely comprised of symbolic labels held in the consciousness of individuals but woven into the intersubjective awareness of the many, thereby defining and organizing reality for us. We become human as we assimilate the world of others into our minds and create its representation.

Each one of us is a pulsing node in a glowing network of interconnected others – replicating the beliefs that surround us, interacting with others in world building and creation, and adding something of our own oddity to our presence as a commodity in the world of others.

Money, like language, is created in the intersubjective world of others and represented in our minds. There is no "money" without other people, just as there is no language without other people. Money and language need more than one person to exist.

Because of the fundamental ignorance of the individual, we really cannot know anything about reality except as it is mediated through our trust in others we rely on. Only a group sharing experience can gain accepted knowledge.

Money is the group-experience par-excellence as it is drawn on the faith of a community, and without that faith it is empty of any value.

BIBLIOGRAPHY

Alvaredo, F. Chancel, L., Piketty, T., Saez, E. and Zucman, G. (2018). *World Inequality Report 2018*. World Inequality Lab.

Archer, J. (1979). *Kane & Abel*. St. Martin's Paperbacks.

Auster, P. (1997). *Hand to Mouth*. Faber and Faber.

Ayres, J., Garcia, M. Guillén, D.A. & Kehoe, P.J. (2019). *The Monetary and Fiscal History of Brazil* 1960-2016. NBER Working Paper No. 25421.

Banner, S. (2017). *Speculation: a history of the fine line between gambling and investing*. Oxford University Press.

Bernholz, P. (2003). *Monetary regimes and inflation: History, economic and political relationships*. Edward Elgar Publishing.

Bertram, C. D. I. (2013). *Property in the Moral Life of Human Beings.* Explore Bristol Research.

Bertran. M., Mullainathan, S. & Shafir E. (2004). "A behavioral-economics view of poverty". *The American Economic Review*. 94 (2): 419–423.

Casey, M. (2012). *The unfair trade: how our broken global financial system destroys the middle class*. Crown.

Clarke, G. S. (2018). *Thinking through Fairbairn: Exploring the object relations model of mind.* Routledge.

Colander, D., Holt, R. and Rosser, B. (2003). The Changing Face of Mainstream Economics. *Middlebury College Economics Discussion Paper* 3-27.

Crafts, N. and Fearon, P. (2013). *The Great Depression of the 1930s Lessons for Today*. Oxford University Press.

Ferguson, N. (2008). *The Ascent of Money: A financial history of the world.* Penguin.

Fine, B. & Milonakis, D. (2009). *From Economics Imperialism to Freakonomics: The Shifting Boundaries between Economics and Other Social Sciences. Economics as Social Theory*. Routledge.

Franklin, B. (1729). *A Modest Enquiry into the Nature and Necessity of a Paper Currency.*

Friedman, M. (1985). Monetary Policy in a Fiat World. *BOJ Monetary and Economic Studies.* September.

Fullbrook, E. (Ed.). (2004). *A guide to what's wrong with economics*. Anthem Press.

Gleeson-White, J. (2011). *Double Entry: How the Merchants of Venice Shaped the Modern World – and how their invention could make or break the planet.* Allen & Unwin.

Graeber, D. (2001). *Toward an Anthropological Theory of Value: The False Coin of Our Own Dreams*. Palgrave.

Hayek, F.A. (1976, 2007). *Denationalization of Money*. Institute of Economic Affairs.

Heine, B. (1997). *Possession: Cognitive Sources, Forces, and Grammaticalization.* Cambridge University Press.

Heinsohn, G., Steiger, O. & Decker, F. (2013). *Ownership Economics: On the Foundations of Interest, Money, Markets, Business Cycles and Economic Development.* Routledge.

Ingham, G. (2004). *The Nature of Money*. Polity Press.

Jarvis, C. (2000). The Rise and Fall of Albania's Pyramid Schemes Finance and Development – *Quarterly Magazine of the IMF*. March 2000, Vol. 37, No. 1.

Joseph, P. (2017). *The new human rights movement: reinventing the economy to end oppression*. BenBella Books.

Kennedy, M. (1995). *Interest and inflation free money: Creating an exchange medium that works for everybody and protects the earth*. Stranger Journalism.

Keyes, M. (2017). *The Break*. Penguin.

Kiyotaki, N. & Moore, J. (2001), *Evil is the Root of all Money* Clarendon Lectures - Lecture 1.

Koo, R.C. (2015). *The Escape from Balance Sheet Recession and the QE Trap: A Hazardous Road for the World Economy*. Wiley.

Kornai, J. (1992). *The* socialist *system: The political economy of communism*. Princeton University Press.

Landes, D. S., Mokyr, J., & Baumol, W. J. (Eds.). (2012). *The invention of enterprise: Entrepreneurship from ancient Mesopotamia to modern times*. Princeton University Press.

Lawson, T. (1997). *Economics and Reality*. Routledge.

Leithart, P.J., (2014). *Gratitude : an intellectual history*. Baylor University Press.

Leontief, W. (1982). Academic Economics. *Science*, Vol. 217, Issue 4555, pp. 104-107.

Levitt, S. and Dubner, S.J. (2007). *Freakonomics: A Rogue Economist Explores the Hidden Side of Everything*. William Morrow.

Lincoln, A. (1863). *The Gettysburg Address*.

Locke, J. (1689). *Second Treatise of Government.*

Lyons, J., & John, L. (1995). *Linguistic semantics: An introduction.* Cambridge University Press.

Mallaby, S. (2010). *More money than God: hedge funds and the making of a new elite*. Penguin Press.

Maxwell, S. (2008). *The price is wrong: understanding what makes a price seem fair and the true cost of unfair pricing*. Wiley & Sons.

Mazzucato, M. (2018). *The Value of Everything. Making and Taking in the Global Economy*. Penguin.

McAndrew, C. (2010). *Fine art and high finance: expert advice on the economics of ownership.* Bloomberg Press.

McKenzie, R. B. (2008). *Why Popcorn Costs so Much at the Movies.* Copernicus Books.

Menkhoff, L., & Tolksdorf, N. (2000). *Financial market drift: Decoupling of the financial sector from the real economy?* Springer Science & Business Media.

Menninger, K. (2013). *Number words and number symbols: A cultural history of numbers*. Courier Corporation.

Mildenberger, M. (2019). The Tragedy of the Tragedy of the Commons, *Scientific American*.
North, P. (2007). *Money and Liberation: The Micropolitics of Alternative Currency Movements*. University of Minnesota Press
Ogden, T. H. (2018). *The matrix of the mind: Object relations and the psychoanalytic dialogue*. Routledge.
Ostrom, E. (2015). Governing the Commons: *The Evolution of Institutions for Collective Action.* Cambridge University Press.
Posner, E. A. & Weyl, E. G. (2018). *Radical Markets*. Princeton University Press.
Poppendieck, Janet (1986). *Breadlines Knee Deep in Wheat: Food Assistance in the Great Depression*. Brunswick, New Jersey: Rutgers University Press.
Prins, N. (2022). *Permanent distortion: how the financial markets abandoned the real economy.* Hachette Book Group.
Rose, C.M. (1994). *Property and Persuasion: Essays On The History, Theory, And Rhetoric of Ownership*. Westview Press.
Schmandt-Besserat, D. (1992). *Before writing, vol. I: from counting to cuneiform (Vol. 1)*. University of Texas press.
Seiler, H. (1983). *Possession as an operational dimension of language*. (Language Universals Series, 2.) Tubingen: Gunter Narr.
Sieroń, A. (2019). *Money, inflation and business cycles: the Cantillon effect and the economy*. Routledge.
Shapin, S. (1995). "Trust, Honesty, and the Authority of Science." Institute of Medicine. *Society's Choices: Social and Ethical Decision Making in Biomedicine*. Washington, DC: The National Academies Press.
Shepard, W. (2015). *Ghost Cities of China: The Story of Cities without People in the World's Most Populated Country*. Zed Books.
Shiller, R. J. (2000). *Irrational exuberance*. Princeton University Press.
Smith, A. (1776) (1977). *An inquiry into the nature and causes of the wealth of Nations.* University of Chicago Press.
Soros, G. (2000). *Open Society Reforming Global Capitalism.* Public Affairs.
Steinbeck, J. (1939) *The Grapes of Wrath.* Viking Press.
Sugden, R. (2005). *The economics of rights, co-operation, and welfare*. Palgrave.
Turner, A. (2017). *Between Debt and the Devil*. Princeton University Press.
Veblen, T. (1899). *The Theory of the Leisure Class: An Economic Study of Institutions*. B.W. Huebsch.
Weatherford, J.M. (1997). *The History of Money.* Crown Publications.
Wilson, B. J. (2020). *The Property Species: Mine, Yours, and the Human Mind.* Oxford University Press
Wilson, B. J. (2021). *Respecting Property takes Two*.
Winnicott, D.W. (2005). *Playing and Reality*. Routledge Classics.

www.ingramcontent.com/pod-product-compliance
Lightning Source LLC
Chambersburg PA
CBHW051400240926
51852CB00002B/71
9786197628401